...an educational odyssey

HNS

[Continued from front flap]
struggles to enrich and ennoble the lives of the people. His vivid description of events which shaped his life and movements which claimed his support brings alive an important phase of American intellectual development. It portrays the whole pattern of education south of the Potomac during a crucial period, revealing much that is significant in the history of such great institutions as Vanderbilt and Duke universities, such widespread movements as the Chautauqua lectures and the Ogden campaigns for popular education. Through it all this staunch classicist expounds a common-sense theory of education which finds much to condemn in the modern scene, and he upholds his views with vigor and courage. Especially interesting is his excellent discussion of the type of education imported from Germany during the last century.

As Dr. Snyder takes the reader into the "goodly fellowship" he has enjoyed along the way of his educational pilgrimage, he acquaints him with the often inspiring "little people" and underprivileged of the land as well as with the nation's favored and great.

From first to last this humane teacher speaks a strong word for the educational methods of "Mark Hopkins and his log" as he traces his own education and searches out the reasons for the profound influence of little Wofford College in South Carolina.

The life story of this beloved educator breathes the enthusiasm and evangelistic zeal which he early brought to books and early and late has put into the getting and giving of education, even as it reflects the charm and easy grace of a man recognized as an accomplished lecturer in a region where oratory is still cultivated as an art.

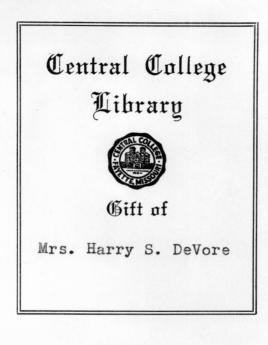

An Educational Odyssey

HENRY NELSON SNYDER

President of Wofford College
Spartanburg, South Carolina
1902-42

ABINGDON-COKESBURY PRESS

New York • Nashville

AN EDUCATIONAL ODYSSEY
COPYRIGHT, MCMXLVII
BY STONE & PIERCE

x

To the Dear Comrade and Perfect Lady
who has kept alight the long road with the wisdom of love

FOREWORD

WHOLE BATTALIONS of capital "I's" marching across the pages that follow announce that the book is an autobiography of a sort—one man's talk about himself and his experiences. Well, it is that, though what is written will not warrant anyone's giving it the title "Great Men Who Have Known Me."

I may have dined with presidents and have had at least a speaking acquaintance with not a few of the nation's great, yet my official duties as president of a small but important southern college have also given me much companionship with the little people of the land, the underprivileged, the "forgotten men," about whom so much ado has been made in the last half century. As a churchman I have felt it my business to do what I could for them educationally as well as religiously. So to the humble places I have gone with something of the zeal of an evangelist, and what I have seen is set down as nearly as possible in terms of the realism of life itself. This is to say that the incidents recorded and the persons described are meant to be representative of various strata in southern society.

So, then, the book might also be taken as something of a sociological treatise—written, though, by one who is not a sociologist—for in it are "cases" illustrative of the folkways, habits of thought, and standards of living of a people far more "solid" in their racial and social unity than even that well-worn phrase "the solid South" suggests.

This means further that what is written has plenty of history in it without necessarily being a book of history. In trying to understand why the southern section of the Union is what it is, for better or worse, one must always hold in

7

mind the historic forces that have shaped its destiny through all its past and today are determining its future. Even an autobiographer cannot escape history, though he may have to account only for himself. What makes history also makes him.

But the chief emphasis in what history is used in this book must of necessity be on the educational aspects of my own life as well as on the educational aspects of the section of which I am a product. To whatever educational processes and movements there were in the South I have been subject, and, in addition, have shared actively in them as teacher and college president for sixty years. All these, moreover, have been stirring, exciting years, with hardly a dull moment in any of them. They have been all the way along of the nature of adventurous pioneering and continual discovery, as if the South were a new frontier.

Of course, out of such experiences have come views, opinions, convictions, faiths concerning the whole big business of helping youth find its best for the uses of life—a process vaguely called "getting an education." There will be in these pages, therefore, much about this process and those who carry it on—presidents, deans, instructors, and even the students, who are too often forgotten in the rattle of administrative machinery.

Then, too, there is the fact that I have been connected, of my own will, with one small denominational college for fifty-two years, forty of these as its president. Consequently, much has to be said about Wofford College itself, particularly because of the way it has had of training a noteworthy leadership quite out of proportion to its size, equipment, and resources. If there is any "problem" in this book, it is just here: How has a small institution like Wofford been able so profoundly to influence southern life and education during the past sixty years? Maybe I have given the answer as I have woven into the total pattern of the book the story of this small college of the liberal arts and sciences, and in so doing maybe I have also told the story of others of its kind.

Anyway, to have taken part in the making of this story leads me to disbelieve that "academic shades" and "cloistered walls" are either quiet or tranquil. The implications of these ancient phrases represent the dreams of a world the scholar would like to live in if only youth and life's urgencies would let him. But they will not; and though, surrounded by his books, enveloped in the blue haze of the smoke from his pipe and in the soft light from his shaded lamp, he will persist in his dreams, tomorrow will bring him to the noisy realities of campus and classroom and the hurly-burly of the football game. He too will join the cheering crowds, and when the occasion offers will lustily sing the Alma Mater. No, I have found higher education quite something else than that suggested by "academic shades" and "cloistered walls." To me it has been the most exciting thing in the world, the most alive, the closest to the heart and soul of life itself in all its ways.

And now by way of summary, I may be permitted to say that in this account of the people and the land south of the Potomac there will appear reasons why they are so beloved of the investigators, the researchers, the regionalists, the reformers. For all such this South has been the happy hunting grounds for book material of many kinds. What, for instance, would the storytellers have done without its dialects, its sheer ugliness in spots, the terrifying tragedies of its social conflicts, and even its magnolias, its roses, and its moonlight on white-columned mansions? As I have recalled various aspects in the life of this very American section of the nation, most of these matters I have somehow felt as "peculiar," as so many have found them to be.

Without imputing to them any responsibility for the faults of this book, I must express to Dr. Weldon Myers, head of the English Department of Converse College, my appreciation for his reading of the manuscript and his valuable suggestions, and to Professor K. D. Coates of the English faculty of Wofford College, for his generous service in reading the proofs.

HENRY NELSON SNYDER

CONTENTS

11

1

A MIDDLE TENNESSEE BOYHOOD

1865-83

THERE IS SOMETHING freakish about the things we remember out of the farthest past when we first became citizens of this planet. Perhaps the Freudists and Behaviorists have the answer to why we recall one thing out of what must have been a multitude of various experiences and forget blankly all the rest. My earliest recollection goes back to the time when I was two years old and was carried on the shoulders of a tall, stalwart black man over a newly plowed field—I was in dresses; boys didn't discard them for pants and blouse in those far days until they were four, five, or six years old. Just that experience and nothing else remains of the several years we lived in the country some three miles out from Nashville on the Dickerson pike on the Edgefield side of the Cumberland River in the heart of the bluegrass country of Middle Tennessee.

I was to learn later that this Big John, on whose broad shoulders I was eased over the rough furrows, was one of our Negroes who after the war had drifted back to take up life with his "white folks" under unfamiliar relationships which both he and they were slow to understand, and to which it was not easy to make adjustments. And the "drifters" kept coming in. All through my early boyhood I would hear their soft voices in intimate talk with my mother and other members of the family. They were usually women, who had also "belonged," if not to our own family, to some other branch. They would take the little boy on their cushiony laps and wrap their big arms around him, exuding strong body odors mixed with the heaviest of cheap perfumes, chiefly musk. They would discuss with my mother whom I looked like, or rather whom I "took after." When they had settled all family matters, they would retire to the kitchen, from which would soon come song and laughter, and I knew the dinner was going to be better and more profuse on that day.

But a day came when the drifting stopped except in the case of a few older ones who had to have "spells" of going over with my mother the days when they were in a true sense of the family, not even feeling that they were slaves. They walk before me now, gentle, kindly, loyal, affectionate; and it is good to think that the arms they threw around me in my childhood were arms of love and loyalty. I "belonged" to them, I am sure, even in that freedom into which they were trying to fit themselves. Just the other day a colored woman who has been a part of our home for many years— so many that the relations between her and Mrs. Snyder are not those of hired servant and mistress, but rather those of two women whose difference in color is no barrier to trust and affection—suddenly asked in the midst of a talk about what the war had done to disarrange these relationships: "Do you know what the colored people say about Dr. Snyder?" No, she didn't know. "They say, 'He don't look down on anybody.' " And I have been proud ever since, thinking back into a distant boyhood for the sources of my attitudes toward this race that will contribute much to enrich American life if the "reformers" fail in their efforts to sow the seeds of hate and prejudice among them.

The next thing I recall happened when I was perhaps four years old. I was marching up and down on the big dining-room table in the presence of the whole family, a little Confederate soldier, clad in gray uniform with brass buttons down the front of the jacket. I had stepped out of dresses and was wearing my first suit of clothes—trousers, blouse, and coat—made out of the last uniform my father wore. About a year before the war ended the family had bought the cloth for $1,500, and the women with their own hands had made the suit and sent it to him. My father and brother were looking very solemn as the very young, proud soldier paraded up and down the table, but my mother and sister were in tears. It was long afterward before I understood the meaning of the tears and sober looks while the soldier was strutting so bravely. The guns had been silenced only yesterday, the memory of the dead lying on the battlefields was still poignantly fresh, and the streets of Nashville were, on occasion, thronged with blue-clad soldiers, living symbols of the humiliation of a very proud people.

Out of the next year or two I recall that my mother said to me in her quiet, even voice—I never heard her raise her voice in anger or impatience, for to do so would be "common"—"Now, Henry, you may play with Negro children, but don't ever let me see you playing with the children of these Yankee soldiers!" She need not have issued this order even to the youngest of us. With the laughing, friendly children of former slaves, yes, but not with the white children of those soldiers that walked the streets. For these it was already the throwing of stones, and no suggestions from our parents were needed. In the heart of childhood the war had not yet ended.

Now these incidents out of the memory book of a far distant childhood—a little boy on the shoulders of a big black man; the drifting into his life of others who seemed to be intimately and affectionately of the family, though of different color; the little Confederate soldier on the dining-room table; his gentle mother's command as to his playmates—these things out of the book may seem trivial enough, but even now, with all that has come in between, there are few experiences more significant as I think back on them. They represent the historic forces of an old order that was passing beyond recall and their influence on that new generation which, without any choice of its own, was having its way of life, its moods, its attitudes, shaped and channeled for that future which one day it would have to take over.

The incidents here related, vividly recalled as the only things I remember, were therefore essential elements in preparing me and my generation, the children of the immediate postwar era, for the kind of men and women we should be in the years thereafter. All the social, political, economic, and spiritual adjustments that would have to be made as life unfolded for us are in these experiences of a childhood lived between 1865 and 1875. That we cannot forget them—and indeed that they are about all we can recall with any degree of reality—registers their supreme importance in the early training of the generation which was mine.

There is one other incident from these earliest days that stands out yet with undimmed vividness. The Methodist pastor used to visit our home, in line with his ministerial duties, I assume. He would awe me with his height and the size of his feet—the tallest man I had ever seen and with the biggest feet, and they have lost nothing of their size with the long lapse of years. He would always greet me with three nicknames— "Goober-grabber," "Duke of Sorghum," and "Georgia Cracker." Small boy that I was, I resented these names, feeling he was poking fun at me for being a Tennessean born out of place—Macon, Georgia.

When Nashville fell to the Federals in 1862 my father was a captain in the quartermaster's department of the Army of Tennessee, with headquarters at Macon, and my mother was living on a farm some fourteen miles south of Nashville with four small children and several slaves. Greatly harassed by stragglers of both armies, she must move into Nashville but could remain there only on the condition that she take the "oath of allegiance" to the Federal government. This she would not do; and she and a group of other Nashville ladies were given passes through to the Confederate lines at Dalton, Georgia. At Bridgeport, Alabama, General Grant and his staff came aboard the train. With them he very courteously paid his respects to the Nashville ladies, furnishing them at Chattanooga with an ambulance and an escort of cavalry under a flag of truce through to the Confederate lines.

Later my mother used this chance acquaintance to secure from President Grant a pardon for a young kinsman who had run into trouble with the Federal authorities during reconstruction days and got himself a considerable term in the penitentiary. The president based his pardon on the condition that the young man—he was only eighteen years old—should never return to Tennessee. This he never did, but lived a long, successful, and useful life in Louisiana. General Grant was the only man who wore a blue uniform for whom my gentle mother ever had any kindly feelings, going even so far as to say she thought he might be "a gentleman."

She joined my father at Macon for the duration of the war, serving as superintendent of a Confederate hospital for two years, seeing the war in its most tragic aspects, and gathering out of her experiences stories of its pathos, its terror, and its horror, which by the fireside, as they were growing up, she would tell her children, not in bitterness, but as something about war she thought they ought to know. To this day as I happen to go through the wards of a modern hospital, so clean and sanitary, I must think of the kind of hospitals in which the wounded and the sick of the South died, their endurance under suffering, their gallant acceptance of conditions little short of unbelievable, their appreciation of small favors, the letters they would want written home, and the dear little trinkets sent to sweetheart, wife, or mother. Such stories as my mother would tell didn't hurt a growing boy by filling his mind with dark, gruesome images, but rather served to increase his appreciation of human nature's capacity to face the worst things with a shining nobility of spirit. Maybe it was the way my mother related these experiences that produced this effect upon her children.

Though coats of arms, family trees, portraits chiefly of women—rather handsome ones, too—did hang on the parlor

17

walls in my own home and in the homes of other branches of the family, I didn't take much to genealogies. Questions concerning such matters came to be, even when I was but a boy, so serious to the women folk as to seem to me a bit ridiculous, something essentially feminine and not for men. As I was growing up I would be constantly introduced to new cousins, that is, new to me but not to my mother. When they were gone, she would try to explain just how the "cousin" relationship could be established. But it was all too complicated to understand, though some names do even yet stick in memory—Robertson, Reeves, Hill, Harrison, Rains, Craighead, Cheatham, Cockrill, Taliaferro, Nelson, Beck, Van Leer, Gower, Mayes, Paine, Blount, and no doubt many others that failed to stick in memory. Later I was to find out it was not a bad array of family names; and when I also discovered that my great-great-grandparents had twelve children and my next two sets of grandparents had ten each, I could understand that a society that developed from frontier conditions would produce these multiple relationships. Further, when my history books noted the immigration movements from 1825 to 1860, I could understand why so many of our cousin visitors came up from Mississippi, Louisiana, and even Texas.

But all the talk would begin and end with General James Robertson, "Grandpa Robertson," who seemed to be the original head and founder of this numerous and widely scattered clan that kept moving from one frontier to another, after the manner of the first of them. Stories about him filled my boyish imagination—how he came with his young wife from Brunswick County, Virginia, to eastern North Carolina back in 1750; how he moved, after a little stop, to the Watauga in Tennessee, to found there, with John Sevier, one of the most romantic figures in all the frontier, a miniature free commonwealth in the wilderness; how, after achieving success and prosperity, with all his goods and chattels and some two hundred friends and neighbors, he followed Boone's

18

trail through the Great Gap of the Wilderness Road, turning left, however, away from Kentucky to found another wilderness commonwealth on the banks of the Cumberland in the rich lands of Middle Tennessee; and how but a few years later with Sevier he merged the two wilderness commonwealths into the proud state of Tennessee. I was told of the exploits of the backwoodsman, Indian fighter, and frontier statesman; of the diplomatist to Spaniards and Indians becoming once again successful and prosperous, owning 30,000 acres of land, building on a knoll by a winding stream the first brick house in what is now Davidson County—and a stately home it was, compared with the log houses in which he had spent most of his life—of his drastic destruction of all the Cherokee towns along the Tennessee in vengeance for their slaying and scalping his son, a boy hardly out of his teens; of his dying at last among the Chickasaws at the spot where Memphis now stands, while on a mission from the federal government, of a wound he had received in a battle with Indians at Kanawha Falls far off in what is now West Virginia.

As a very small boy I used to look at two portraits that hung on the walls of my grandmother's parlor, portraits of James Robertson and his wife Charlotte Reeves, the comrade of his journeyings and sharer in all his hardships. A strong-faced couple they were, and yet there was a certain kindliness in their faces with all the strength the painter had to see. I would wonder and wonder if these could be the hero and heroine of those stories of courage and endurance, of suffering and bitter hardship, I had heard so much about, and I wonder yet.

These stories colored our Middle Tennessee boyhood, giving direction to our games and sports. We were frontiersmen, backwoodsmen, fighting men, organized into warring bands of Indians and whites, armed with bows and arrows, wooden guns, tomahawks, and knives. The woods and fields, the deep valleys cut by swift-flowing streams, the high hills, were our playgrounds, or rather the mimic battlefields and ambushes for stealthy trailings by scouts and for all the arts of courage and cunning displayed by our ancestors in defending their homes from the red savages.

Beadle's "Yellow-Back Dime Novels" made even more vividly real the fireside stories of pioneer ancestors. Carried about hidden next to the skin beneath the blouse and read clandestinely, these books were passed on to the next secret reader in spite of the terrible things the preacher and the Sunday-school teacher said would happen to sinful boys who read them. Lewis Wetzel the Scout, Simon Girty the Renegade, Kit Carson, and a long succession of great but worthy killers walked side by side with those ancestral heroes of the Cumberland settlements.

But other heroes, more recent ones, were with us also both by reading and by word of mouth. Lee and Jackson, Stuart and Pelham, Longstreet and Early, Ewell and Hill, Joe Johnson, Albert Sidney Johnston, Forrest and Morgan—these, too, were the familiars of our imagination, furnishing shining examples of what to live by and of what to die for, and how to do it gallantly. Those Middle Tennessee boys were not conscious of much humiliation in the thought of defeat, for when they called the roll of such names, their swelling pride would put down all other emotions, though their young cheeks would flame hot with anger at the sight of blue-clad men swaggering, as they thought, along the streets of their city. In the main, however, the nobler emotions that stir the heart of a boy who is taught to honor men of great and valiant achievements, particularly where courage is called for, would erase all less worthy emotions, and he could pay tribute to them without being mean for long toward his enemies who wore that blue uniform.

Now much that has been here set down was more than hearsay—it assumes reading and a degree of formal education. For instance, those yellow-backed novels, and others whose backs were not yellow, had to be read, of course, and before I was twelve I must have been absorbed in the glorious panorama of John Esten Cooke's *Surrey of the Eagle's Nest* and *Mohun, or the Last Days of Lee and His Paladins.* I am sure, moreover, that I was hardly in my teens, certainly not beyond fourteen, when I was reading Bulwer-Lytton's *Last Days of Pompeii* and *Rienzi, the Last of the Roman Tribunes;* Jane Porter's *Scottish Chiefs;* Wyss's *Swiss Family Robinson;* Defoe's *Robinson Crusoe;* Day's *Sandford and Merton;* and Scott's *Ivanhoe, Waverley, Old Mortality, Kenilworth,* and *Quentin Durward*—all favorites of mine, as were also Cooper's "Leatherstocking Tales." Scott's narrative poems, all of them, I fairly devoured, the swift-moving meter adding to the interest of the stories. Over and over again I read them, the fighting parts especially, and without effort many couplets stuck in my memory. Can anybody beat the Wizard of the North in telling a moving story of strong feelings, courage, and romantic achievement? His mailclad knights were not unlike their buckskin-clad brothers in the qualities that make men men. At least it must have been this kinship that I recognized in spite of all differences in time, place, and costume.

Then came Byron! For some reason—just what it was I don't recall—I bought a cheap copy of his selected poems. His dark, mysterious heroes with a strange past which must never be uncovered but always hinted at—Lara, the Corsair, the Bride of Abydos—entered into possession of the imagination of early adolescence. And those moon-eyed, melting ladies of the East —were they not more alluring than all the fair daughters of the North? At any rate, for a time at least one boy thought so, and was sorry he found none like them near at hand. Perhaps it was better for him that they lived only as creatures of his dreams. With his school geography he tried to follow the pilgrimage of Childe Harold on the maps. Here, too, was the romance of strange and unfamiliar places and persons. By way of contrast the lush sentimentalism of Thomas Moore's poetry and Owen Meredith's *Lucile* got hold of him for reading and rereading. And Shakespeare, too, he read, especially *Julius Caesar, Macbeth, The Merchant of Venice, Romeo and Juliet,* though he always felt he would like to rewrite the closing scenes—it wasn't fair to let two such glorious lovers die by their own hands when it would be so easy to save them.

To this miscellany of more or less narrative literature should be added Macaulay's essays—perhaps it was a certain narrative element in them that attracted him. He read them avidly, discovering doubtless for the first time that there was such a thing as "style," though he had never heard the word used in its rhetorical sense. As he read "Milton," "Lord Clive," "Warren Hastings," "Bunyan," he knew only that he liked the way they were written and wished very much that he could write that way himself.

Later, in the middle of his college course, when he was taken by the cool, dry, oracular manner of Matthew Arnold, the brilliant glitter of Macaulay's prose shone forth once again by way of contrast. Even yet when some writer of history, whose phrasing is as dry as last year's cornstalk in the field and who can record earthshaking events with as little emphasis as the summer's weather reports, discounts Macaulay's facts because he states them with color and interest and emphasis, I want to say: "Dear Professor, nobody believes what you say for the reason that you say it in such a way that it seems not worth believing, not important enough for you to feel a microscopic glow from the greatness of the happenings." Moreover, when a very modern instructor of the course in "Creative Writing," in language as colloquially sloppy as the boys sitting in front of him with tousled hair, wide-open shirt collars, the tails of their shirts outside trousers more baggy than a sailor's, jeers at my favorite's "artificial affectations" as a style that is out of date, I am up in arms again to affirm a faith in the superiority of my adolescent taste for "fine" writing.

Now where were Dickens and Thackeray and the New Englanders in the interests of a Middle Tennessee boy in the seventies? They were not on my reading lists, though I do recall faintly discussions among the elders as to which was better, and I think they were mainly on the side of Thackeray. I

22

recollect hearing the word "common" applied to the life depicted by Dickens and the characters he was making so familiar. Dimly, too, I remember some poking of fun at the young ladies of the family connection for weeping over *David Copperfield* and *Old Curiosity Shop*, and indignation over American life as drawn in *Martin Chuzzlewit*. But these were not for me until I became a freshman in college, when they were a part of my assigned reading. The New Englanders I did catch in scraps in the readers in school; and those from Longfellow, Whittier, and Bryant were good "scraps"—so good that I memorized parts of some of them.

Now this account of what a boy had read by the time he was fourteen does, in retrospect, seem to make up a formidable list. But it was not so to him or to his family. That he should have read these books must have been a matter of course. His older brother and sister did the same, no doubt, in their day. In a word, I was no infant prodigy in my own or anybody else's eyes, but just a normal boy who had all the diseases in order and played rather expertly all the games in season—marbles (and "for keeps"), tops, kites, baseball, shinny, long-run, fox and hounds. Neither do I recall that it was regarded as a particularly noteworthy performance when I completed the nine grades of the free public school in five years, finishing at fourteen, ready for business or college. The skilled instruction of my mother made this possible and easy. She took me over at eight, and for the next year the curriculum was the multiplication table and Webster's Blue-Backed Speller. Through and through, back and forth, she carried me till both were mastered—and I mean mastered—impressing upon me the conviction that, unless arithmetic and spelling were really mastered, nothing else counted much. And so my formal education began in a one-teacher school, but my mother was the teacher and I was the only pupil.

At nine years old, then, I entered school with a swarm of my kind, and with girls, too, for whom my special kind had little respect, approving their separation in the classrooms

23

and on the playground. But for that prim, blonde, blue-eyed, fluffy-haired teacher, sitting so upright behind the table on the raised platform, we had the greatest respect. Our own home training had taught us that such as she was due all the chivalrous courtesy of which a gentleman was capable, and though he might be only nine years old, he could at least be a little gentleman in the presence of ladies. And he generally was. Any disorder in the classroom was on the side of the girls, who were not bound by the same code.

And so from Miss Addie we went on to Miss Lizzie, beautiful with her black hair and eyes and the soft, persuasive appeal to knowledge in her voice. Here again was accorded to her a gentleman's consideration for a lady, and there was no misbehavior in spite of the instinctive urge toward it in those boyish breasts. To yield to the urge would be violating the rules of both heredity and environment.

But when we passed from the sixth grade into the last three, and found Miss Maggie and Miss Sallie, other restraints besides youth and eyes and beauty and the code were needed. These two were well beyond middle age, had taught their own private schools before the war, and bore the marks of time on face and figure and hair. They were skilled, experienced teachers of the advanced courses in grammar, geography, reading, history, arithmetic, algebra, and Latin, and the fourteen weeks in natural philosophy. Precise, exacting, thorough in their methods, they brought over from another day a spirit of discipline that assumed that all boys were stupid and bad and must never be allowed to slip the leash in the classroom. They got the respect due them and the restraint needed for the orderly ongoing of their programs. They commanded with a manner that always implied the use of violent methods in case of necessity, and we learned what they taught in the way they wanted it learned—exactly as it was in the books. It was good for boys between eleven and fourteen to sense the meaning of real discipline, for without knowing its value, that was what we were getting.

24

But the superintendent—he was the school! Carrying a heavy stick, he walked with a dragging limb due to a wound in one of his knees. This wound helped in the history course, for we studied more closely each of the great battles of the war with the idea that it was this one where that bullet or piece of shell struck him—Shiloh, Chickamauga, Antietam, Chancellorsville, Resaca, Seven Pines, or Gettysburg. Which? We usually selected the bloodiest, that is, the one in which the number of Federal dead was disproportionately larger than the number of dead on the side of the Confederates, for "our captain" must certainly make the enemy pay dearly for the hurt they gave him!

Bursting suddenly into a classroom, without the formality of knocking, he might pick up a textbook and proceed to hear the lesson, or he might start talking about the business we were in, "getting an education." "It is a battle all the way: our books are the enemy to be beaten, killed as it were; those in advance are spelling, writing, grammar, reading, arithmetic—these must be slain first before you can get at those in the next line, history, Latin, algebra, geography, science; but these, too, must be overcome without quarter and with all speed; to hesitate, to count the costs, to be sick when the call to battle comes, may be fatal, and the victory will be lost." Here was no lock step with everybody moving together, the slow pacing the fast, but a hastening through with all the speed we had, defeating our enemies of war, the books, in five years instead of nine, and "ready for the battle of life," as the saying went, even then. A wounded soldier's "pep talk" did it, stirring the martial spirit of youth. Reverberating in memory yet, it sounds not unlike the talk of a modern football coach before the big game.

I recur to the reading done through these five school years to say that no part of it was directly inspired by the school itself. Of course, there was no parallel or supplementary reading—so many books to be "studied" and so many more to be "read." I had to wait for college to be surprised by that sort of

25

thing, particularly so when not a few of the books assigned I knew, as it were, by heart. Between recitations, though, in the schoolroom I would read in a few weeks quite through the McGuffey's readers, borrowing from a deskmate his reader, if it was of the next grade ahead.

But during the first year it did not occur to me that the reading skill I was acquiring in the classroom could be transferred to reading outside, to those Beadle Yellow-Backs my older brother sometimes read to us. One day when the hero of one of them was in a predicament from which there seemed no escape—prone on his back; blood trickling from a wound in his forehead; a powerful redskin, his arch enemy, astride him with tomahawk raised to strike the fatal blow—this brother nonchalantly folded up the tattered little book, put it in his pocket, and walked away, leaving a group of listeners breathless with suspense. This was too much to endure, so I trailed him like a sleuth till the book was mine. It was open where he had left off, and to my amazement I could read on until I heard the sharp crack of a rifle from the dim recesses of the forest and saw the Indian slump forward with blood gushing from a ghastly wound in his head, and the hero was saved for the waiting heroine! I could read, and for the first time I knew it. It was a coronation moment of experience, and from then on a new world opened—a world almost as real as, and at times far more satisfying than, that world of daily commonplace living from which it was often a way of glorious escape, furnishing the Fortunatus cap and seven-league boots for voyaging into "realms of gold."

But it was not "realms of gold" for a Middle Tennessee boy, aged fourteen, who had just finished school. It was college, of course, the new Methodist university, made possible by the munificence of Cornelius Vanderbilt, located in the western suburbs of Nashville, and opened for students only three years before. But the boy was too young, and would not be accepted until he was sixteen. So he faced the reality of going to work as all his classmates did. The years between 1865 and 1880

26

matured boys fast, and a fourteen-year-old boy looked at life with no little of a man's viewpoint, having no doubt that his first business was to begin to "earn a living," as the phrase went. An advertisement in the local daily for a boy in a large new and secondhand bookstore caught my eye, and I applied for and got the job, the only position I ever asked for. The wages were $2.50 a week!

But the job was in a bookstore, and the compensation in money didn't matter. I didn't really need it anyway. It was the books that mattered, even the very smell of them. The understanding that the clerks might take out overnight any second-hand book for home reading made this store for me a vast circulating library, and I at once entered upon a debauch of miscellaneous reading and even began to be a purchaser of books "at cost," building a library of my very own. Under such surroundings I felt no humiliation that my first three months were given to sweeping floors, washing windows, and dusting and rearranging books in order "to learn the stock." The day I was let into the secret of the price marks in cryptic letters and told that I was a salesman also is one of those days remembered as red-letter days, and no elder salesman put more zest into the selling or more knowledge of the book to be sold than this latest and youngest recruit. He became a propagandist as well as a seller of goods, because he somehow felt that everybody should love books as he did.

About a year later, on a rainy day when there were no customers in the store except the stray browsers who read but never bought, on a stepladder I was dusting the books on the higher shelves when I let an armful slip to the floor with a crash. At a second happening, the proprietor came rushing from his desk in the rear of the store to say with much irritation, "Damn it, Henry, you'll break me!" In a sort of quiet, cold anger I followed him back to his desk to announce, with a dignity I have never been able to muster since, that I was leaving and desired a settlement at once, that nobody could speak to me in the manner he used. I was just fifteen and was putting an elderly man in his place! But wasn't I a "gentleman" who knew what was due from one gentleman to another? No amount of persuasion on his part could change me, the code by which I was living being too strong to warrant my risking a similar experience again.

I didn't have to wait long for another position. Not more than two days later the manager of the Methodist Publishing House sent for me, and I accepted the job he offered at a considerable increase in compensation, that is, from $2.50 a week to $4.00. I was much flattered, feeling that somehow I had been rewarded for my attitude toward my employer's language when his clerk accidentally dropped an armful of books from the top of a ladder! My new duties, however, were quite different. Having hardly any local trade, the Publishing House did a large mail-order business in religious books and periodicals throughout the entire South. Orders would be distributed to a half dozen clerks to be filled and laid on a big rectangular table. My job was to wrap the books, paste on the labels carrying the addresses, and put the packages in a box, stamped and ready for mailing. In a little while I became expert in the wrapping of packages, acquiring considerable speed and skill, for it took both to keep up with the work of the six clerks. By the end of the year I was getting $6.00 a week, and I seemed to be receiving "big money." And it was for a sixteen-year-old boy.

One rigid rule I must observe in my duties: If the paste was thin and my brush should smear the label so that another had to be written, under no circumstances was I to rewrite it, but must have the clerk who was filling the order do another label. But late one evening when everybody was anxious to finish the day's work in order to get off, I smeared the label. Seeing the responsible man nowhere in sight, I went to the nearest desk and made out a label myself, thus breaking the rules of the game. The manager passed, looked over my shoulder, and asked me back into his office. I followed, feeling perfectly sure that I was to receive a ticket of dismissal. To my surprise, though, he began to tell me how well I was doing my work, how much pleased he was that I always seemed willing to do more than was expected of me, closing his eulogy with words that fairly took my breath: "I noticed also your handwriting. Fingers that can write as good a hand as yours do have no business tying strings around bundles. I am promoting you to a desk, and your salary will be $40 a month." "Salary," not "wages" any more, and a "desk," doing the work that men were doing! I really believe that under the influence of unexpected praise and promotion a seventeen-year-old boy was born a man on that day in the back office of the manager of the Methodist Publishing House.

That year was a maturing year. Associating with men twice my age and sharing with them daily the same tasks and responsibilities tended to make me older than the calendar's eighteen years. Indeed I am afraid that I deliberately assumed a maturity that should not have been mine. Doing what really was a man's work doubtless flattered me into trying to be more of a man than I was. So when at the end of the year I was again called into conference in the now familiar back office, I really was not particularly surprised when I was told by the manager that he was sending me up into the bookkeeping department at a salary of $60 a month. Now I was really in the men's class, for in 1882 in Middle Tennessee did not men marry, buy a home, and start a family on $60 a month? They did, and I knew it from the talk I heard among them. Though flattered, I was not tempted. I had other plans that included, first, at least two years at the new university on the city's western border, then a lawyer's office for study and the practice of law. The manager was disappointed when I declined his offer. Belittling the law as a career and glowingly depicting the business advantages in Nashville at that particular time, he tried to dissuade me from the course I had marked out for myself with the consent and approval of my parents. The "consent and approval" of parents really meant something in the 1880's, though the boy might be eighteen years old and self-supporting. I resigned, and my business career was at an end, though its lessons of promptness, orderliness, respect for facts and figures, and the necessity of group co-operativeness in common tasks never ended.

But these four years in business did not abate my interests in some other things, though they did put a stop to what my friends called a "promising career" in baseball. The sand-lot prodigy in the newly discovered art of curve pitching had to surrender something he loved very much, taking his part in this game only by watching—when he could get off on a summer afternoon—professional games. He still remembers seeing those ancient worthies of this sport in action—"Pop" Anson, Mike Kelly, Clarkson, Billy Sunday, Williamson.

Then there was an occasional visit to the theater to see James O'Neil in *The Count of Monte Cristo;* robustious John McCullough tearing a passion to tatters in *Virginius,* and liking it; Joseph Jefferson in *Rip Van Winkle,* bringing tears rather than laughter; Buffalo Bill in *The Danites* when he was a reality as a scout and Indian killer and a marvelous shooter with rifle and revolver, and had not yet become the aged, pallid legend of Wild West exhibitions. Then, too, for two hours and a half I forgot the world when I saw Richard Mansfield in *Richard III,* Fanny Janauschek as Lady Macbeth, and Edwin Booth as Brutus in *Julius Caesar,* supported by Lawrence Barrett as Cassius. During the first two acts I was all on the side of Barrett; his noisy, energetic manner seemed to me what acting ought to be. But as the play went on, even my immature judgment was caught and held by the quieter, simpler art of Booth. I knew he *was* Brutus and not a man playing the part, and ever afterward in all manner of public speaking, on the stage, at the bar, on the hustings, in the pulpit, I had a standard of excellence that demanded simplicity, naturalness, restraint.

I think it well that I had the opportunity of seeing such plays and actors in the unspoiled period of youth before a critical attitude had been developed to sickly "o'er with the pale cast of thought" the sheer emotional delight I found in witnessing them. The great of the stage I have seen in this country and Europe, their greatness assisted by all that modern science, mechanical art, and scholarship could do in the way of creating a perfect background as the stage setting, and yet somehow they have never seemed as great as did Mansfield, Jefferson, McCullough, Janauschek, Barrett, and Booth, on that all but bare stage in the little city of Nashville in the 1870's and early 1880's. Was it that the imagination of youth doesn't need the externals to make a play real, because for it "the play's the thing"?

Nothing diverted my purpose from the college direction during these four years, neither work nor recreation. Knowing I would have to have it for entrance, I "read" plane geometry, not working the theorems so much as literally reading the processes of demonstration because it seemed to me that most of them were too obviously true to need any proof, the lettered figures being sufficient proof in themselves. And, by the way, this attitude persisted all through the courses in the so-called higher mathematics to give me no end of trouble. I kept myself fresh in what Latin I knew and added to my knowledge by reading Cicero's orations against Cataline. They really interested me, and nobody had to tell me that here was great oratory. Not even the barrier of a foreign tongue could hide this from me, and as I went along in a necessarily sort of fumbling way I must stop to repeat aloud some of the moving passages in the Latin, and they remain with me yet.

Somewhere along this road, that is, before I was eighteen, I discovered three books, or rather they discovered me, and did something to me I never got over. They were Emerson's *Essays*, and Carlyle's *Heroes and Hero Worship* and *The French Revolution*. I owned them in cheap reprints in small type on bad paper. In the main, Emerson's *Essays* startled and stimulated me without any too great understanding on my part of just what he was trying to say. I was much pleased later during my college course when I read in a criticism of his writings that he himself did not always understand what he was saying,

. 31

but that young James Russell Lowell, after hearing one of his lectures, had declared that something great and beautiful had passed his way. However, "The American Scholar" stirred me, and still does, as does the reading of the Declaration of Independence. "The American Scholar" made me feel that as an American I must be somebody and the way to be somebody was to be yourself, independent, self-reliant, original, learning the methods and catching the spirit of those who had been the great of the earth but in no sense aping them or cringing in their presence. How much of this philosophy I tried to practice, I don't know, but it was good in the days of one's youth to feel its inspiration and challenge, there being in it a clarion call to battle for one's right to be a free man intellectually and spiritually, and that was something for a seventeen-year-old boy to hear just before entering college.

This mood was reinforced by *Heroes and Hero Worship*. It interpreted the significance of sheer human greatness in history and released that strain of the heroic latent in youth when it goes into high counsel with itself in those secret moments of aspiration while it is looking into its future at the kind of life it would care most to live. One may not live the great life, but a reading of *Heroes and Hero Worship* does leave an unforgettable admiration for it and maybe an all too brief purpose to live it, and that may serve as a protective against some of the low things that forever threaten youth as it struggles through the perilous twilight zone that comes before manhood. Thank you, grim, dour old Scotchman, whose Covenanter ancestors left enough of their heroism for you, the writer man, to recognize its power and glory and to paint in living phrases the portraits of those who changed the course of history because they possessed the heroic in rich measure, and to do this for youth when youth most needed it to be done!

But *The French Revolution* was a transforming influence for other reasons. Somehow I had associated the French Revolution with our own revolution. Its "liberty, equality, fraternity" were of a piece with our "life, liberty, and the pur-

32

suit of happiness," and here in Carlyle's book was the mighty drama of the French battle for freedom from oppression within, as ours had been for freedom from oppression without. I was so deeply and irrevocably on the side of freedom that the guillotine, the terror and horror of the wholesale blood-letting, did not offend me, and I do not recall that I had much sympathy even for the fair Marie Antoinette, though I had read, in my McGuffey's Reader, Burke's magnificent appeal in her behalf. The verbal pyrotechnics, the lurid coloring, and the always-dramatic presentation of Carlyle's kept me in a state of excitement entirely in the mood of the emotional tension of his superheated pages. If I had known Wordsworth's couplet while I was reading *The French Revolution*, I would have made it entirely mine:

> Bliss was it in that dawn to be alive,
> But to be young was very heaven!

And so this is the way one boy grew up in Middle Tennessee from 1865 to 1883, and was looking forward, with an eagerness which amounted to a passion, to what college had to offer. For four years he had really thought of nothing else, and for better or worse as to his preparation for it, the gate was open, the fair country of his dreams beckoned. But his educational odyssey was well begun, and he had already found it exciting.

2

A UNIVERSITY IN THE MAKING

Now THAT NEW university I was entering in 1883—how it got its name and how it came into being constitute as romantic a story as ever put a splash of color on the pages of the history of American higher education. It was opened with much fanfare and great talk on the part of Southern Methodist dignitaries in the first week of October, 1875. John Wesley, the founder of the church, was a son of Oxford, as great a scholar as there was in all that eighteenth-century England. But somehow his mission seemed to be chiefly to the poor, the unlettered, the underprivileged of his England; and, indeed, most of his helpers in the great enterprise of transforming spiritually the forgotten men and women of his day were from the very class he and they were trying to lift. The Oxford don knew better than anybody else that, if the results of his revivalism were to be permanent and the "societies" he was organizing were to be effective, education must join with religion in the process. So he set up schools and sent forth from the printing press more books and pamphlets for popular enlightenment than did any other man of his time. He was a resourceful, untiring distributor of useful knowledge in cheap, readable form.

Francis Asbury, the first American bishop, whose bronze statue on a tired horse stands in the center of the nation's capital, rode up and down the settled seaboard from Maine to Georgia, and after the Revolution followed all the immigrant trails over the mountains into the great valleys beyond. He himself had no college training, but made himself a lover of learning and a scholar, as did not a few of the "circuit riders," who went wherever the farthest settler might go westward.

34

In America, as in England, the appeal of the Methodist faith and policy seemed to be mainly to the poor and the unlettered. So Asbury and his colaborers in the gospel vineyard promoted education along with religion. In fact, in connection with the highly emotional tone of their spiritual efforts, at their primitive log meetinghouses, they offered free instruction in spelling, figuring, and reading, feeling it a Christian duty to try to cure illiteracy at least in the fundamentals. But they and those who came after went farther, and by 1860 they had the South dotted with colleges of the liberal arts, some good and others not so good, but all representing the church's sense of educational responsibility to the needs of a rapidly growing constituency.

In January, 1872, at Memphis, Tennessee, delegates from seven southern states met. This assembly had been authorized by the general conference of the Southern Methodist Church two years before to take steps looking toward the establishment of a university for the youth of the church and the entire section. The Memphis convention, under the leadership of the ablest men of the church, dared to appoint a board of trustees and get out a charter under the laws of Tennessee for Central University to be located in this state, to be of "the highest grade" for "theological, literary, scientific, and professional studies," and to announce that "the sum of one million dollars is necessary to assure the object desired." I said "dared" because it was a sheer soaring expression of human faith, with very little, if any, solid ground of realism from which to take its flight. All the rules of practical consideration were against it, and their only dream of success lay in the faith of Christian men that Providence, God, must be on the side of those who would minister to great human needs—and surely this was one of the greatest—and that he would somehow bring his own supernatural power to their aid. And so they made a venture of faith greater perhaps than any other in the history of American education. They who made it, it must be recalled, were not starry-eyed visionaries, but in their own fields practical, successful men, great men, some of them, and all God-fearing, God-trusting, devout men who rarely doubted the final accomplishment of any task to which their church might commit itself.

But with all their faith in the intangibles, the imponderables, their world was against them when they set out to raise their million dollars for Central University. In 1872 in the South, the wounds of war were still fresh; reconstruction was at its worst; misguided, unscrupulous outsiders were arrogantly in the saddle, corrupting everything they touched and offending all the decencies the southern people had been accustomed to; former slaves were in positions of power; dire poverty, gaunt and grim, stalked the land, a money panic adding its confusion to an already wrecked economic system; there was secret and even open opposition from the smaller Methodist colleges; a yellow fever epidemic was desolating the leading cities of the South. What were men thinking of, men wise in the ways of life, even to dream of raising a million dollars for a university, however great the need? Yes, they were thinking, but the motive behind this thinking was faith in a Divinity that shapes worthy ends.

This they never gave up in spite of the initial failure to secure even enough funds to pay the expenses of the agents they sent out, and some of these agents were the most influential men in the church. In particular, there was one who never surrendered, Holland N. McTyeire, born in South Carolina, prepared for college at old Cokesbury Academy, finishing at Randolph-Macon College in Virginia, and finding his field of service in Alabama. As pastor of the Methodist church in Mobile he had in his membership the two Crawford cousins, lovely and intelligent, and as close in their comradeship as if they had been sisters. He took one of them to be his wife, and the other later married Cornelius Vanderbilt of New York, the "Old Commodore," chief among the financial barons in their golden age of power. The young preacher, by the various processes of ecclesiastical promotion, came at last to be a bishop of his church, and was called its leading "ecclesiastical statesman," with more prestige than perhaps any other of its bishops had and with the reputation of exercising the powers given him by church law rather ruthlessly when it seemed to him the thing to do.

The great bishop became ill and had to go to New York for treatment. During convalescence he was the guest of his wife's cousin, the Alabama wife of the Commodore. "Central University" was still on the bishop's heart, and he asked Mrs. Vanderbilt to talk to her husband about his university. No, but she would suggest to him that he speak to the bishop about the project. And here is the legend, though there is no reason to doubt its essential truth: The Commodore went up to his guest's room, and two men not unlike in temperament and ways of getting things done faced each other. The bishop could, under similar circumstances, have said, "The public be damned," and the Commodore could have summarily dismissed a group of professors whom he didn't like, as the bishop did later. The legend is that the talk went on until four o'clock in the morning, and closed with Cornelius Vanderbilt handing Holland McTyeire a check for $500,000. Chauncey M. Depew, the Commodore's confidential lawyer, reported Mr. Vanderbilt as saying as he made his gift: "I want to unite this country, and all sections of it, so all people shall be one, and a common country as they were before. Though I have never had any education, no man has felt the lack of it more than I have, and no man appreciates the value of it more than I do and believes more than I do in what it will do in the future. How much do you want?" And the bishop came back to Nashville with a check for $500,000 in his pocket, which assured him the buildings and grounds and apparatus for his university, to be increased within the next three years by $600,000 for its endowment.

And a church's dream based on faith came true in 1875. Cornelius Vanderbilt was so taken with the great bishop that he put certain conditions on his gift, conditions that assured him that the bishop would manage the affairs of the university as he himself managed his railroad enterprises; that is, the bishop must be president of the board of trustees for life, with veto power over the board's actions, at a salary of $3,000 a year in addition to his bishop's salary, a generous salary for any position in the South in 1873. Here was power, great power, put into the hands of one man in the carrying out of an important educational project. Fortunately, the bishop chose wise, experienced Landon C. Garland, his old teacher at Randolph-Macon College in Virginia, for the university's first chancellor. Dr. Garland had been president of three southern colleges—Randolph-Macon, the University of Alabama, and the University of Mississippi—and had taught at Washington College (Washington and Lee) in the valley of Virginia. Besides, in these different institutions he had taught English, philosophy, chemistry, mathematics, physics, and astronomy, the latter two being his specialties, and the legend about him is that he taught them all as a master. However, he put a strange condition on his acceptance—that there should never be dormitories during his administration of the institution, dormitories being a "curse" to college education.

These two, McTyeire and Garland, brought together in the first faculty an all-star team of men already made and widely known: LeRoy Broun in mathematics from the University of Georgia; James M. Safford from Tennessee in geology and botany; Alexander Winchell from Syracuse in geology; M. W. Humphries in Greek and E. S. Joynes in modern languages from Washington College (Washington and Lee); Andrew Adgate Lipscomb, ex-chancellor of the University of Georgia in criticism and philosophy; Nathaniel T. Lupton from the University of Alabama in chemistry; J. William Dodd, a famed Latinist from Kentucky; A. M. Shipp from the presidency of Wofford College in South Carolina. Here was what might be regarded as a great array of proved talent to greet the more than four hundred students who matriculated in October, 1875. There was much trumpeting, of course, over the sig-

38

nificance of the event, and deservedly so, because this opening of Vanderbilt was more significant, in the long run of its place and influence in southern education, than any other event since the Confederate war, and few events since have counted for so much.

The university was eight years old when I entered in 1883. Much simmering and settling down had gone on in these years, and a few storms had disturbed the serenity of these fresh academic shades. Tradition was in the making, however, and all-star teams do not get along together as they might. The players are apt to leave their appointed orbits and clash. The student body itself, as I found it in 1883, was a miscellaneous assortment of boys from all the southern states, not as miscellaneous in speech, social habits, and standards of living as in the variety of preparation to do college work in a way to meet the exacting demands of instructors who felt as one man that this new institution must do a better grade of work than any other southern institution. Vanderbilt had to live up to its finer buildings, its more adequate equipment, its larger endowment. It must be different in the quality of its work, and I believe it was. Indeed, with its yet-to-be-established educational policies, as a student I felt from the beginning something of an intellectual atmosphere congenial to sound scholarship, and I had the conviction that the loafers—and there were plenty of them—could not get by with shoddy work and would be finally eliminated for failure to meet accepted standards.

All in all, I found myself in a really exciting world from the start. There was no hazing in the sense of laying violent hands on the person of a new student. The sentiment of the student body would not have countenanced this method of initiating a new member into an older group. A man's person being sacred, he would have been justified in using his gun against even a prankish assault. Of course, though, there were other ways of making the stranger in the midst as uncomfortable as possible— for instance, going to his room, a dozen strong, giving him the silent treatment by gazing at him for fifteen minutes and then solemnly, unsmilingly filing out without having uttered a word. With some temperaments this could be even worse than a ducking, a shaving of the head, or a beating with paddles. There was a famous case in which a country boy was held up at the point of a pistol in a lonely hollow near the university and robbed of his watch and money. Recognizing some of the pretended bandits, he reported it to the police, and a lot of begging and explaining had to be done to prove it was just a "joke." It was the subject of mighty "bull sessions" for a while, with the general opinion that that was carrying things too far, and the perpetrators should have been required to pay a substantial fine instead of being let off. Yes, you might tease a new man, but there must be no laying on of hands. That sort of thing was to come later, but not in my day.

Greek-letter fraternities, secret societies, kept the institution, trustees, faculty, and student body in a subdued but tense state of near-explosive excitement. Such organizations were strictly forbidden by the laws of the university, and yet in the promenades through its very halls a demure maiden would mince her way along, wearing on her gentle bosom a fraternity pin that gleamed on a rosette of colored ribbons. The condemned societies were there, and everybody knew it except the authorities of the institution, and they were so blind that the more daring among the students wore their pins and bright-hued ribbons on all gala occasions. But the students were fighting, protesting all the time, charging that no group of men, trustees or faculty, had the right to forbid other men, especially college *men*, from joining any society they pleased so long as it was not guilty of breaking the laws of the land or violating the accepted code of morals. Thus youth was standing up for what it conceived to be its constitutional rights. I myself had my name on a petition for a charter from one of the national groups, with the understanding, however, that we would not accept *sub rosa* relationships, taking the position that we did not have to come to Vanderbilt, but if we did, we could not honorably do otherwise than accept its rules. I think we were right, and to their credit the heads of the fraternity to which we were applying for a charter agreed with us.

But by Christmas of the year of my entrance, 1883, the ban against fraternities was unexpectedly removed, and all the hidden chapters burst into the open in a blaze of glory to celebrate their victory over the powers of darkness and foes of the university's progress toward taking its proper place among the great institutions of the nation, from which place it had been kept so long by its failure to recognize the patent fact that there could be no real university without Greek-letter fraternities! I believe I was one of the noisy celebrants.

But there was never a dull moment on that campus when there was an election up. From every southern state the students had come, trained in the dark, devious, and sometimes violent ways by which their fathers and elder brothers had redeemed their state from scalawag and ex-slave, and had salvaged what war had left of a civilization which in their eyes grew increasingly fair the less of it that survived. To college they brought an enthusiasm for politics *per se*, and skill in not always scrupulous methods of accomplishing their ends. Each fraternity was a little Tammany club, whose leaders could have taught the sachems of New York wigwams how to get their man elected. Like night prowlers, groups would be in and out of the rooms of every boardinghouse, canvassing for their man as if his election were a life-or-death matter. To be in these campaigns was an exhilarating experience, though they did sometimes develop into near riots and did result once in a "free-for-all" in the main hall in front of the chapel while the faculty were sitting in judgment to select eight men to compete for oratorical honors, having taken out of the hands of the literary societies such selections because their choices were not on a merit basis, but on a partisan basis—not whether the man had oratorical ability, but whether his friends could gather enough votes for him!

Once they even went off the campus to help a Democratic club in a doubtful precinct redeem the city from the threat of a Negro or Republican alderman. The distress signal for about twenty voters was got to the students; and a young Mississippian, already wise in the ways of counting in some and counting out others, gathered the required number, regardless of their eligibility under the laws of the land. There was a lane of Negroes at the polling booth, noting particularly each white voter. As the boy from the black belt of the deepest South started in to vote with his group that had themselves assumed the rights of citizenship in a time of need, he was halted by a Negro leader with the inquiry, "Where's yo' credentials, white folks?" The Missisippian drew from his right hip pocket a long black revolver and from his left upper vest pocket a long-bladed knife, and presented them in the face of the Negro challenger with, "Will these do?" "Yas suh, Cap'n, dey'll do!" And they did, and the young South had brought to college another experience learned down home, lessons in practical politics which have even yet not been unlearned.

But withal these campus campaigns were stirring and warming to the blood of youth, and I do not recall that anybody found much fault with them—not even the defeated factions. Apparently it was the only way anybody knew of carrying on the business of the literary societies and those activities that pertained to the general interest of the student body. But when it came to handling such a matter as cheating on examinations, at once there was unity of spirit and purpose that fused all factions into one. So strong, moreover, was the sentiment of the whole student group against cheating that it was really neglible as a practice. It was not even talked of as a campus vice. There were only two or three cases of it during my entire career, and these were dealt with promptly and ruthlessly, and no one had a condoning word or even sympathy for the guilty. This sense of honor could not have been created as an institutional tradition in the few brief years of the history of Vanderbilt. No, it was something the students brought with them from their homes that made it easy for them to apply these standards to college life. I say "college life" because the sense of honor extended to other things where truthfulness was involved. There were drunkenness, gambling, and prostitution in that student body—alas! too much!—but when one was "hauled up" before the chancellor for an offense, he was expected to admit it, if guilty, and he usually did as far as his fellow students knew.

This attitude of loyalty to a sense of honor—not always sound, of course, among young students—showed itself acutely around an article that appeared in the first annual gotten out by the students at Vanderbilt. In it was a drastically critical attack on one of the departments of the university, which greatly offended the faculty and the trustees, who were meeting at commencement time. These demanded the name of the author, or heavy discipline for the whole staff, and this, in some cases, amounted to a withholding of diplomas. I had been appointed teaching fellow in Latin for the coming year; one of the trustees sent for me to say that my fellowship would not be awarded unless the name of the writer of the offending editorial was revealed. I think my reply to him was quite in keeping with the spirit of that student body. I told him I would be sorry to lose the fellowship, having looked forward to it for a long time, but I should be proud to lose it rather than break an honorable agreement entered into by the editorial staff of the annual—that what was printed in it was the united responsibility of all. But no discipline was inflicted on the staff, and the reasons for it leaked out. Our "old" chancellor stood before the board, saying that he for one would not be "a party toward having any one of these young gentlemen violate what he might regard as an honorable pledge. There are more important things than printing unfounded attacks on a department of the university, and one of them is to preserve a loyalty to a sense of honor among its students." The whole matter was dropped at once.

Dear Mr. Chancellor, your words, remembered after sixty years, got into young hearts on that far June day, to stay with them as a steadying influence through their lives. And there

43

were no drastic criticisms in the next annual or in the next, not because its editors feared the discipline of faculties or boards of trustees, but because you spoke of something which even they, in the heedlessness of their youth, knew might be more important than the university itself, and which it dared not leave out of the training of the students. Then, as always in life and speech, honor was the subject of your story. We knew, too, Mr. Chancellor, when you said those great words to the governing body of your institution, angered as they were at what they thought was an unjustifiable assault on the university, you lifted that frail, bent little body of yours till it became straight, and you seemed for the moment even a tall man, as we noted when you said great things to us in the chapel on Wednesday mornings. You were a sort of granite foundation on which were built enduring influences while the university was in the uncertain ferment of its young days. The providences that watch over the beginnings of universities were kind to Vanderbilt when they let you be chosen its first chancellor!

By 1883 that all-star team was already scattered into other orbits. The rumors rife on the campus were that most of them went away under pressure due to clashes with the administration, and the administration was Bishop Holland N. McTyeire, and everybody knew it. By temperament, aided and abetted by the provisions under which he held office, he could not do otherwise than exercise a one-man rule over the affairs of the university. Perhaps in that stage of its existence it was well that a man of his type was in control. Otherwise such a heterogeneous group of trustees and faculty as was brought together in 1875 could not have functioned effectively in shaping the destinies of the new institution. What was really needed was a strong, courageous, guiding hand, and the university found it in the bishop. Though he was like a rock when he once made up his mind, he could and did change it when the occasion demanded. The important thing is that by 1883 he was replacing the "stars" with whom he began with young men whose fortunes were yet to make. He created a chair of English and brought young W. M. Baskerville, Ph.D., Leipzig, from Wofford to fill it; he employed Charles Forster Smith, Ph.D., Leipzig, a Wofford graduate and instructor in the classics before going to Harvard and Germany to succeed Humphries in Greek when he went to Texas, carrying with him the only honorary degree ever conferred by Vanderbilt; and in 1886 he called W. F. Tillett to the deanship of the school of theology, and W. L. Dudley from Cincinnati to the chair of chemistry to follow Lupton, one of the elder "stars," and then in the same year James H. Kirkland, Ph.D., Leipzig, a student under Baskerville and Smith at Wofford and an instructor there before going to Germany. My guess is that these two men, Kirkland and Dudley, were under thirty.

Here was evidently a deliberate change in policy on the part of McTyeire and Garland, and with almost breathless speed which even the students felt, though they may not have known what it was all about, this change of policy began to show results. These men in the spirit of the daring of youth proved to be not only great and inspiring teachers, maintaining instructional standards of the very highest, but also men who at once proceeded to plan for the educational advancement of the institution—to make it what its founders dreamed it might be if it really served the South, a university. In less than ten years this group had abolished the old "school system" and substituted the class system, had done away with all introductory or preparatory classes, and had set up standards of entrance equal to those of the best eastern colleges; it had dared to be willing to wait on the establishment throughout the South of private preparatory schools and the development of the public high school, seeing the academic department reduced for several years to a mere token attendance, organizing intercollegiate athletics on such a basis as to give to them their educational values. These men drew within the range of influence every reputable institution in the southern states, and

45

propagandized for such standards as would separate college, university, and preparatory education, sharply and definitely—a propagandizing that resulted in the Southern Association of Secondary Schools and Colleges in 1895. Potent beyond any other influence in southern education, I believe, was this extraordinary group of young men brought together at Vanderbilt from 1881 to 1886.

And we, the students, were aware that something was happening on the campus, and through the leadership of this group of youngish men. The overly dignified aloofness of the older group was replaced by an easy friendliness. Any of them might stop you on the campus for a sort of man-to-man chat about the last promenade or oratorical contest or the recent baseball game with Sewanee, or the coming track meet. Dudley, the bachelor, a handsome, fascinating man, the very last word in stylish dress, kept open house in his apartments on the campus. There would be on his table pipes, cigarettes, cigars, chewing tobacco (*sic!*), and he would indulge in any way with you. The talk would be about your work with him—he was a brilliant lecturer and was growing into fame by things he was doing in the field of industrial chemistry—or about anything a young student might be interested in.

At the end of my second year Charles Forster Smith, to whom I had never before spoken, called me aside in the hall as I was going into the office to matriculate. "Why aren't you taking Greek? I understand you are good in languages." I was no little flattered by his recognition of a sort of knack I had at learning a foreign language. My reply was, "Why, Doctor, I don't even know the Greek alphabet!"

"Get you a copy of Goodwin's Grammar, Xenophon's *Anabasis*, selections from Herodotus, and enter the second introductory class for the *Anabasis* and my first-year class for the Herodotus, and see what you can do."

I did, completing both the subclass and the first-year class in a year, and his second- and third-year classes the next year. And what reading and writing of Greek during these two

46

years! Homer, parts of both the *Iliad* and *Odyssey*, Xenophon, Herodotus, Thucidydes, selections from Plato, a play each from Aristophanes, Euripides, Sophocles, some lyrics from Pindar, an oration or two from Demosthenes and Lysias. There it is. Believe me or not, it can be done in two years if you have a teacher like Charles Forster Smith who believes you can and helps you do it! Anyway, that's the kind of man who was teaching Greek at Vanderbilt, and it was a very much alive subject because he was very much alive.

William J. Vaughan was the last of the "stars" called to Vanderbilt. He came in 1882 from the University of Alabama after a long period of distinguished service there. An extraordinary man in personality and scholarship, he had the spirit of eternal youth; and, though well past middle age, he fitted into the new group as one of them. He knew twelve languages, including Russian, was an authority in Sanskrit and Semitic philology, and had a collection of Napoleonic and American history material hardly surpassed by any private library in America. His students who went for their doctorates to the eastern universities would say he knew more math than any of the famous men under whom they got their degrees. A wise, kindly, humorous man he was, whom all students honored for his patience, his sympathetic understanding of their troubles in mathematics, and yet also for high requirements of achievement. I was never a star man in his department, and yet when the final grades were posted on the bulletin board, he had given me a 2, a high grade. I knew I hadn't earned it. It must be a mistake! I went to him to ask if the grade was not a mistake and if it was already posted on the university books. He said it was already posted and was no mistake.

"Now, Doctor, how did you make that grade for me? *I* didn't." "Snyder," he replied, with that engaging smile and twinkle of his eyes, "I gave you that grade for the brilliancy of your ignorance—you went wrong in more intelligent ways than any other man I have ever taught!"

From then on he admitted a boy into his friendship, and as the boy grew and matured and as his understanding professor went on into the sunset, he was to be grateful that he had known William J. Vaughan. He, too, was of the forces making for unity as a new university was in process of becoming —when it needed all the unifying influences that emanate from great and wise human personalities.

Any sensitive student could not help being aware in those days of the middle eighties that there was developing around the institution what might well be called "a literary atmosphere." Baskerville, Germany-trained philologist, had by nature and a cultivated taste a rare and sure appreciation of literary values not only in English literature but also in Greek, Roman, German, and French literatures; and what is more, he was a watchman always on the lookout for what was promising in current literature, especially if it was by Southerners and had to do with southern life. He was among the first to recognize and approve the new stars rising so fast and in such numbers in the firmamant of literary effort in this section— Charles Egbert Craddock, Joel Chandler Harris, Sidney Lanier, George W. Cable, Richard Malcolm Johnson, Maurice Thompson, Thomas Nelson Page, James Lane Allen. He might come into the classroom on almost any day, those fine eyes of his all ashine and that handsome face aglow, pulling nervously at his moustache in his excitement, and there would be no recitation on historical English grammar that day; or if it were *Hamlet*, even that would be forgotten, for he would say: "Young gentlemen, you just must read that latest story in *Scribner's*, *The Century*, or *Harper's*, by Craddock, or Page, or Allen—it has the qualities of real literature." And then, in a manner that made one eager to read the story, he would tell what these qualities were, passing into a vivid discussion of what he called the "Southern Renascence." His own interest was contagious with many of us, contagious enough to be the topic of many a "bull session" and of not a few articles in the college monthly. Baskerville himself wrote a series of booklets on southern writers, and after his death his old students of the eighties completed the series as a memorial volume to their old teacher who showed that their South was up and coming not only in the industrial way but in the intellectual and literary way as well. In fact, he added greatly to his service in this respect by bringing to the campus for readings and lectures some of the very men who were then making southern literature of a superior sort—Cable, Maurice Thompson, and Thomas Nelson Page I recall, but I am sure there were others. So Vanderbilt was offering its students a variety of excitements to make life interesting and memorable.

On an early morning in the latter part of May in 1886 I was crossing the campus. I was well content because I had settled a matter that had troubled me for some time. The manager of the Methodist Publishing House had sent for me again, this time to offer me the position of assistant bookkeeper at a salary of $75 per month—not a bad salary for a twenty-one-year-old youth in 1886. I had made up my mind to accept it—just why I do not now recall, but perhaps the family fortunes were at a low ebb. Certainly my acceptance could not be due to anything at the university. The three years had been happy years. I really believe I loved books and the study of them. To many a class have I gone with eager expectancy, and examinations didn't scare or irk me. The truth is I rather liked the challenge of them, wanting to see what the "old man" could do to us. I had settled it that I was not going to be a lawyer or a minister, though these decisions had nothing to do with my going again into business. I think in one of our student talk sessions I advanced the big idea that I liked being in college because it "ministered to the intellectual life." No one challenged me to a definition, and I am not sure I could have given one. All I probably meant was that I liked books and the men who taught them and I did find very great satisfaction in my association with both. Then, too, I think I fairly reveled in the comradeship with my fellow students, and I know I resolutely refused to confine myself to the small group that made up my fraternity as I had seen many others deliberately do. In a word, college life suited me, and I was getting on well in it.

Suddenly a big, deep voice boomed out from a bench under a maple tree: "Oh, Henry, come here!" It was Bishop Mc-Tyeire, between whose family and mine had been a long friendship. "Sit down. What's this I hear about your quitting the university?" With something of the pride of a boy who has been flattered I told my story. He had in his hand a long shepherd's crook, which he brought down with force, sending it six or eight inches deep into the soft bluegrass turf; in a voice of command that those who knew always expected when he wanted something, he issued his orders: "No, you will not do it! I have other plans for you. My son-in-law Baskerville wants you for his fellow in English when you finish next year, and after being a year or two with him, you could go to Germany for your Ph.D. Baskerville thinks you would make a real English scholar." Now, flattered again, what was a youngster to do with a great bishop wanting to make a scholar of him! It was that conversation under the maples on that May morning that fixed my career and set the whole course of my future. I not only do not regret the change brought about by that conversation, but I am grateful to the bishop for it. His son-in-law took me in charge, and with him I was to remain not just another student, but rather a young disciple to whom he gave unfailing guidance and friendship.

In that last undergraduate year it was Baskerville, Smith, John J. Tigert, and Edward E. Barnard. Tigert was a young minister teaching political economy, logic, and mental and moral philosophy, carrying in his small head—about which he was sensitive—mounted on a large vigorous body, the best set of usable brains I have ever encountered. The ease with which he could handle the great things of philosophical thinking produced a sense of awe among his students. It was fairly exhilarating to see a mind like his in action.

Now Barnard didn't rank above an instructor in astronomy,

50

but was probably the most widely known man on the campus. With the best pair of eyes then looking toward the starry heavens through a telescope, he was making discoveries that labeled his name all over the skies, carrying his fame around the world. Seeing my teacher late one night by his telescope on the back campus, I politely asked him how he was getting on. "Paying the mortgage on my home," was the answer. A few weeks later the newspapers announced that he had seen and recorded a strange visitor in the night skies that nobody in all the world had seen before, and had received an award of several thousand dollars.

Smith in Greek, Baskerville in English, Tigert in philosophy, and Barnard in astronomy—any institution, young or old, that gave its students a chance to study with four such men during their last undergraduate year was a great institution, and Vanderbilt was only twelve years old!

Out of a sort of chaos inevitable in the founding of a new university the students themselves were sensing that order was evolving, and they were beginning to take a pride in their university in spite of much grumbling and faultfinding. It was finding itself while they were discovering it in the able men of its faculty, none abler anywhere, in the standards of scholarship required, and in the foundation-building and far-reaching reforms being advocated. They closed the foreword of their first annual, named *The Comet* in honor of the young astronomer who was bringing fame to the university as well as to himself, with these words:

If we succeed in causing our friends in the North and East to understand that in Vanderbilt they have a future rival, and, above all, if we succeed in making Southern men realize that here in their doors is a growing institution devoted to true university training, we shall be more than satisfied, and shall feel that our work has been well done.

We knew we were a part of something big in the making and felt called to tell the world so. I, as editor of the students' monthly magazine in '87, did it, as also did others. For did we not have all the departments that great universities have— academic, theological, medical, dental, engineering, law, and pharmacy? Then we had fraternities and intercollegiate athletics, and clubs were springing up fast—bachelors' club, eating clubs, tennis clubs, glee club.

And also, as young as we were, didn't we already have legends and traditions? That ablest of professors with the smallest head—with him didn't we refute the contention of the famous phrenologist Fowler that big heads meant big brains, which, in turn, meant the highest intelligence? Did not our professor with the little head have the top intelligence among all the rest? Shall we ever forget the morning when two white Republicans, Senator John Sherman of Ohio and Governor Hawkins, appeared in our chapel when they were fresh from conferences with Negro politicians? They looked unexpectedly decent, too, but couldn't be since they were Republicans! That visit of Grover Cleveland, a Democrat at last in the White House, to our campus, accompanied by his beautiful new bride! "They tell" that the carriage stopped in front of the stone steps of Wesley Hall, from which platform our aged chancellor, a gentleman if there ever was one, made a gallantly chivalrous address, chiefly to the lady sitting by the president's side in the carriage. From her husband came no other response than a gruff, grunted "Drive on!" to the coachman, and it was decided then and there that the radical Populist-Democrats were probably right—*he* was no Democrat. but a Republican "wolf in sheep's clothing," and no "gentleman." Add to this the account of how the midget of the campus, flanked by two stalwart bodyguards, horsewhipped one of its giants; the famous political campaigns in electing men to the Bachelor of Ugliness degree; and the epic story of the "big fight" in the main hall in front of the chapel, in which several professors got facial bruises and one a lovely "shiner" in their efforts to separate the combatants. Could older universities, those even a hundred and more years old, do any better than this in the way of legendary lore that gives romantic, human continuity to an institution's history? And yet we were only twelve years old, but we were coming fast in accumulating the memories that make a university great with its alumni.

One other story is still told—how a Mississippian, still rather wild in his cups on a Sunday morning, boarded the mule-drawn street car, ejected the driver, who was also the conductor—allowing him, however, to run along beside his car—and proceeded to deliver with an excessive show of courtesy his church-going passengers to their appropriate churches. This was too much for the university authorities—and on Sunday, too. So our Mississippian was given a permanent ticket of leave back home, where such things were not taken too seriously. He was to have represented Vanderbilt in the coming state oratorical contest. I yielded to the patriotic pressure of both fraternity and literary society and accepted the position of emergency substitute, just ten days before the contest. I wrote my speech in one day, memorized it the next, rehearsed it before the professor of "elocution" the third. I was awarded the medal as "the best college orator in the state" for that year, was carried out of the hall of the House of Representatives in the state capitol down the stone steps on the shoulders of my admirers, the noisy, boisterous group being escorted out of town by a squad of policemen. So, in the words of my friends, I closed my undergraduate years "in a blaze of glory"; but, believe it or not, neither then nor since have I had any special vanity over any skill I may have as a public speaker.

But to my disappointment I did not get the position of teaching fellow in English under Baskerville, the graduate student holding it deciding to stay on another year. However, Kirkland sent for me to offer me a teaching fellowship in Latin with him, and this I am sure was better for me. I had never had a course under him, having completed the undergraduate requirements in Latin before he came to Vanderbilt. It was a good change for me in many ways, particularly in beginning to learn something of the art of teaching through the close, careful, definite, syntactical methods then in vogue in Latin instruction.

For the three years that followed there were only two of us taking advanced graduate work in Latin, Greek, and English. Our four instructors were all Leipzig Ph.D.'s, and I am sure if two men were ever completely "Leipzigized" they were Chiles Clifton Ferrell and Henry Nelson Snyder. Smith in Greek, Kirkland in Latin, Baskerville in English, and Walter Deering in Gothic gave us huge doses of classical, Germanic, and English philology that I am sure was precisely what was poured into them at Leipzig. All reference books recommended were written by German scholars. Indeed, Deering conducted his course in Gothic entirely in the German language to make this impression of being "Leipzigized" even more real. The truth is, if the spirit and methods of the German universities were the important thing in American graduate instruction, I doubt whether any other two men in any other university got more of it or from more competent scholars than did Ferrell and I. And we were exhilarated by it, for neither of us had yet come to the doubting, critical stage with reference to much of what we were getting.

But it was not all Leipzig—no, not by a good deal. In a little house back of the campus a South Carolina mother was making a home for her bachelor son Jimmie. After being put through the rubbers for two hours by her "Jimmie"—our Dr. Kirkland—which included all sorts of excursions into Latin lore, concluding with thirty minutes of conversation in Latin, we would be called in to dinner. We would hear from that gentle lady of the Old South how she had still the original first silver dollar which this great scholar, her boy, gave to her to save for that Leipzig degree, and we would see a mist in the eyes of our hard, exacting professor and a gleam in the mother's eyes that told of a sacred romance of love and sacrifice. We were graduate students for the time in the deeper meanings of human relationships, and our professor, even as a scholar, gained in influence over us.

Then Smith might casually say to us one day, "You will have tea with us tonight after the seminar," and we knew what that meant. After we had gone meticulously through a half dozen lines of Homer in a way that lifted the curtain on the secrets of an ancient language and culture, his South Carolina wife, the daughter of a member of the first faculty of Wofford, herself a campus product, would appear to call us to tea with an unaffected grace and charm that made two young students feel quite at home. At that table our professor of Greek became the South Carolina gentleman from Abbeville County.

Baskerville in that princely way he had, after one of his most scientific discussions of some disputed passage in *Beowulf* or *Andreas*, would have a message from Mrs. Baskerville inviting us, just the two of us, to dinner tomorrow, which was Sunday. Mrs. Baskerville was the daughter of Bishop Mc-Tyeire, himself born and bred in South Carolina and educated in Virginia. Her mother was from Mobile, Alabama, and she herself was a woman of exceptional attractiveness and intelligence. That dinner in its abundance, in the beauty and taste of its serving, and in the scintillating talk from our professor and his lady furnished experiences that were of the nature of graduate courses in aspects of life that each of us was to need.

Ferrell was a Kentuckian, and I a Middle Tennessean. He went to Leipzig, and there brilliantly achieved his doctorate. The University of Mississippi called him to its service. At the end of my third year of graduate work and teaching, I had made all my arrangements for going to Göttingen, not Leipzig. Then, only a month before I was to leave, came that telegram from Wofford in South Carolina, stating I had been elected professor of English, and Göttingen was postponed till a few years later.

W. M. Baskerville, Charles Forster Smith, and James H. Kirkland, you were great scholars, and we knew it, Ferrell

55

and I. We learned much from you in the way of scholarship that is unforgettable; but that other course, when each of you was yourself in the gracious atmosphere of your home, is also unforgettable. If I have raised the question as to whether any other two graduate students in America ever had more competent instructors in the fields of English, Latin, and Greek, I raise also the question as to whether any other students were taken into the friendship of three such princely gentlemen while they were getting ready to live as well as teach.

3

CURRICULUM, FACULTY, STUDENTS—
"OLD STYLE"

IN MIDSUMMER of 1890 I was elected professor of English and German at Wofford College, Spartanburg, South Carolina, at a salary of $1,500 and a house, rent free, after the first year. I accepted the position.

It was in the late afternoon of September 19, 1890, when my wife and I stepped off the train from Atlanta. The amosphere with the help of the sun was softly golden with the dust that came from the deep-red earth. The rolling red hills, the scraggy pines of the forests along the way, the scrawny stalks of corn in the fields, the leaves of the cotton already brown while its snowy harvest was bursting into bloom—these together presented a rather vivid contrast to the lush greenness of the Middle Tennessee landscape even in the late September days. My first impression was that we had come into a barren land, lacking in that rich beauty which is the mark of the dark earth where the bluegrass grows.

And when we stepped out on the platform of the little station, I felt we had come to a country town. To be sure, Nashville then was not a big city, but still it was a city. But Spartanburg as I first saw it fifty-six years ago looked like a sprawling village. This view was confirmed by the rickety hack in which we rode to the home where we were to spend our first twelve months in South Carolina. The streets were narrow, crooked, unpaved, dusty; the buildings along the way were small, ramshackle, and greatly needing paint. However, when we drew up to the home in which we were to be paying guests, we saw an ancient white house in the best traditions of southern architecture—three stories in height, piazzas on the second and third stories, stretching almost the entire length of the front, four great square columns supporting the roof of the piazzas. Here were dignity and distinction, reminding one of the time when the South built homes for both comfort and beauty. I felt better, though my impression was that this stately home had no place on a narrow side street of a small town but should have been set on a green knoll, encompassed with great oaks and pines and hickories and overlooking a winding river.

September 20 was not only another day, but a different day. During the night a fall rain had come up. The golden haze of the afternoon before was all swept away by a bitter east wind that blew gusts of cold rain beneath your umbrella and made your overcoat not much protection. It was a gray, dreary, drippy day to step out into. The sidewalks on the street were unpaved, and the walks on the campus no better than just paths. And such mud! Red and sticky beyond any I have known.

It was a bleak campus that I entered. The buildings, the main building and five professors' homes, seemed old and uncared for. But these homes were distinguished-looking buildings in the best traditions of early American architecture— red brick, two stories high, square, with a columned piazza nearly across the front of each. They stood in a sort of parabolic curve on the flanks of the main building. It was plastered with a dingy yellow stucco, but its spacious frontage, with a noble piazza and lofty twin towers, was all distinction and dignity—an academic structure appealingly appropriate in design and beauty. I had to stop in front of it for a while in spite of the chill and the wet. Its sheer impressiveness held me —an impressiveness which was to grow with the years.

Walking up what was no better than a muddy pathway to the broad piazza, supported by square columns and thickly covered at each end with rambler rosebushes, I knocked on the door of the home of the president who was to be my chief for the next twelve years and my neighbor for the next seventeen. A faded red brick house it was, looking somehow much older than its thirty-seven years, but on a smaller scale it had the unassuming dignity of the main building itself. Already it was one of the famous homes of South Carolina. And I mean famous, for if you asked any intelligent South Carolinian of that day who were the three "great" of the state, he would promptly inform you: John C. Calhoun, Wade Hampton, and James H. Carlisle. Yet when someone wanted to write his "Life," he refused to permit it with the remark: "What is there to write? I have been only a teacher." "A mere teacher," yes, but one who, though he rarely left the campus of this small college and though he was known by sight only to his students—and those not many—and a few others, had so profoundly impressed himself upon the life of the state that he was honored and reverenced as no other living South Carolinian was—one other illustration of the miracle of the influence of a great human personality.

Something of this I felt as he himself met me at the door, conducted me into his study through a wide hall, almost bare of furnishings, and with a gentle, old-world simple courtesy quickly made the young recruit to his faculty feel quite at home. He towered above me, six feet four and one-half inches in height. A long black coat hanging loosely about a large angular frame made him appear even taller. He had a florid complexion; full iron-gray beard, thin enough, though, for one to see the contour of his face through it; hair that hung over his collar to his shoulders; and a pair of large deep-blue eyes that illuminated his whole countenance when he smiled. I knew I was in the presence of real greatness, though I realized that he was taking the measure of the youngest man he had ever welcomed to a full professorship at Wofford. I was just twenty-five.

When our brief hour of conversation was over, I found that we had talked little about myself and my new duties, but much about his old friends: Bishop McTyeire, the president of the board of trustees of Vanderbilt, and his former Wofford colleagues and students there—Dean Shipp, Smith, Baskerville, and Kirkland. Possibly this was his way of testing the intelligence quotient of his new instructor. At any rate, I do not recall that I thought for a moment of the impression I was making on him. If I had any self-consciousness in this direction—which would have been natural enough in the case of a young man for the first time in the presence of his college president—it all vanished in the impression he was making on me—an impression of sheer simple human greatness that, with a sort of natural humility, never seemed aware of itself.

I did take time, though, as a lover of books, to glance around at those book-lined walls. It was a large room, eighteen by twenty feet, and the height of the ceiling was at least fifteen feet. Each wall was lined with books quite to the ceiling. A ladder stood against one set of shelves. I was later to discover that it was an amazing miscellaneous collection, covering almost every field of knowledge; basic in it however, were standard books in the fields in which he taught and in which naturally he was most deeply interested—mathematics, ethics, astronomy, and the Bible. There were only a few works of fiction, and these few were of a religious flavor, if not directly of religious intent.

And so these were my first impressions of the man under whom I was to serve. It didn't take much insight to divine that he was a man richly endowed intellectually and possessed beyond most of those unbeatable qualities of wisdom and goodness—a man who did not know he was richly endowed and certainly did not suspect that he was either good or wise, though everybody else might know him for what he was and reverence him for it. I venture to raise the question right here: Are we growing men of his sort in the academic world now? Or do they, like other forms of greatness, come but rarely—once in a generation or so and then as a sort of miracle to surprise us with their rarity?

Then, too, are such men recognized now or even appreciated when they appear as unfamiliar visitors on a college campus, strangers among a faculty group of hard, conventionalized academic specialists to whom teaching in a real sense is an interruption or even an irritating burden? Mark Hopkins and his famous log are coming in for no little sneering lambasting as educational sinners of the first rank. The lawyer president of a large mid-western university is loudly blowing taps over their graves, clamorously proclaiming that such men as Mark Hopkins are sheer poison in the field of education and should be promptly eliminated from the present scheme of higher education. Over at Annapolis an exuberantly cocksure educational Columbus wants to be in at the killing off of such men. No, the "Hopkinses" and the "Carlisles" didn't have time to shriek much about their educational reforms; they were too busy making men and scholars—men who, when they left the classrooms of such teachers to go to the graduate and professional schools, knew enough to measure some of the instructors they found there—specialists that seemed little in contrast with the men they had known in their undergraduate days.

Yes, it will be a tragic day when American education ceases to grow men of the Mark Hopkins sort; and those who will suffer most from their lack will be the students themselves, for the college will be an intellectual as well as an emotional desert unless there are instructors who are both scholars and men of contagious greatness of personality. Well will it be with any college that has even a few. For such as these there is simply no substitute under heaven. I say this with a conviction that started with my college days, sixty-one years ago, and has grown in strength through my years as instructor, professor, college president, and as one who to the best of his ability has tried to study trends and pressures through more than half a century.

I have watched these trends and pressures, not as a sideline quarterback, but as a player in the heat and dust and fight of the game, and I have seen most of them come and go, and come and go, again and again. The threat of the junior college, private and public; the menacing shadow of the great state universities and the huge endowed university foundations; the invasion of the vocational conception of education; the "elective" disease that for a long time undermined the health of American higher education; the unremitting assaults of every known form of fantastic faddism upon the curriculum and aims of the college; the cult of numbers and bigness; the ear-splitting trumpet blowing of the promotionist presidents and hired public relations men in the interest of the side lines of campus life; the struggle to preserve academic freedom and institutional individuality against mechanized death at the hands of the standardizing agencies—these all came and went, and came again whenever the colleges were controlled by the aberrations of one mind, and that mind enveloped with the halo around a man called "the president," who might feel that nobody had learned anything in all the long yesterdays in the history of education, but that it was given to him by some special dispensation of insight and understanding to rectify the educational errors of the past and substitute "the light that never was, on sea or land."

And yet the great teacher, "the notorious Mark Hopkins," to quote from one of them, is still the high man on any campus, big or little—Kittredge at Harvard, Shorey at Chicago, Trent at Columbia, Phelps at Yale, Wilson at Princeton, Corson at Cornell, and, no anticlimax, Carlisle at Wofford. These are not local but national figures in the field of higher education. Wherever they were, or are, there is education at its best; and where they are not, there isn't any except when the student himself takes the bit in his teeth, so to speak, and, in spite of the obstacle courses in his way, on his own becomes an educated man. It can be done; it is done on every college campus in America by students who fail to find a leadership where they have a right to expect it.

Now this excursion in praise of the tribe of Hopkins is neither a diversion nor an interlude in what I have in mind, but a proper introduction to my colleagues of the Wofford faculty of 1890. The June meeting of the board of trustees seemed to have been signalized by a faculty house cleaning, the resignations of four out of six having been accepted and a sort of new deal started. When F. C. Woodward left in 1888 to head the department of English at the University of South Carolina, it looked as if Wofford's line of great teachers had been broken. Two years before, Professor W. W. Duncan had been elected bishop in the Southern Methodist Church, and one year later Dr. A. Coke Smith had been called to Vanderbilt to teach mental and moral science to academic students, and to be an example to the ministerial students of how a real preacher should preach. And so, with one exception, the successors did not measure up to Wofford standards; a group of relatively small men rattled around in chairs occupied not so long ago by Smith, Baskerville, Kirkland, and the men I have just named. When the wreckage was cleared away, all that was left of the faculty of 1889-90 were the president, Dr. Carlisle, who had been professor since the opening of the college in 1854 and president since 1875, Daniel Alston DuPré, and Joseph Augustus Gamewell.

These three men were of the Wofford family, so to speak, DuPré being the son of Dr. Warren DuPré, a member of the original faculty as professor of the natural sciences, who went to Martha Washington College, Abingdon, Virginia, as its president, and Gamewell being the son of a member of the first board of trustees of the college. DuPré came to the campus as an eight-year-old boy and grew up on it, while Gamewell was present as a four-year-old youngster at the laying of the cornerstone of the college. Both as sixteen-year-old boys had served in the Confederate army in its very last days. So the saving remnant of the faculty might be described as an all-Wofford team of veterans, who were graduates of the college. DuPré was of the class of '69 and Gamewell of the class of '71. When I first came to know them in faculty meetings around the table in the library, called the "reading room," they were in their early forties, each having come up from the "Subcollegiate Department." Ancestrally and of course habitually they were "gentlemen" in the very best sense of that greatly abused word. But the fact is they simply couldn't be anything else. They were of old low-country South Carolina stock, English and Huguenot, possessing those qualities that Southerners used to expect of their men of class—"breeding, courage, and piety." DuPré, professor of natural philosophy, spent a year studying physics, chemistry, and geology in Edinburgh, not a bad place to study science of any kind in the early eighties; while Gamewell took time out every now and then in the summer to go to Cornell or Hopkins "to brush up," as he called it, on his Latin! With the years these two men became "Uncle Dan" and "Uncle Gus" to their students, and taught them the art of gracious and gentle living, winning, without effort, love and reverence. One felt they earned their salary by being who they were as much as by their teaching in the classrooms.

There was one other Wofford man on the faculty, the financial agent of the college and acting professor of metaphysics and political science, the Rev. John Carlisle Kilgo. He had been in the service of the college only one year when I first met him. Having left the institution at the end of the sophomore year because of bad eyes, he joined the South Carolina conference of the Methodist Church, and in four or five years was recognized as the most promising of its younger members. He was about thirty when we came together on the Wofford campus. Not tall, five feet seven inches perhaps, very thin, a little stooped, with one shoulder lifted above the other, he was not an impressive figure of a man. But when one looked into his face, particularly when thought and feeling were aroused, that was decidedly something else. With clear-cut, classic lines, high cheekbones, mobile mouth, lips not too thin, fine gray eyes under a spacious forehead, his face had everything an ambitious actor in big roles might covet. And he was an actor by nature, and because of this about the best raconteur

I have ever known. A mimic of the first rank, he could drama-
tize to perfection the voice and gestures of almost anyone;
and, with an amazing fund of firsthand experiences, he was a
teller of tales, humorous, witty, sentimental, and pathetic, that
would have brought fame and fortune on stage or platform
had he chosen to sell his gifts for money. But he was "called to
preach," and the pulpit became his throne of power.

To the gifts that I have named he brought a sincerely search-
ing and uplifting eloquence. Without any previous training,
with perhaps only a background of reading—though it should
be said that he was a voracious reader, devouring with a fierce
intensity whatever he set his mind to—with the intellectual
daring that was his by nature, he took over the department
of metaphysics and political science—three hours in the junior
year and four in the senior. And I found that there were no
soft spots either in the texts or the methods he used. A "natural"
he was in the way he had of stirring other minds, not a bad
quality in a teacher.

After about a year's association, he asked me if I would go
through my English course with him as it was laid down in
the catalogue. Not really knowing what I was about, but acting under the impulse I had then to teach anybody English who
would let me, I said, "Come along." And he came. I shall never
forget the fighting seances we had, some of them lasting until
two in the morning. I had to defend all the high gods of English literature from his assaults upon their right to their thrones.
He accepted nothing, took nothing for granted, but waded in
with sarcasm and ridicule to topple them from the seats of the
mighty. Tennyson was "just sweetened water," Browning
"hiding kindergarten religious stuff in words jumbled so that
nobody could understand what they meant." "Dickens, Thackeray, George Eliot were trying to draw human beings that
never existed except in the sentimental slush created by the
writers themselves." Matthew Arnold was "a bloodless infidel
that hadn't the courage to say out loud that he believed in
nothing but himself." Shakespeare was "too much sound and

65

fury." Carlyle—"Now there was somebody. What a preacher he might have made, had he not fooled himself into being a writer, a wordmonger." The young English instructor had his hands full trying to keep the citadel of English literature from being overthrown, but it was a greatly worth-while experience. Kilgo went to Trinity College in 1892 as president, to become the stormy petrel of North Carolina education for twenty years until elected bishop of the Methodist Church in 1911.

Then there was Edsin Boone Craighead, a big, blustery, energetic Midwesterner from Missouri—a graduate of Central College at Fayette, an institution of the same general type as Wofford. He had his M.A. in the classics from Vanderbilt, went to Germany for further study, but didn't take to the philological, scientific approach to his favorite fields, Greek and Latin, in vogue there. Hating the German universities and their methods, he wound up at the University of Paris, where he stayed for a year, thoroughly appreciative of the more or less literary treatment of his favorites. He was fresh from Paris when he came to Wofford at the same time with me.

In addition to his classroom interests in Greek and French —and they were strong and active—he carried a side line in the way of oratory. He considered De Quincey the greatest prose writer in the English language; and William E. Munsey, an East Tennessee Methodist preacher, who concealed the spiritual message of his sermons in the coruscating stardust of brilliant rhetoric, Craighead esteemed only second to De Quincey and would often affirm that, had Munsey been born in London or Boston, he would have been ranked with the great masters of English prose. By a proper mixture of De Quinceyan rhythms and cadences with splashes of the Munseyan starry rhetoric, in the three years he was at Wofford he became famous as a public speaker, widely sought after and heard with generous approval by South Carolina audiences.

His was a restless soul, and I soon divined that the four walls of any classroom would be too confining for him. And so after only three years at Wofford he was called in 1893 to the presidency of the newly opened Clemson Agricultural and Mechanical College—a classicist at the head of a technological trades school. Then in succession during the next twenty years he held the presidency of his alma mater, Central; the State Teachers College at Warrensburg, Missouri; Tulane University; and the University of Montana—a quite varied career, but in keeping with his ambitious restlessness in the field of education.

The third new outsider to join me at Wofford at this time, 1890, was Samuel R. Pritchard, M.A. from the University of South Carolina and formerly an instructor there. He was a quiet, low-voiced, dry, precise, exacting, competent man, just the kind of man who ought to be the professor of mathematics that he was, though he was a constant source of surprise by knowing more of other things than one would suspect in a mathematician. Mathematics became a highly respected study at Wofford under his teaching. But he, too, didn't stay long— only four years—going to the Virginia Polytechnic Institute as professor of physics. He was later promoted to the deanship of that important Virginia institution.

I must name here another man who also came to Wofford in 1890 as a teacher of English in the preparatory department ("Fitting School," as it was then called)—a tall, thin, shy, timid man who had graduated in 1889—William Preston Few. He wanted to go to Harvard, but was a little short on Old English, he said, and asked if I would not help him out in this phase of English. Of course I would, and every Saturday during the year 1890 we worked at it, and I knew I was helping in the making of a scholar. After assisting me with the freshmen for two years, he went on to Harvard, receiving his Ph.D. He found a place as professor of English at Trinity College, Durham, later to become its president when Kilgo was elected bishop. Then in 1924 it was he who organized and developed Duke University when James Buchanan Duke poured forth his millions. President Few will take permanent rank among the educational statesmen of the South.

Now I have named these seven men that I found at Wofford to give emphasis to a conviction from which nothing has been able to shake me during all the years of my experience and observation, and that is, *a college is its faculty*. It may have everything else, buildings whose stately towers point to the stars, libraries, laboratories of more than adequate proportions, endowments and financial resources heaped into the millions, but if it is not rich in great teachers, with all its wealth it is poor indeed, and its greatness is not as an educational institution, but as a splendid physical plant, and that is something else. But this Wofford to which I came in 1890 was a little college by every material standard of measurement—student body, buildings, equipment, financial resources—but it was a great college in its way of conserving and handing on spiritual and intellectual values to aspiring youth and at the same time giving them an austere discipline in the processes of thinking. This Wofford did because it had on its faculty Carlisle, DuPré, Gamewell, Kilgo, Craighead, Pritchard, Few, and their kind before and since. When I sit in on educational forums, panels, work conferences, as I frequently do, and listen to the brittle, hesitant, fumbling speech of "experts," using a conventionalized jargon that may mean much to them but little to the rest of us, these men whose names I have called walk again in the flesh to indict education of high crimes and misdemeanors, chief among them being the thought that any kind of mechanized contrivance of method or aim can take the place of—Mark Hopkins, if you please.

4

EUROPEAN INTERLUDE

1900

AFTER TEN YEARS of teaching—and they were enthusiastic, happy years—I began to be a little uneasy about my "extra-curricular activities," what they might in the end do to my scholarship. About this I was always sensitive, feeling that a teacher who let anything cause a relaxation in it was in peril of losing his academic soul. Such a feeling was of my very temperament, but, in addition, it had been ingrained into me at Vanderbilt. Any man with the instructors I had had who wavered at this point was a sinner in their sight and guilty of disloyalty of a base sort. Now women's clubs were beginning to flourish right and left, and, whatever their aims, they had to have now and then a "lecture." Even the men were having their clubs with an intellectual flavor, as the women were; and they, too, wanted lecturers for the open meetings. Also the multiplying luncheon clubs were entering into the epidemic stage. Then the churches were calling me into their pulpits, and the young people's societies had to have a speaker. What few high schools there were thought they must have commencement, with some outsider to mimic the colleges with a literary address. So I was in demand over South Carolina and near-by states.

As I faced the future, there were reasons enough why it should be Europe for the next year. My going was to be no vacation, no moving with the tourist tide of American sightseers just then beginning to swarm abroad in great numbers. Ambitious school teachers were filling the cheaper ships in answer to the appeals of the travel agencies. On a day in early September, 1900, one of these ships, the "Waesland" of the Red Star Line, out of Philadelphia, a small ancient vessel of not more than five thousand tons, found me aboard—fare for the trip over, $35, which included food, lodging, and transportation. That it could ever have been so low is inconceivable now. But the quarters were comfortable enough, the food good, the service efficient, and one's companions agreeable. After ten days, wind-tossed and wave-beaten, the little ship rounded the green coasts of Ireland under a glorious September sun and soon docked at Liverpool. Two days later I was in Göttingen.

But to get settled promptly in order to give to the study of the language the next three weeks before the opening of the university was the main business. After a day or two of shopping around I managed to secure a sunny front room, looking out on a generous yard well supplied with shrubbery and a modest tree or two, sitting well back from the street. A pension it was, Herzberger Chaussée, 19, located almost on the edge of the suburbs among agreeable surroundings. This was evidently a good neighborhood, with several university professors living near by to give it a final touch of respectability. The house was kept by a dear old Fräulein who was continually bemoaning the fact that she hadn't gone in her youth to America, that "paradise for women," as she called it. In addition to the individual *café au lait* and rye bread in the morning, she furnished two meals *en famille* to about eight of us, mostly Germans with several transient foreigners mixed in, a Greek and a Swiss. It was the opportunity of learning the language the hard way, I may say, because it was used in the give-and-take of general conversation with nobody much concerned as to whether you understood it or not.

So I put an advertisement the next morning for an "exchange" (*Austausch*) student, and by late afternoon a short, squat, swarthy little German, displaying a gallant attempt at a Kaiser Wilhelm moustache—the kind that turns sharply up at both ends, which are plastered to the face—was admitted to my room. Hat, cane, and gloves held in his left hand, he broke himself at the middle with a formal bow and handed me his card in a manner intended to be ceremoniously polite. The card bore this inscription—Frederick Schmidt, Ph.D., Berlin. I tried to be as stiffly ceremonious in my efforts as he was, and we were soon getting at the business in hand, but with some difficulty, his English being no better than my German. Before accepting final arrangements, he asked for time to consult the professor of English at the university concerning my English, inasmuch as I was an American! I could not resist saying that I also should make inquiry in regard to the quality of German spoken in the neighborhood of Berlin. In fact, I told him I had been advised to get a Hanoverian if I could—and I had been so advised.

He reported promptly at the appointed hour the next afternoon, and in a speech which he had evidently memorized and practiced with much care he managed to let me know that he might risk exchanging with me for a while anyway, provided he was very watchful of certain peculiarities of American accent and pronunciation. And so we began circumspectly, talking only German one afternoon and only English the next. For my part, I tried to keep the conversations close to Göttingen, the city itself, the university, the professors—who were good and who were not so good—the students and their ways. Then more generally, as best I could, I probed him about his country, its social life, its political procedures, its aims. A solemn, stolid, not so bright young man he was, limited in his knowledge and ideas beyond the narrow field of his specialty, Germanic philology. The questions he put to me naturally followed the lines of my questions to him. In a hesitant, awkward way, with not much apparent interest in the matter, he would want to know something about life in America and education in particular.

I found it difficult to get into his mind the place of the standard four-year American college of the liberal arts, how it dif-

71

fered from the German Gymnasium, and why the two extra years were necessary before the student was ready for graduate and professional studies. I do not think I ever succeeded in bringing him to understand this or, indeed, many other things, for that matter. Of course, my failure might be due either to my limited skill with the German language or with his density and slowness of mind; I am inclined to think it was due to the latter, for I was to find later that this young man was typical of a considerable group of German university students—plodding, slowgoing youngsters mentally, just capable of doing thoroughly and accurately and with a certain degree of independence what might be required in a restricted field of investigation—men from a lower stratum of German society with ambitious dreams of lifting themselves up and out into a Gymnasium professorship or even into a university professorship with the Ph.D. degree. Nor is this type confined to Germany. Our own graduate schools are cluttered with them, and even after the sifting process in these schools, some of them come through with their degrees to be the problem children of many a college president as he futilely tries to educate them into effective college instructors and socially adjusted human beings.

Anyway, in the three weeks I was with him I learned much from Herr Doktor Frederick Schmidt. In his slow, heavy way, he was patient and courteous. Not once did I detect a smile on his face at my terrific attempts to make myself understood in his native language. Maybe he was lacking in a sense of humor, which I always suspected. Nevertheless, he calmly let my blunders pass when he should have shrieked out loud with laughter at my unwitting assaults on the grammar, use of words, and pronunciation of the German language. Behind my back, when among friends, my guess is he exploded with gusto by quoting some of my violent perversions of German as a foreigner speaks it. But withal the three weeks were profitable to the foreigner. The visits with one another in our rooms; walking the main streets of the city, now crowded with returning students with their *corps* colors, their canes, their dogs; the long hikes through the twilight gloom of heavily wooded forests, climbing mountain trails, viewing the ruins of ancient castles, resting in country inns listening to the guttural, idiomatic talk of German farmer folk—these gave topics enough for practice for both of us. I was satisfied, and even after the lapse of the long years I hope he was.

So I felt I was getting along reasonably well in the matter of the language. Indeed, some of my newly made friends at the pension had assured me that my progress had been *colossal*, and when I visited the three professors under whom I was to study, to have them sign my matriculation book, I seemed to myself to get along amazingly well in the rather limited talk needed to complete such a formality, though I couldn't escape the suspicion that, on their part, they were explaining things to me about as a grown person does to a little child, whose vocabulary is limited. I was to hear Gustav Roethe on the German romantic movement, Moriz Heyne on wordbuilding, and Lorenz Morsbach on the poetry of Robert Burns. I chose Roethe because I had a letter of introduction, but chiefly because he had the reputation of being an exceptionally brilliant lecturer; Heyne because he was a philologist of the old school, whose translation of *Beowulf* I had read; and Morsbach because I had no other choice, he being the only man in the university offering anything in English. I was also admitted to Roethe's proseminar in Middle High German, and to Morsbach's seminar on the Middle English poem of Havelock the Dane after a preliminary testing based on a passage or two from Chaucer.

With eager expectancy I attended the first lectures; and as they unfolded, each in succession, but for the foreignness of the language of the lecturers and of certain mannerisms of delivery, characteristic of them because they were German and not American, it didn't take me long to feel quite at home. Professor Heyne was a roly-poly type—gray of hair and moustache, with a protuberant roundness below the waistband—

a fine old soul, speaking his lecture in soft, guttural, mushy German in a way that led one to believe he wanted each hearer to catch every word, not so much for the importance of what he was saying as for the ease of understanding on the part of his students. I could follow him so well that I flattered myself into thinking I had mastered the German language, and to this day a feeling of affection rises in me, whenever I think of him, for this temporary satisfaction while I was struggling with the language.

I needed this feeling of satisfaction to bolster me up a little when I heard Roethe. He was an explosive, rapid-fire lecturer even in the proseminar course in Middle High German, based on one of the minnesingers; but when he came to the lectures on the German romantic movement, he was simply pyrotechnic in the machine-gun rapidity of his delivery, with accent and pronunciation sharp, hard, clicking, spluttery at times, when he got excited, as he frequently did. He flung the door open violently, entered the room talking, talked all the way down the aisle to the rostrum, then faced his hearers, kicking the wall with first one foot and then another—a dark, medium-sized man, with a shock of black hair, a thin short moustache, the straggly ends of which turned up á la Kaiser, clad always in a modest gray cutaway, the tails turning up as he leaned over his desk, producing the impression of a bird of prey ready to pounce on his victim. He was always caustically "pouncing" on some other historian or interpreter of the romantics. He was a brilliant lecturer, a surprising exception to every other German professor I heard, and I visited around a good deal during my stay in Göttingen.

Now Morsbach, the English man, was a tall, distinguished-looking blond Rhinelander, rosily apple-cheeked, with fine blue eyes. His straw-colored hair, though it had made a considerable retreat back from his forehead, was pompadoured high enough to add some two inches to his height. A solemn, dry, meticulously careful lecturer he was, and in dress and manner he was the same.

I have said that, despite the strangeness of my surroundings and the barriers presented for a while by the language itself, I soon felt I was at home in these lecture rooms and familiar with the methods, aims, and spirit of these professors. When Heyne and Roethe began with the Gothic and traced the sound shiftings of the German tongue in the tribal wanderings, located geographically their variations, I was back at Vanderbilt again hearing Waller Deering, fresh from Leipzig, a guest lecturer to whom Baskerville turned over his graduate students for a session. When Morsbach began his course with a discriminating discussion of the manuscripts and editions of Burns's poems, studying these poems not as examples of lyric art but as survivals of the Old English Anglian dialect, I knew I had little to learn—I had been this way before. In these matters I had already been thoroughly indoctrinated, or Germanized. I was merely at the sources whence my undergraduate and graduate instructors had drawn their inspiration and conceptions of scholarship. At times it seemed to me that they were no better than imitators, but on closer thinking I concluded that they imitated so well that they were as good as, or even better than, their originals. Then there would arise the further thought: Why should I come so far to acquire what I already had? This thought created for a time a sense of dissatisfaction that kept me in an extremely critical mood, particularly when I found it was shared by about all my American student friends who had had a year of graduate work at an American university. To hear them talking one might predict an exodus tomorrow. But not so. While one might wander off to release his protests by a bit of travel, to Switzerland or Italy maybe, or stray to another university, they stayed on, especially the mathematics and chemistry men. Just to walk through Nerns' laboratory, as crude and ill-kept as it was, was in itself to receive an accolade; and to study under David Hilbert and Felix Klein, the mathematicians, was the dream of aspiring youngsters in this field and the future hope of mature professors in colleges and universities, the result being that the hearers

75

of these two men were a large, cosmopolitan, enthusiastic group from the ends of the world. It was they, Hilbert and Klein, who gave to Göttingen a fame above that of any other German university. And by the way, Klein, being a Jew, is today either in a concentration camp or in exile. That's the superior race's way with its gifted children.

Considering these two men who were conferring distinction on this comparatively small university brought to mind, as I had never thought of it before, the profound and far-reaching influence of the German universities upon higher education in the United States during the last sixty years of the nineteenth century. I was, of course, familiar in a way with what this influence stood for, not only as a graduate student, but also as an undergraduate. Germany began to work on me in the first year of college in an institution set up but yesterday in a small city in the central provincial South. There were no dormitories, no deans to coddle us into good habits; but there was freedom of election as to what one wanted to study, and there was much lecturing even to freshmen. I wonder how the standard four-year liberal arts college, with its roots back in Oxford and Cambridge, managed to survive. It did so by sheer force of tradition perhaps, but the graduate schools were completely made over according to the German pattern.

In 1904 we were dedicating a modest science building at Wofford. As far as it went, it was well-equipped as to apparatus and laboratories, adequate for the uses of a small college, and we were proud of it. Dr. Ira Remsen, of Johns Hopkins, a distinguished chemist, with his doctorate from Göttingen, made the dedicatory address. But in it he punctured the gleaming bubble of our pride by reciting the stories of famous chemists and physicists who had astonished the world with their epoch-making discoveries, and yet had done so in laboratories no better than cluttered lumber rooms or even kitchens, and with crude apparatus fashioned by their own hands. As I listened to him, I knew he was back in Göttingen again and was interpreting the methods and spirit of the German universities—that it was, finally, not buildings that created these methods and this spirit, not even laboratories and apparatus supplied with every shining gadget that technical skill could furnish, but men, the professors themselves. I sensed also that he might be thinking of his own Johns Hopkins—the Johns Hopkins created by Gilman, who resisted the temptation of most universities for Gothic buildings and put his money in men—in Gildersleeve, Roland, Warren, Bright, Ely, Adams, and others of their kind—so much of his money that Hopkins might be called a university without even a roof to shelter it from the weather.

But of this basis what a university it was! If ever an enterprise justified the purposes and ideals of its founder, it was Johns Hopkins. The purposes and ideals of German universities were transplanted to America to be mightily potent in influencing American university instruction. It drew at once to itself during its first two decades the finest group of aspiring young scholars, not a crowd of them, but enough so superior in quality as to lift permanently the levels of higher education in this country. The Hopkins Ph.D. matched, as a symbol of scholarly training, that from any of the ancient seats of learning of the Old World, because even there it is doubtful whether there was as able a group of scholars as the men who constituted the first faculty of Hopkins, or as capable a group of young scholars in the making who came to sit at their feet, afterward to spread their standards of scholarship into every leading institution in America. A naming of the alumni of Johns Hopkins would be, I am sure, a roll call of the great, not only in scholarship, but also in other fields during the last quarter of the nineteenth century. It was at Göttingen that I learned to understand what Gilman was trying to do and to appreciate what he actually accomplished in the way of centralizing in one institution the sporadic influence of the German universities as it was scattered in spots in various American institutions.

Alas! With the passing of Gilman, the stars in their courses fought against Hopkins. With the spectacular rise of the school of medicine to topmost leadership in American medical and surgical training, drawing to its support money that might have gone to the continued development of other divisions, and after much fumbling and experimentation with an undergraduate department, Hopkins has at last housed itself in a suburban plant of some architectural distinction, becoming just one other American institution of higher learning with no particularly distinguishing features, certainly not those with which it began its career of extraordinary influence. But it should be insisted that at least in the medical school the spirit and purpose of Gilman go marching on, and there Hopkins is still a name to charm with, because what I recognized at Göttingen as German scholarship is vital and controlling. However, it should be further insisted that the influence of the medical school and its service to mankind are what they have been and are because of the methods, spirit, and aims that permeated Johns Hopkins at its founding about seventy years ago.

But to return to Göttingen—or have I really been away in this pointing to Johns Hopkins as the example at its best of what I found at one of the smaller universities of Germany? Probably not. As the months passed and the language barriers fell away and I became acquainted in a personal way with the professors, I was more and more made aware of the debt of America to Germany as it was shaping its standards and methods of graduate and professional instruction. The result was that I grew more interested in my work, not because of what I might be actually learning but because of the *how* of the processes and the spirit that directed and controlled them. Here was something that went deeper than that presentation of facts which at times seemed childishly trivial. It was the discovery that truth itself was based on facts, all of which must be found and marshaled in the search after it. So an enthusiasm, a kind of glow would hold me as I listened to the men lecture. To hear Roethe, for instance, take a half dozen

verses from a medieval German poet and fan out all over
Europe to connect them with other romances, following by-
paths into the Greek romances; then, selecting a few words,
come back into the Gothic, linguistically, and go with these
words with the German tribes in their wanderings, winding up
with modern German—this would constitute a sample of the
thoroughness and completeness that characterized German
scholarship; and though I had been made familiar enough with
it before I went to Göttingen, it still had the virtue of strength-
ening in me the conviction that no kind of teaching is worthy
of respect that is not grounded in this kind of scholarship.

Morsbach's seminar was different in methods, though the
spirit and aims were the same. Its student personnel consisted
of about twelve or fifteen young Germans well on their way
toward the doctorate, two or three who had already achieved
it, and a few others who were preparing anxiously for their
orals, which were close at hand. In turn each took a short passage and interpreted it after the manner of Roethe. The rest
of us challenged—and criticized where there was any doubt,
keeping the leader on the defensive. When my turn came,
Morsbach asked me to conduct in English as he wanted the
discussion to be in English. I told him I could use the "correct"
English of the American dictionary, or I could put on a good
imitation of "Oxford" English, or I could use the language of
the southern part of the United States, the last being my pre-
ference as it was natural and normal to me. "My God," he
said, "use the last. Language is really alive only as a dialect."
Then he said he had a man to take his degree with him last
year, whose English accent was very different from mine.
This man, he thought, was from Chicago. "But why the difference?" he inquired. I reminded him of the size of the United
States and the racial differences in the population, and could
not resist adding that his Chicago friend didn't speak English,
but "Chicagoese." I don't think he caught the point as to what
the West can do to the English language, or some other sections of America for that matter. Anyway, my English,

learned in Tennessee and South Carolina, didn't seem to trouble much my hearers as I tried to illustrate that I, too, had had no little training in the ways of German scholarship, though I had been in Göttingen only a few months.

One could run into all sorts of interesting persons in Göttingen. The English were there in great force and for a variety of purposes—some to learn the language, others to study, and still others for plain loafing after the stolid, self-centered English manner—a manner that brought no love to England and the English, but served rather to deepen the already traditional, continental prejudice toward this island folk. They stuck together, and one had to break through the barriers of their insularity, particularly when away from home, to get at them. It should be noted, though, that when the barriers were once down, they were not a bad lot. Then there were the German students who, many of them, were friendly and easily accessible; and my letters of introduction gave me the entree to a few substantial German homes, and these out of sheer kindness spread me around generously among their friends. So I was privileged to see the Germans at home and to meet them on both formal and informal occasions. I found them a hospitable, friendly people, sensitive and egotistic to be sure, but generous socially to the stranger within their gates, at least to one who brought with him letters from kinsmen and friends living on this side of the Atlantic. As one recalls these gentle folk, it is hard to realize the modern Germany that under Hitler ran amuck to threaten the freedom and civilization of the whole world. Yet it is the children and grandchildren of these very people that he whipped into a fanatical frenzy of savage conquest!

The "American colony" at Göttingen was a miscellaneous collection, some of whom one could always meet at a little cubbyhole of a place on the Weender Strasse, reading American newspapers and telling each other how very superior everything American was to everything German, getting much satisfaction out of their affirmations of patriotic faith.

Among them, however, were at least a few of obviously exceptional promise. There were Brown, who took his Göttingen chemistry training to the service of the Standard Oil Company; Hyde, the archaeologist, who returned to a professorship at the University of Pennsylvania; and the three mathematicians who subsequently went high in this field: Hedrick at the University of Michigan, Noble at the University of California, Max Mason at Wisconsin and from there to the presidency of the University of Chicago and thence to the presidency of the Rockefeller Foundation.

But the one who was to be in the future probably the most famous American of them all dropped suddenly in on me one morning at Herzherger Chaussée 19. He was a tallish, well-built man, with small, black, shining, dancing eyes and a shock of touseled uncombed black hair above a high broad forehead. Rather shabbily dressed, at first he produced the impression of just another stranded American who, if he had only a few more dollars, even one, could get to Bremen and thence work his way home. I waited for the usual hard-luck story, prepared to buy release with my standard price of one dollar. But no, not this time.

"I'm Leonard," he said.

"I'm Snyder. Sit down, Leonard."

And he was opposite me at my table pouring forth a rapid-fire, picturesque assault upon the whole business of higher education in Germany, in language heard from no other wandering American. He had tested it all out—the vaunted classical training of the Gymnasia wasn't in the same class with what he had had at a small American college; and as for the universities, the lectures there weren't any better than those he had heard at Harvard if as good. All this and more he said with great energy of voice and manner and much nervous snuffling and twisting of a fine beak of a nose. As he paused for breath, I interrupted to ask for his academic background. He had an A.B. from Boston University and an M.A. from Harvard.

"You know I'm New England all the way through, for look what my parents tagged me with, William Ellery Channing Leonard!"

"It's bad enough," I said, "to be 'New England all the way through,' but to be weighted with a label like that is to doom you to the receiving end of jokes through all your days. Your parents must have dreamed great things for you when they placed all that in front of so modest a name as Leonard."

"They did," he commented with a burst of sardonic laughter that filled the room. "But wouldn't you like to hear something?"

Without waiting for a reply, he went into an inside coat pocket and, drawing forth a fat bundle of papers, proceeded to read first a translation from the *Aeneid*, and then one of the odes of Pindar. With my knowledge of both poets, I was able to sense that these were translations that caught not only the thought but the rhythms, cadences, and even the moods of the two poets. So from me to him: "Where did you get that, Boy?" He touched his head as if to say here, and proceeded to read on in a sort of singsong manner, not translations, but now original poems, and there was beauty in each. To be sure, through them all there were echoes of Tennyson, Keats, Shelley, Browning, but they were good echoes, with, however, a flavor, freshness, and a newness that did not belong to any other. "Where did these come from?" Once more his hand went to his head in a gesture to say, "They are mine," and I knew that, where I had expected a tramp, I had found a poet, at least one whose budding genius promised a rich flowering.

Two hours had passed, and, having something else to do, I suggested that we go in the afternoon to the Bismarck Tower for another reading. Under the trees on the slope of a little mountain overlooking Göttingen, I saw the sun go down and the twilight melt into darkness as I listened to what I knew was real poetry. Another American poet was on the way. He glowed and swelled under my praise, mixed as it was with equally honest criticism. He grew so enthusiastic over my recognition that he was going to chuck everything at once, plans for a degree and a college professorship, and live by poetry alone. From then on I fought the idea, insisting that he would starve, not live, if he leaned on such a frail reed for a livelihood, that he had better stick to the professorship, letting poetry be but a side line in the business of earning a living. I won the argument. He remained in Germany a year, then went to Columbia in New York, and finally to a professorship in the University of Wisconsin—a professorship he made famous both by the sheer scholarship he displayed and by publishing from time to time poetry that ranks with the best in recent American literature.

It was a dreary, drippy morning in midsummer of 1901, too cold for the season, that I saw Leonard, his coat collar turned up, waving me wistfully good-by as my train moved away to Bremen, where I was to catch my boat for America. I recall that it was with real regret I was leaving him, for if anyone needed a counselor, guide, and friend, it was this highly gifted man. I was hoping that some understanding woman with the deep wisdom of love might get hold of him to save him from the logic of his temperament. Many years were to go by before I should see him again. By then he had published two strange books, *Two Lives* (poetry) and *The Locomotive God* (prose). From them I knew that tragedy had stalked his footsteps and had caught up with him. Being in Madison to interview a prospective instructor, I went around to his apartment to see him, and was shocked at the changes. The bushy hair of yesterday was still there, but now it was a disordered crown of snowy white; the lines were deep in his face, and nervous nasal snuffings had greatly increased. His wife appeared to be a wholesome blond Norwegian woman, and it seemed he might have found a quiet haven in the home she was making. I don't know, though he did seem reasonably contented. But it was not of the intimacies of the more recent years he talked —he would have done so had I permitted it—but of those happy months we spent together at Göttingen. Deliberately I kept the conversation there; and soon, in spite of what time had done to him in appearance, he was quite the Leonard of those days, with the same wistful look in his eyes he had when we parted in Göttingen on that rainy summer morning twoscore years before. His is a life story worth recording, and his poetry is worth interpreting as among the glories of American literature. I hope a competent person will do both.

On a Sunday morning late in February, I was paying a friendly visit to Morsbach in his home. I always had the idea that he liked these visits because it gave him an opportunity of practicing his English on me and at the same time of studying in my own speech another dialect of English, that spoken in the southern section of the United States. At any rate, he always seemed pleased at the visits. The subject of Byron came up, as I recall it, because of one of those periodic controversial storms raised in England by somebody's proposing that the poet's ashes be placed in Westminster Abbey among the other men of letters of the nation. Of course it was not done, the moral sense of the people protesting successfully against the inclusion in the Abbey of one whose whole life had been a deliberate flouting of their moral standards and their social conventions. The storm in England over this issue brought repercussions in all continental Europe, which were expressed by the usual assaults on the pretensions, self-righteousness, and downright hyprocrisy of the English. In the course of our conversation Morsbach remarked that a study of Byron in English literary criticism might be a good subject for a doctor's dissertation, suggesting that, as long as I was in Göttingen, I take it. He further suggested that with the training I already had I would have little trouble in doing the dissertation and getting the degree in a couple of semesters. The subject interested me greatly as a possible fruitful study in the whole matter of the attitude of England toward certain ethical qualities in its literature from *Beowulf* all the way down the line. And when he said the investigation couldn't be adequately done outside the British Museum, I jumped at the project. It would at least give me the long-desired excuse for an indefinite stay in England.

In the early days of March, I was in London, settled in a boardinghouse in easy walking distance of the British Museum. When I went down to my first dinner clad in a dark brown German-made sack suit, I felt quite out of place, everybody else being in tuxedos or full dress and my landlady or hostess sitting at the head of the table in the last word in an evening gown, herself generously sprinkled with diamonds on the fingers, in the ears, and around the neck. The chill of the arctic regions settled around me, and I knew I was out of place. The next day as tactfully as she could she let me know that I mustn't do it again; and as tactfully as I could I let her know I had a fine dress suit in Göttingen, locked, however, in my trunk, so that it could not be sent to me, and I wouldn't buy another. I asked her to permit me to try it again. Reluctantly she consented, after delivering a mild lecture on the carelessness of Americans in adjusting themselves to fine European customs.

I began that evening by calling attention to how busy and hard-working Americans had to be in the fiercely competitive world in which they lived, too busy for the leisure to cultivate certain formalities of life; and, indeed, without our being aware of it, maybe some of the rough and ready manners of the vanished frontiers were still with us. A middle-aged Englishman at the table, thinking to come to my defense, in the throatiest of English said: "Yes, to be sure, and how can one expect from Americans the culture and manners of the ancient European civilizations? Culture, what there is of it, is too young in America. With time, they may acquire those amenities that give a grace and diginity to life in the Old World."

A good long speech it was for an Englishman in mixed company. It got the nodding approval of his fellow countrymen. But I had to add a comment: "It is not strictly correct to say that America is too young. The truth is that in a sense America was born old, never really having a youth. Its history is the story of the transplanting of ancient cultures to new conditions, and departures from the old ways are of the nature of protests against the uselessness of many Old World habits and customs—efforts at successful improvements, more direct, more simple, more natural, more in keeping with the everyday requirements of practical living." From then on I was accepted without formal evening clothes.

The group at the dinner table, all men, grew increasingly interesting. There were three or four English "regulars," and two American regulars, as completely American as two men could be—both tall and stalwart, speaking an exaggerated western dialect of the English language. One was a veterinarian from Ames, Iowa, whose official business was to inspect for contagious diseases cattle shipped to the United States. The other, from somewhere in Kansas, was a sort of detective for checking on the declared value of art objects. His stories as to what wealthy Americans actually paid and what they should have paid legally were unpleasant accounts of wholesale chiseling which deprived Uncle Sam of his customs money. Then there were the transients at the table—Australians, New Zealanders, Canadians, South Africans, men returning from India, and nearly always an American promoter of some stock-selling enterprise, chiefly mining. Altogether it was good company, and gave a firsthand experience of the varied interests of this wide empire, the loyalties that bound it together, and the kind of men who carried forward its business. They might be from the most distant commonwealth colony in 1901, yet the ties of language, of social inheritance, and of business, and the mystic bond of Parliament and the monarchy constituted mighty links in a chain that nothing could break.

The dining room at Upper Bedford Place furnished rather enlightening and stimulating experiences at the end of a long day's work. Usually two hours were spent together after dinner before the group broke up. The talk was good, the talk of practical men who knew the world, at least their part of it, at first hand and in the raw, mine being the only academic mind present. And yet all had visited the literary and historic shrines, and I couldn't escape the feeling that, in spite of geographical differences and deeper differences due to the varying ways of living in widely separated parts of the world, here was a group of men with intellectual and spiritual kinships which none of us could quite define and yet which constituted strong bonds of real unity. For example, on the occasion of my return from a little excursion to Stratford, the question of Shakespeare naturally came up. Henry Irving and Ellen Terry were then playing Shakespearean roles in London. I had seen them, and so had most of the group. In addition I could bring out that during my student days at Vanderbilt I had heard Edwin Booth and Lawrence Barrett in *Julius Caesar*. And so Shakespeare was the subject of discussion till far into the night. Theirs was the layman's point of view and the layman's direct unacademic way of expressing it—both mightily refreshing to the instructor in English, who was declaring all the time to himself that, if God would forgive him his past sins in the use of language, he would in the future try to interpret Shakespeare more nearly in the speech of the man in the street than in the conventionalized jargon of the man in the teacher's chair.

Then I thought, too, of what Thomas Carlyle said somewhere, in effect this: "Stupid parliaments and mad kings may separate into different governments the widely sundered branches of this English race, but here is a king, King Shakespeare, who despite all political crimes will hold them together. He belongs to them all, and to him all pay allegiance in speech and understanding." And still, nearly fifty years after these conversations here referred to, men from the far places of the earth are striving to preserve the heritage that gave them Shakespeare as a common possession, and they speak his language still when the deep controlling emotions of life struggle forth for utterance.

These three months in England were happy, fruitful months for a teacher of English. Six or seven hours every day in the British Museum, gathering material for the study of what the critics thought of Byron; visits to all the literary and historical shrines in London; excursions to Oxford, Cambridge, Warwick, Kenilworth, the Lake Country, Edinburgh, and the Scott and Burns country! What more could one ask as a year's interlude in his life and as a further preparation for the better teaching of the subject very dear to his heart, the English language and literature? Already I was fairly itching to be back at it. Plans of new courses and fresh methods were shaping in my mind, and I was full to overflowing with an enthusiasm to make things go as never before when I should face my classes once again. English—why nothing else in the college course counted beside it! But not yet. There were other things to do as an essential part of the training I had laid out for myself. There was a bit of travel both for its own sake and for seeing with my own eyes, though briefly, the backgrounds of two other great European cultures.

The last days of May found me in Paris, trying to absorb as best I could enough of its associations to help me realize Paris as the intellectual and artistic capital of the world. Somehow I didn't particularly like Paris—a terrible confession to make. Maybe a week was too short to touch more than the surface, or to get away from a sort of "Coney Island" impression of it, that it was a show place above everything else. Of course, my almost daily frequenting of the Louvre, Notre Dame, and certain monuments *de la gloire,* such as the tomb of Napoleon, left indelible memories, but I moved on without much regret. Possibly to my shame I say this.

I woke up a bright morning in June in Munich. Here was a city that made an immediate and lasting appeal. The art galleries, the Wagnerian music, the gardens, the cafes, the soft mushy German of its friendly people, the cosmopolitan group at the pension—all conspired to make me a loyal lover forever of this south German city. If I must live anywhere outside of the United States, I believe I should choose Munich.

So my week was too short, and it should have stretched into many weeks. But Italy was to be next. The journey was by way of Lindau, over Lake Konstanz, through the Mount St. Cenis tunnel, with stops at Bern, Zurich, Geneva, Milan, and then Rome itself. I have never been to Athens, but I must say that nowhere else does one get such an overwhelming sense of the past as in Rome. Both the ancient Christian world and the pagan world of the Caesars were everywhere. The very atmosphere seemed murky and moldy with the past. In its ruins I recalled my Latin studies, and walking over its highways I heard the tramp of the legions again going to conquest to the ends of the world, and I was stirred anew by the grandeur that was Rome.

This was enough to take to Florence with me, there to learn once more the significance of art to the human spirit and to appreciate its immortality on canvas and in bronze and marble. I could understand, too, all the better why the Brownings loved Florence, as indeed do all who value man's effort to make real his dreams of beauty as he aspires after the permanent in the midst of the fitful, fugitive, quickly ending fever called life.

At Florence I wanted to stay, but I had at last become just another tourist who must hasten on, satisfying himself with fleeting glimpses of glories which he would like to live with always. Venice was next for just a day—a muggy, hot, soggy day—the black waters of the canals filled with floating debris and emitting their worst odors. Certainly St. Mark's and its square were all that Ruskin or anybody else had said they were, and the storied splendors of this Queen of the Adriatic still called to the imagination, but the flesh was weak enough to be asking for cooler and cleaner air, and in the night I went to Verona. I couldn't pass it by without walking its streets with the ghosts of the Capulets and Montagues, and sharing that tragedy of the two who loved so blindly, young Romeo and Juliet, and at the same time paying tribute to an English dramatist whose art made their tragedy known wherever English is spoken. At Ravenna in the gathering dusk of a summer evening, with the heavy shadows of the mountains adding a touch of gloom, I looked up into the face of the bronze image of Dante, thinking of that grimmer portrait in the Pitti Palace of Florence, of the women of Ravenna who pointed him out to their children as the man who had been in hell, and of Thomas Carlyle's estimate of him as the voice of ten silent centuries. In the gathering gloom, with lofty peaks behind it, the statue had in very truth a singularly appropriate background, a Dantesque setting.

Over the Alps through the Brenner Pass in a snowstorm, by way of Innsbruck, I traveled back to Munich. With difficulty I withhold any comment on the Tyrolean Alps, as well as the Swiss Alps. A saturation with John Ruskin's gorgeous ecstasies on Alpine beauty and grandeur render it impossible for me to do more than recall them, adopting as my own his descriptive language at its best (or worst). It took me three restful days in Munich to recover my breath.

Three days later, the warm days of mid-June found me once more in Göttingen, renewing old acquaintances and beginning to work fiercely on my Byron material to see how it would shape up. To do this properly and turn it into a small book seemed to me to require at least a year. So I decided to return home, where I could find library facilities as good as those in Göttingen, and to come back in the summer of 1903 for the degree if I so desired. By the middle of August I was on the "Koln," a mixed passenger and freighter boat of the North German Lloyd Line out of Bremen, headed for Baltimore. It was an exceedingly pleasant voyage of fourteen days over quiet seas, the Atlantic behaving beautifully. The cabin passengers were an agreeable company, about forty in all, though in the steerage was a whole Polish village of approximately five hundred souls, cheap labor for the coal mines of Pennsylvania. There were only two other Americans aboard besides me—a young tourist from Chicago and an American doctor who had spent a year in the hospitals of Vienna, bringing back with him, in addition to increased medical knowledge, a quite charming Jewish wife to introduce to his Washington family, who had not been informed of his venture into marriage. The rest of the ship's company were Germans, elderly people returning from visits to their kindred in the fatherland and young Germans who were coming to America to gather that fortune that grew on trees and could be had for the reaching.

The night before we were to land the pilot came aboard to guide us into port. I followed him into the dining salon, saw him drop into one chair at a table and lift his big feet into another chair. This familiar gesture touched something deep within me. I knew I was at home once again. I felt more so when, turning to me, he said, "Do you speak the lingo of these Dutchmen?" I told him I did. Then, "Tell 'em to bring everything they have, and be quick about it," and I felt more at home. And his nasalized English! I never thought that I, who had been brought up with the soft drawling speech of the South, would find music in such a voice and such an accent, but I did, for long absence from it had somehow endeared it to me as the distinctive English of my own land and people. So I stayed with him to hear him talk, as he put away a colossal meal of "everything they had," and his talk was as music in my ears.

The next morning was heavy with clouds as I peered wistfully across a gray sea to catch a first glimpse of the shore line. Soon there was a strong offshore wind twisting and tumbling the clouds about. I looked up, and there floated in gleaming colors the flag of the "free heart's only hope and home" against a background of a patch of deepest blue, and beyond were Maryland and the buildings of Baltimore, still under the glory of the morning sun, and my interlude was behind me.

Now, nearly fifty years after, again I am thinking back on the days and experiences of that interlude in Germany and England, but thinking also in terms of the horror that was Europe after 1939, of the unmeasurable death and destruction of the years following, of great cities bombed to rubbish heaps, of the leveling beyond repair of shrines symbolic of the spiritual progress of mankind, of the enslaving of men and women, of savage slaying of women and children from the air. Can it be that the children and grandchildren of those dear, kindly, hospitable folk of those happy fruitful Göttingen days did these things? Yes, they did, as unbelievable as it seems. It was they who brewed this devil's broth, and with primitive brutality poured it forth on the civilized world—a world that wanted, only too blindly, too strongly, to live in peace and freedom.

I recall the subjects that would come in for conversation around every café table, at dinner parties, at social gatherings, at student meetings also, and obtrude themselves as seeming side remarks but usually made with great feeling. That word *Lebensraum* would always start things exploding —Germany must have room to expand. Then there would be *Drang nach Osten*, the Bagdad railroad, the "push toward the East," the "Germanization" of Poland by peaceful means if possible, by force, if not; the glorification and invincibility of the German Army; the *Emkreisung*, the "encirclement," with Russia on one side and France thirsting for revenge on the other; and finally, the menace of the British Navy blocking all the sea lanes of the world, but "just wait till we complete our naval program and then, and then! But there are the Jews—they are the real enemies of the German people, corrupting everything they touch, a gang of unscrupulous internationalists, hoarding our wealth to send it out of the country."

The years went by, and the little Bavarian Corporal came along to add to this brew the alleged wrongs of Versailles and the gigantic egotism of race, and to superheat the mixture with flames of an insane lust of world conquest, and the Germany I knew and loved stalked the earth a Frankenstein of terror and a threat to all the fair dreams of civilized people. He was a mighty schoolmaster to do so much in less than a generation, an evil artist in a humane craft.

5

ON MAKING A COLLEGE PRESIDENT

1902

THE AX AND the saw brought it down with a crash—the great wild cherry tree that stood not more than thirty feet from the southwest corner of my piazza. Its topmost limbs had gone into obvious decay, constituting a major threat to passers-by when a little stronger wind than usual might be blowing. The fact that it had to come down didn't ease the hurt of its fall or the sorrow over the end of its days. Its grace, its beauty, its characteristic ways of growing through more than fifty years had entered into the affections of all who lived in the old "red brick house," as we called that ancient place of gentle, tranquil, happy living.

When we first began to love this tree, its trunk was no better than six or eight inches in diameter, forking into two prongs some six feet from the ground. But as time went on, these two prongs clung close together in a sort of Siamese twin fashion, and the tree grew tall with little spread of branches. The reason for this was its neighbors. In the first place, the house itself was near it; then a great oak by the side and a little toward the front of the house hemmed it in. On one flank was a group of hickories, with a single competing hickory on the other flank. So the cherry tree, thus crowded, was throughout its days engaged in nature's ruthless struggle for survival. It had to fight its way upward for the sunlight that gives life. This kept it a slender tree. It grew tall and graceful reaching for the sun above the surrounding competitions—an inspiring tree lifting itself high for the sources of its living.

This tree had a way of shedding its leaves long before the others, even before they showed any signs of autumn's sear and yellow leaf. It didn't wait for the bite of the frost and November's winds to strip it bare. By mid-September its pale gold leaves had already littered the yet green grass. When I first noted this, now more than fifty years ago, I wrote my lady, who was away at the time, that our tree was dying. When she returned, we stood by it for a while in a session of real grief and regret, concluding to wait, however, to see what spring might do before cutting it down to replace it with another. And once more spring performed its usual miracle. It was again the firstling of the year, with its delicate leaves well in advance of those of all the others, announcing that winter was over and spring and summer were here.

Now what has this rather sentimental account of a tree to do with how a college president was appointed forty years and more ago, why he accepted the appointment, and what he thought about the duties of the office then? Maybe not much to do with anybody but the president himself. Anyway, with the sound of ax and saw and the first crash of the upper limbs as they fell, strangely enough something did happen to him. It brought the memory of a warm summer night forty-two years before when he was sitting in the corner of the piazza, watching the fireflies light up the tree and match the glitter of the stars beyond through its leaves. At the time he was waiting for his commencement guest, a member of the board of trustees of Wofford College, who were then meeting in annual session. About twelve o'clock the guest came down the walk and up the steps, and abruptly said: "Well, you have been unanimously elected president of Wofford College!"

"President of Wofford College!" I almost shouted back. "I don't want to be president of any college. What's happened to Dr. Carlisle? Why can't he go on? He's pretty old, to be sure, but there's nothing wrong with his mind or body. He's as much a president as he ever was. Besides, nobody has ever spoken to me about the position, certainly no member of the board."

And they hadn't, not a single one of them. The faculty hadn't discussed the matter among themselves, though they knew Dr. Carlisle's resignation had been with the board of trustees for three years. There were only a half dozen of us, and it was probably respect and reverence for him that kept us from raising questions about his successor so long as he was in office. Besides, as I look back on the kind of men then in the faculty, my guess is that they thought the choice of a president was strictly a matter to be handled by the board of trustees and nobody else. Therefore it was not quite the proper thing for a faculty to meddle in matters of this kind; there were considerations of ethics and of future official relationships involved—considerations that seemed to make it at least not good form to busy ourselves about the choice of a president. Of course, it's hardly conceivable that college professors should once have taken such attitudes! But they did, and such attitudes may have been just a sort of academic by-product of the code of a gentleman, still pretty real in the South forty years ago. A gentleman would be instinctively sensitive about official as well as personal relationships that might grow out of any activities on his part in the election of a president.

"Well," my friend went on, "everybody wanted you for the position. A trial ballot [the word "tentative" had not yet been invented for such procedures] without nominations was taken, and you got all the votes but two, eleven out of thirteen, and then on a real ballot you were unaminously elected. You'll take the job. You are to meet with the trustees at nine in the morning. Good night."

With this brusque finality my trustee friend left me standing more or less stunned by what had happened. The summer winds were still rustling the leaves of the cherry tree, the fire-

flies were turning on their lights, and far beyond, but seeming near, the stars were shining in the glory of the June night.
But I wasn't seeing and feeling all these any more. The second
crisis of my adult life had come, and I sensed acutely, though
vaguely as yet, that for me life was at the crossroads. I had
already declined the presidency of a worthy woman's college and a professorship of English at an important southern
college.

Then began an all-night session with the gallant lady whose
clear wisdom has lighted our pathway with a steady flame for
fifty-seven years. The session opened with the possibility of
our going to Leland Stanford. An old Vanderbilt friend on
the faculty there had started gestures toward me for a position
in the English department. We pushed this prospect aside for
the time on these grounds: First, Wofford had given me a
year's leave of absence, and I had been back only a year, and
therefore if my eighteen months in Göttingen had added anything to the quality of my service, a little more of it was due
Wofford before I should consider going elsewhere. Second,
I had my doctoral thesis nearly complete and was planning to
return to Göttingen the next summer (1903) to stand my
final examination for the degree.

So we let the Stanford gesture go, and turned to the effect
the presidency might have on my own teaching. I was "ter-
ribly" (this is the right word) in "love" (and so is this one)
with teaching English. No man had ever had a more respon-
sive group of students. Most of them would do about anything I wanted them to do, and almost every classroom hour
brought some thrilling experience to their teacher and, he always believed, to them as well. Besides, I offered voluntary
courses in Anglo-Saxon and Middle English, and could be sure
of a select group of a dozen or more boys to take these courses
without college credit, just for the love of the language itself.
Then, I also had a class of young women who came out to
the college once a week for a study of one of the great English authors or a restricted phase of English literature. In ad-

dition there was the Shakespeare club, which I conducted once a month downtown in a succession of homes—as intelligent a coterie of aspiring young men and women as one could meet anywhere. I was also lecturing here, there, and yonder on my favorite subjects, and in some instances people would even pay to hear the lecturer!

And so the major question came to be, "What would the presidency of Wofford College do to all this?" This led to a consideration of the duties and activities of my predecessor in office for a guide, Dr. James H. Carlisle. He sat as chairman of the faculty, and had no administrative functions whatever, and nobody expected him to have any. He taught some phases of mathematics, astronomy, and ethics to each of the four college classes, but above all he was the greatest inspirer of men to be and do their best I have ever known. It would have been a waste of time for such a man to be cluttered with the details of administrative duties. He was profoundly an educator, with that mystery and miracle of personality from which young men, and their elders for that matter, caught the contagion of high ambitions that worked out practically into worthy living.

This kind of president I never dreamed of being. Nobody who knew him could think of stepping into this man's shoes in his way of influencing growing boys. However, as we talked on through the night, it developed that I might still teach my beloved English, preside over a small faculty of seven or eight men, maintain the standards of scholarship that had been the glory of this little college from its foundation, and possibly do some pioneering in new directions. And so I was being persuaded to do something I didn't want to do—take up the duties of a college president at a time when they seemed simple. Then: "Let's try it for a year anyway. We don't have to keep it; and if we don't like our successor, we can move. There are other places." Thus youth, with its spirit of adventure, its courage of ignorance, cast the deciding vote, and the decision was unanimous. Then a little sleep, and the dawn—a new day of opportunities that grew and grew so rapidly through the years that I wonder now how I met even half of them. But that's another story.

A little after nine o'clock on a bright June day, the tenth it was, I left my home to report to the board of trustees. They were meeting in the small faculty room in the main building. Going along, absorbed in formulating what I might say to them, I do not recall that I felt "flattered" at what had come my way unsought, nor that I had been in any sense "honored." I do know, however, that I was in a pretty solemn mood, that I was thinking mainly of what I might be giving up, without any elation over what everybody would be calling a great "promotion."

Whatever thoughts I might have had were interrupted by a Western Union messenger boy, who handed me a telegram. It was not a first message of congratulation but a message from the chairman of the board of trustees of a respectable midwestern college, asking if I would consider its presidency. Here was another shock, which suggested that fate, or providence, was again taking a hand in my future to change all my ways from what they had been: I had been merely a teacher of English, carrying no side lines, except perhaps an all too ready willingness to take English to a public that greatly needed its cultural influence, as I thought. What did three boards of trustees see in me as a possible president, who from my own standpoint was just a happy evangel of something the world could not well do without—an understanding of the English language and its proper use and an appreciation of the greatness of its literature?

It was with a thought like this that I was ushered into the presence of the board of trustees. There were thirteen of them, all rather oldish men, as it seemed to me then. With a fine courtesy they rose to their feet to greet me, while the chairman, Bishop Wallace W. Duncan, took my hand and led me to a seat by his side at the head of the oaken table at which I had so often sat as a member of the faculty. He looked

98

more like a bishop than any other man I have ever known. There were grace, dignity, and distinction in his manner, and an impression of high integrity and piety that no man could put on. Without resuming his seat, in a few simple, direct, and very earnest words, he told me his colleagues had chosen me to be president of "our" college—I recall the emphasis he put on this word "our"—that they felt they had made a wise choice, and that they pledged their full co-operation and support. With equally simple, direct words I replied I would do the best I could to prove worthy of the trust they had in me, though I was a bit uneasy when I considered the great men who had been presidents of Wofford—Bishop Wightman, Dr. Shipp, and particularly Dr. Carlisle whom I was succeeding.

It was as informal as that, a sort of matter-of-courseness pervading the whole preceedings. The next twenty minutes were spent in general conversation, as if the new president and his governing board needed to get better acquainted with one another. Soon there was a glancing at watches, and the bishop announced it was time for the commencement exercises to begin. The procession was formed, no academic costumes, college life being too unaffectedly simple for that in those days—thirteen trustees, seven members of the faculty, twenty-five members of the graduating class, a few "distinguished" visitors, and the speaker, the Rev. Olin Watson, who was to deliver the "literary address," as it was then described, and properly so.

This group filed down the aisle and took places on the high rostrum, six feet from the floor, that stretched quite across—forty feet at least—the spacious rectangular chapel. Each of the seniors made an original speech, five minutes in length, on a subject of his own choosing; this rapid-fire battery was followed by the literary address on "The Bible as Literature"; then the delivery of diplomas and Bibles was made by the retiring president. As usual he gave a final charge to the graduates in a moving impressiveness of thought and feeling such as I have not heard from the lips of any other man. It was unforgettable as always. And the exercises were ended except for the formal report of the chairman of the board of trustees. This time, however, one could sense throughout the audience an air of expectancy. The story of what the board had done had "leaked" out, and the atmosphere was tense. The chairman arose, and with a voice choked and broken with emotion, all the more impressive because any display of feeling was rare with him, paid a tender and appreciative tribute to the great man who by his service had put something of his own bigness into a little college to make it, too, big beyond most institutions of its kind anywhere. Then simply, without comment, he announced that Professor Henry N. Snyder had been elected to succeed him.

And this was as it should be. The outgoing president had proved himself worthy of the gratitude of men for the high service he had rendered, and by every token of what is best in human nature, recognition, fine and unstinted, should be given him. This should be his hour of triumph, though there was a humility in his greatness that always made him seem surprised whenever anybody praised him or his works to his face. Still after a brief pause the audience broke into generous approval of the choice the trustees had made in his successor. Then came the benediction, friends and students crowding around, and the new president felt he was starting with a reasonable capital of good will and loyalty. He was thirty-seven years old, and at that age the spirit of adventure is still strong with the impulses of a man's first youth and with something, too, of its blindness to the difficulties and burdens that lie ahead. And well it is that youth is this way.

The guests had gone; the children were in bed asleep; the exercises of the morning, the congratulations, the warm voices of friends promising support and co-operation, the youthful enthusiasm of students over their new president had melted into silence. We sat in our favorite corner of the piazza nearest the cherry tree. The familiar summer winds whispered in the leaves, the fireflies were doing their best, and the light of the stars seemed close enough to mingle with theirs. We were talking things over. What had been placed into our hands, just what sort of trust had we accepted? Strangely, we did not discuss what might be the most obvious thing— the ragged, unkempt campus and a group of buildings in a depressing state of disrepair, inside and out. But somehow we looked deeper than these physical appearances to those invisible realities that were Wofford College, that had kept it alive during the terrible days of the Confederate war and the gray and haggard period of reconstruction that followed.

We talked first of my predecessors, Dr. W. M. Wightman, who left Wofford in 1859 to become president of Southern University in Alabama and later bishop of the Methodist Church; Dr. A. M. Shipp, who in 1875 went to Vanderbilt as dean of the theological department; and Dr. James H. Carlisle, who stood with Calhoun and Wade Hampton as the three greatest creative forces in the history of South Carolina. We talked also of three other men who as financial agents of the college from 1870 to 1890, those grim years of defeat and desolation, traveled this state, preaching a gospel of Christian education, holding the Methodists loyal to their college in spite of adverse conditions, and bringing in a trickling stream of financial support even in those lean years. These three men were very able men from every standard of measurement. Each was subsequently chosen bishop in the Southern Methodist Church: Bishop Wallace Duncan, Bishop Coke Smith, and Bishop John C. Kilgo. The latter went from Wofford to little Trinity College at Durham, North Carolina, as president, to be the first to tap the resources of the Duke family for higher education and thereby to become, in a sense, the founder of Duke University.

I decided that in men like these was an endowment that accounted in part for the extraordinary influence of this little college in the number and quality of the men it turned out—men who, though few, represented the important leadership of South Carolina. Wightman, Shipp, Carlisle, Duncan, Smith, Kilgo—through them I knew whoever succeeded to the presidency was the heir to a spiritual wealth that had infused into the life of this college worthy standards of character, conduct, and service, guided by the religious motives of a great church. I know I became very humble when I thought of myself and them, but I did highly resolve to do the best I could to carry on in education what their leadership had stood for at Wofford.

In addition to certain specialized duties all these men taught college classes—mental and moral philosophy or metaphysics. They were not "scholars" in the technical meaning of this word, but they were men of great ability, of impressive personality, wise in a firsthand knowledge of men and life. Such qualities had counted immensely in creating that Wofford I was taking over, and I knew it.

But in assessing Wofford College further I was aware also that it had never been without real scholars in its classrooms—men, themselves trained in its processes and spirit, who with all their souls believed in scholarship for its own sake as well as in scholarship as an indispensable instrument for the discipline and culture of youth. Among these were Warren DuPré, A.B. from Randolph-Macon, M.A. from Yale, teaching the natural sciences; David Duncan, M.A., University of Glasgow, teaching the classics; Charles Forster Smith, Ph.D., Leipzig, who was to succeed Duncan but afterward was to go to Vanderbilt and the University of Wisconsin. His own student, J. H. Kirkland, another Leipzig scholar, followed him, going also to Vanderbilt as professor of Latin and later becoming its second chancellor. Then there had been W. M. Baskerville in English, still another Leipzig Ph.D.; and when he left, F. C. Woodard came from Randolph-Macon, a brilliant student of Thomas R. Price, who at the University of Virginia and Columbia University, New York, was to revolutionize English instruction in the United States. Yes, as we talked till far into the night, we held up this other, intangible, element in the endowment of Wofford—its intellectual endowment, given to it by a succession of great scholars. As far as I knew, no other college could muster such an array.

But as I think back, the wonder is that I paid no heed, as I now recall, to the material aspects of the institution—its physical plant and its financial resources. Was it possible that by some sort of intuition I hit upon about all that Wofford had at the time to justify its existence? Or did the intuition go deeper; and did I divine, as I was trying to assess what was mine to preserve and direct, the real secret of education, that nothing else counts—no, nothing—unless a college is the congenial home of intellectual and spiritual values?

Anyway, the new president with something like this in mind entered upon an adventure which was to last twoscore years, through which he tried to keep faith with the vows then made on a summer night in June, 1902. It is to be insisted again, though, that these vows were to the maintenance of the strictly educational aspects of the little institution. My "good demon" kept telling me that here was something really worth preserving, something that seemed to confer on Wofford a sort of greatness in spite of its meager equipment, its poverty of resources, and its little handful of students—a something for which a man could hold his head high and fight. It was well, too, that I took this attitude, for in the Wofford of 1902 in was hard to discover anything else to which a man might give his life with a degree of zest. But this was enough.

And I was confirmed in this two years later in a conversation with Dr. Carlisle. A committee of the trustees of another institution had come to me with a formal offer of its presidency. This institution, from almost every standpoint, would make a stronger appeal to human ambition than Wofford could. This is what Dr. Carlisle said: "I have had to face similar crises in my career. Each time I have raised the same question: Was I by choice an educator or a college administrator? If I chose to be the latter, a college administrator, it didn't matter much whether my stay at a particular institution should be long or short. This would be determined largely by prestige and salary. But if I was to be an *educator*, that was something very different. Education is a process, and requires time, much time, for one to see the results of his labors—five years, ten years, and even twenty years after his students leave college. He has to wait patiently on the slow years to get the measure of what he has been trying to do. For better or worse I've been an educator, not an administrator, and I do not regret the choice."

So, as he made his choice, I must have made mine—not an administrator, but an educator. I do not recall that I deliberately made this choice, but rather that, somehow from the very nature of the institution and that essential vitality of the life it had, it was made for me. Who can say? After all, isn't a college, big or little, an educational institution, and can a president go far wrong if he lets education become his chief business? Anyway, for better or worse, this is what I have tried to make of Wofford—an educational institution.

6

I STUDY WHAT I HAVE UNDERTAKEN

THE SUMMER and fall of 1780 were unquiet, wrangling days in the red hill country of upper South Carolina. Cornwallis had overrun the state and, convinced that he had it subjugated, had moved on into North Carolina toward Virginia. He expected Clinton to come down out of the North, and between them they would be able to crush Washington somewhere in the latter state. But the dimming torch of liberty was kept burning by such hit-and-run partisans as Marion, Sumter, and Pickens, and by bands of patriots, Whig guerrillas, particularly in this upcountry. Here was fratricidal war on a savage level. Burned homes, confiscated lands and property, and ruthless murder were the order of that grim time, 1780. In every community it was a struggle for survival between Whig and Tory, as roving bands bent on destruction went up and down the countryside, members of divided families and neighbors on each side.

On the night of October 18 there were anxious moments in a little log cabin on the south bank of the Tiger River, which the Indians named the River of the Big Cat. Joseph Wofford, a courageous Whig partisan, just had to step in for a visit with his family. But his Tory neighbors on the watch caught and bound him, making ready for the usual hanging. His wife, Martha Llewellyn, a Welsh Quaker out of Pennsylvania, appealed for a respite: "If you hang my husband, you kill three—him and me and the unborn babe I am carrying." They heeded the appeal, leaving the house to come another time to get the husband. In the early hours of the next day, October 19, 1780, the baby was born, and she named him Benjamin Wofford. He was one day to make the largest single gift to higher education ever made by any Methodist to the date of his death in December, 1850.

As I began to study what had come into my hands, one of the first questions that kept arresting my interest for answer was: How did this retired Methodist minister, born in a frontier cabin less than two weeks after the battle of King's Mountain hardly more than thirty miles away, a victory called by Thomas Jefferson the "turning of the tide of the Revolution," and about the same distance from the battle of Cowpens, where Lord Tarleton's army was cut to pieces a few months later, leave a legacy of $100,000 to establish a college, to quote from his will, of "the Liberal Arts and Sciences in my native district of Spartanburg," then no better than a country village in the still crude society of the hill country of upper South Carolina? The deeper I tried to probe for the answer to my question, the more interesting it became. I was to find that the eighteenth-century rationalistic deism; Oxford University; a mighty religious movement started on a May night in 1738, when John Wesley, the greatest Englishman of the eighteenth century, felt his heart "strangely warmed"; Thomas Jefferson and his new university at Charlottesville, Virginia—all entered into the cabin home to make this man do what few others had done in America to forward the cause of Christian education.

Oxford, England, came into this frontier cabin by way of the man of the warm-heart experience on that May night in 1738 who, dying more than fifty years later, left a religious "society" destined to girdle the globe and the record of having saved his country from the bloody excesses of the French Revolution because the people, the masses, who might have been manning barricades in the streets of London, were praying in little chapels throughout the land. This John Wesley was always the Oxford scholar. He sought to elevate these masses by the power of education and succeeded to such an extent that historians say of him that he not only spread

106

"scriptural holiness" throughout the land but by so doing created a "new middle class" out of the underprivileged, the forgotten men and women of that eighteenth century. So great is the power of religion to inspire the virtues of industry, honesty, and thrift.

In 1770 the unresting traveler and passionate seeker after the souls of men seemed to sense the magnitude of the promise in the English colonies in North America. Out of Bristol he chose with something like prophetic insight young Francis Asbury, apprentice to a blacksmith and saddler, to take the message of the warm heart and of Oxford to the New World. He came, and up and down this land he went, following all the wilderness trails from Maine to Louisiana, training a company of helpers—"circuit riders" they were familiarly called. They kept pace with every movement of immigration that struggled up the slopes of the Blue Ridge and spilled over into the great valleys beyond. In fact, the lone pioneer reaching the last fringe of civilization usually found that Asbury's circuit riders had been there before him and were ready to greet him.

In a crowded center of the nation's capital is a significant bronze statue of Francis Asbury on his weary horse. This first bishop of American Methodism has a book in his hand, symbolic of that strain of Oxford that John Wesley had tried to infuse into the life of his unlearned followers. Asbury tried to do the same thing in this young American republic in the process of its formation. He mastered Hebrew in the saddle. In his journal he writes of meeting a certain man, whom he describes as "a man of great piety, great skill in learning, drinks in Greek and Latin swiftly, yet prays much and walks close with God." There we have it—solid piety and sound learning, Oxford and the religion of the warm heart—a union greatly needed because these adherents whom Asbury and his preachers added by the thousands annually during the next half century were mainly unlettered people, pioneers on the move. The "Apostle of the Long Road," traveling more miles horseback than any other man who ever lived, never let the swarming thousands of "lost sheep" get away from him. As he crossed time and again the old Wilderness Trail, up and down which they scattered into Kentucky and Tennessee both before and after the Revolution, meeting them on the march—men, women, and children—he described them in his journal as a "rabble of folk," just the kind he and his circuit riders were divinely commissioned to seek and save.

People of this kind, having fought and won the Revolution, were inspired still by the passion for liberty and freedom, in addition to that other passion for bettering their lot by taking possession of the rich, new lands in the great valleys beyond the Blue Ridge. But they were in the main an ignorant and unlettered folk, it should be insisted; and the great bishop, aware of the Oxford strain John Wesley had infused into the blood of Methodism at its very beginning, had to provide in what ways he could for the education of such a flock, for piety of a highly emotional kind, yes, but also at least for the fundamentals of learning. So in 1784 he had put into the rules for governing the church among the other duties of a minister of the gospel this duty: "Preach especially on education." Some six years later, 1790, he was urging, as one of the important tasks of a "council" he had set up, care for the education of the poor. This is what he said about it:

What can be done in order to instruct poor children, white and black [note the "and *black*"—slaves of course] to read? Let us labor as the heart and soul of one man to establish Sunday Schools in or near the place of public worship. Let persons be appointed to teach *gratis* all that will attend and have a capacity to learn from six o'clock in the morning until ten, and from two o'clock in the afternoon until six, where it does not interfere with public worship. The council shall compile a proper school book to teach them learning and piety.

"Learning and piety"—these two must never be sundered!

But already in the New World this heir of the educational

ideas of John Wesley, fellow of Oxford and founder of the Kingswood School for the education of the youth of the church and "seminary for laborers"—those laymen who were called to minister to the Methodist "societies" in England—had dreams of an educational "system" for the southern section of his rapidly increasing membership. In 1784, twenty-five miles from Baltimore in a beautiful valley by the side of the Susquehanna River, and yet on a hill from which Chesapeake Bay could be seen, he laid the cornerstone of the central institution of Cokesbury College. Thus, when he came for the first time into South Carolina in 1785, his mind was still obsessed with his idea of a system, with academies as feeders to the central institution near Baltimore.

Ten years later, after taking subscriptions throughout South Carolina and Georgia, on March 12, 1795, he dedicated Mount Bethel Academy with a sermon on the text "Rejoice evermore." Consisting of a two-storied main building of roughly hewn stones and a group of log cabins for the instructors, it was located on a rugged hill in Newberry County. For thirty years it was a beacon light of learning, training some of the most significant leadership of the two Carolinas and Georgia, preparing them for the two recently opened colleges established by Georgia and South Carolina. The Oxford leaven was working effectively in the New World through the influence of a religious denomination, whose major service was to the poor of the earth here, as it had been in the motherland across the seas.

Mount Bethel was much more than a teaching place. For a quarter of a century it was an active center of educational propaganda. But when in 1816 the "Apostle of the Long Road" left the lands over which he had ridden for a half century, there was nobody left to solicit funds and students for what he fondly called his "poor school," and it began to languish, finally to die about 1830. Still its influence didn't die. Other schools like it followed in succession in near-by places, Mount Ariel, Tabernacle, and Cokesbury. To Tabernacle there came a young man out of far Vermont, saying in his diary: "I have neither health, money, nor employment in Vermont, and I shall go South in pursuit of all." When he came home to the family with whom he boarded, he overheard the children telling their mother that the new teacher opened the school without a reading from the scriptures or a prayer. He did both the next day, and later under the spreading branches of a great oak something happened in the soul of the roving Vermonter, Stephen Olin. He would call it "conversion" and a "call to preach," in the familiar Methodist words. He became the first president of Randolph-Macon College in Virginia in 1832 and the second president of Wesleyan University at Middletown, Connecticut, and a preacher of great influence throughout American Methodism during the first half of the nineteenth century.

His Tabernacle School passed into the Cokesbury Manual Training School in 1834, set in the midst of a thousand acres, which the students were required to cultivate. For the next twenty-five years this institution drew a wide and influential patronage, and flourished greatly. But the War Between the States gave it a shattering blow, from which it never recovered.

Now let us go back to that cabin on the south bank of the Tiger where Joseph Wofford, battle-scarred soldier of the Revolution, was bringing up a rather considerable family under what might be described as still frontier conditions. Frequently there came into that home a certain George Doherty, a circuit rider out of Georgia, who had the reputation of being a self-made scholar of prodigious learning as well as a preacher of great evangelistic power. Under his preaching in 1802, Benjamin Wofford was "converted" and "called" to preach. Now George Doherty had a passionate zeal for education, and was Bishop Asbury's main support in his Mount Bethel School. Doherty continued his activities in behalf of the other schools that succeeded Mount Bethel—Mount Ariel, Tabernacle, and Cokesbury. May it not be said that through

110

him the early strain in early Methodism found a place in the mind of his young twenty-two-year-old convert, Benjamin Wofford?

Benjamin Wofford, a Methodist circuit rider, in 1805-6 traveled a wilderness circuit that stretched from Nashville on the Cumberland to Cincinnati on the Ohio. At the end of the year at a conference at Ebenezer in East Tennessee, an open letter was addressed to the young minister, informing him that he would not be received even into the relationship of "a preacher on trial" until he got rid of the two slaves he owned in South Carolina. Returning to South Carolina, he kept his slaves and added more. Retiring from the active work of the ministry, he settled down in Spartanburg County for the next thirty-four years of his life to acquire the reputation of a skinflint and miser on account of his talent for making and keeping money. Traditions of miserliness grew around this lean, gaunt man, six feet two inches tall, Lincolnesque in face and figure—his careful picking up of pins and nails, sweeping of every single grain of tobacco into his pipe, letting his candles burn down to the last gasp of light, using of the torn margins of newspapers for keeping his accounts. Yes, it was thrift to the point of miserliness, but with a purpose for future service to his people and church. Ten years before he died he attempted to buy a piece of debt-ridden college property at Gaffney, some twenty-five miles from his home, the Limestone College property. But the trade fell through over a few dollars of interest, and the purpose of this pioneer preacher waited for fruition till his death on December 5, 1850, when he left $100,000 to found a college of the liberal arts in his "native district of Spartanburg"—the equivalent of $500,000 in today's currency.

The meeting of the religion of the "warm heart" and Oxford University had come together in this frontier preacher, and the college that bears his name was the result after a little more than one hundred years. But there was also that other mood of the late eighteenth and early nineteenth centuries—

the intellectual and rationalistic mood and attitudes toward life and its meaning, with special preoccupation with natural philosophy or the physical sciences. As a result the deistic, or naturalistic, interpretation of religion threw a chilling blight over anything like an emotional, instinctive, or imaginative response to religious experience and aspiration—areas from which the rationalistic approach had to be excluded. Protest against the dry, realistic atmosphere of this eighteenth-century intellectualism had to come, and it did come in the romantic period in literature, in the political storms that culminated in the French Revolution, and in the enthusiasms of Wesley's religion of the warm heart that spread like a prairie fire to other dissenting denominations. The masses of the plain people who made up the membership of these churches had to be saved from the soul-destroying influences of the infidelity of the upper or intellectual classes.

Most of the "founding fathers" were under suspicion of being tainted with the disease of scientific agnosticism, or of being adherents of a naturalistic deism as opposed to a divine revelation delivered through a supernaturally inspired book. Thomas Jefferson was among the chief offenders in this respect, and he knew it. Every now and then he complained that after all he had done to free them from the domination of a state church and from taxes for its support, the Baptists, Presbyterians, and Methodists would not send their boys to William and Mary on account of the reported prevailing immorality of its students as a result—so they charged—of the infidelity in the thinking of its faculty. When the Great Liberal opened his university in 1825, and when it was made clear that the instruction and conduct of its students would follow lines of what seemed unlimited freedom, the leading denominations, particularly in the Southeast, became obsessed with the idea that to save themselves and the country they must educate their own constituency as well as their ministry. The result was that colleges sprang up all along the Atlantic seaboard within the dozen years following the opening of

Jefferson's University at Charlottesville. By 1840, the Methodists had founded two colleges in Virginia, Randolph-Macon and Emory and Henry; the Baptists, Richmond College. In North Carolina the Methodists had founded Trinity; the Baptists, Wake Forest; the Presbyterians, Davidson. In South Carolina, the Baptists built Furman; the Associate Reformed Presbyterian, Erskine; Benjamin Wofford was trying to buy a college for the Methodists; and in 1856 the Lutherans set up a college. In Georgia, the Methodists had Emory College; the Presbyterians, Oglethorpe; and the Baptists, Mercer. Thus the recently founded state institutions in all these southeastern states soon found themselves ringed about with religious-educational fortifications against the ungodliness in both their faculties and student bodies. Of course, this does not represent all of the motives in the establishment of these early colleges. There was that other important motive of each denomination's providing for the training of its ministry and its own youth, not risking a separation of religion and education.

Now these were some of the first thoughts that came to mind as I sat down in front of my new job in the summer of 1902. I knew that there was something organic about a college, that therefore it couldn't quite rid itself of the forces and influences that brought it forth and kept it alive during its first years. This is why I wanted to know just how this small denominational (sectarian) institution really came to be and why it refused to die under the devastating shock of the Civil War and the equally menacing days of reconstruction, with the social dislocation and poverty after it. Benjamin Wofford did not just happen to leave a fortune for founding a college in 1850. He did so because of the influences I have been describing, and I was to find that they were still vital enough to keep it going in spite of untoward conditions that were for forty years after 1865 a constant threat to its existence.

There was another matter that I looked into rather closely during that summer of 1902 when I was trying to understand

113

the nature of what I had accepted, and that was the question of who really controlled Wofford College legally and morally. To get a start in this direction I read a copy of Benjamin Wofford's will as printed in one of the early catalogues. I found at once that in ironbound legal terms this control rested in the Methodist Church in South Carolina. There was no doubt here, for the college must report each year to the annual conference of the church for approval or disapproval; its trustees were appointed by the same body every two years; and its faculty and officers, including the president, were elected every four years. This college, then, belonged to the church, and was so controlled by it as to be made to conform absolutely to its purposes, if the church so willed. As I faced my administration, right at its beginning, I was a bit alarmed, for here were the potentials of nagging, of frustration, of petty contentions over matters that didn't count, and of officious meddlings that could become intolerable. I had seen all of these worries in the case of other colleges. There could be the social habits of students in the matters of dancing, card playing, and theatergoing; doctrinal issues raised by ecclesiastical snoopers as to the teaching of a liberal-minded instructor; and barks of the watchdogs guarding the gates of science to keep the satanic serpents of evolution out. These all may now seem trivial things to worry over, but forty years ago they were real issues around every church college in America, and pretty lively in that southern region later described as the "Bible belt."

I dared to take the risk, however, of both threats, that of the ironbound control of the college by the church and that involved in the possible social and intellectual conflicts between the ways of the church and the ways of the world, because I believed profoundly in the indissoluble union of religion and education in the college period. I wanted to make the experiment of seeing whether a great church would allow a reasonably free hand in the working out of such an experiment. How the process of working it out at Wofford

114

may have succeeded is not to be discussed here, but what I wish to affirm at this point is that there has never, in these forty years, been any serious conflict between the administration of the college and the church. Each has trusted the other, but nevertheless here was a relationship that had me hesitating for a while. I had already formed the conviction that a college, however owned and administered, must be first of all an educational institution, not a propaganda organization for specific doctrines and modes of conduct. Besides, I had seen colleges much disturbed by the meddlesome intrusions of ecclesiastical leaders, keeping the college emotionally upset by demanding continuous revivals of the noisy type. Even Methodist colleges had not been free from such disturbances, and there might be this threat so long as the governing body of the church realized that it was in control. On the other hand, while I might approve revivals of a kind, I knew I could never surrender my conviction that there was no substitute under the sun for trained, enlightened intelligence, not even piety, for without intelligence the uses of piety could be limited, darkened, and even perverted. Could the two, "solid piety and sound learning," to use an old Methodist phrase, be united, the one contributing power for living, the other light and guidance?

This was the question I must answer, and for an honest man there could be no dodging. The church, particularly the Methodist Church of 1902, must insist on maintaining certain standards of conduct in a college for which it was responsible on the bases of ownership and a considerable degree of financial support. Otherwise, why should it be at all engaged in the business of higher education? It must put something into education that independent and tax-supported institutions could not, and this something would be the religious motive and the Christian philosophy of life. If it didn't do this, nothing else mattered. Of course, on looking at Wofford College I accepted without reservation this point of view, and I added the belief, firmly held, that in the college period of training it would be little less than a calamity to the church itself and to its service to human society to divorce religion and education. Because I put so much faith in the value of trained, broadened, enlightened intelligence, in its power to shape conduct, I cherished an equal faith in informing this power with religious dynamics and Christian standards of living. In other words, those aspects of intellectual values needed for the service of society and the development of character might be menacing possessions unless they were directed by motives and purposes devoted to the high uses of righteous living, such motives and purposes being the accompaniments of a clear, tolerant, vital religious faith. I had often to ask myself whether the Methodist Church in South Carolina, a state ultraconservative in its religious thinking and standards, would permit me to make such an experiment with its college. I say *its* college, for in all my forty years as president of Wofford I never let myself forget for a moment that it belonged to the church.

I dared to believe that it would permit the experiment, that of maintaining a real college of the liberal arts vitally informed with the spirit and philosophy of the Christian religion. So with that degree of exhilaration which only youth feels when it faces an enterprise in which there are difficulties, dangers, and even the constant threat of failure, I entered upon the adventure of trying to hold together in helpful comradeship those two mighty forces in determining human destiny—religion and education. I knew it wouldn't be easy, but it was greatly worth trying. But, to succeed, the venture had to be carried out in mutual trust on both sides, the college and the church. I made up my mind that there should be no secrets on my part, that at each step along the way I would take the church into my confidence, that Wofford must be first of all an educational institution, that its measure of service to the church and religion should depend on how fully it fulfilled its mission in this respect.

As I went forward in the effort to do this, to make this

small college, within the limits of its resources, a first-class educational institution, the church went with me. The truth is, every request I made to it for increased appropriations was on the basis of improving the strictly educational facilities of the college. Moreover, I should say here that a day soon came when, out of this mutual trust, as president I was permitted to name each member of the board of trustees, and was myself made president of the board of education of the church, whose function it is to nominate the board of trustees of all institutions of the church. I mention these matters with considerable satisfaction because it has been charged so frequently that denominational colleges are hampered by all sorts of narrow sectarian, ecclesiastical restrictions. Certainly, I was given a free hand in the administration of Wofford College by a great church, and whatever its weaknesses and failures as an institution, they were the results, not of the meddling of the church in its affairs, but of the incapacity and unwisdom of the president himself. He had his way for forty years, and he can say it was a freer way than that of most of his friends in other types of colleges, tax-supported institutions for example.

But this is not to say that the going was always easy. There were threats of storms, but no storms; and now and again one might suspect that "booby-traps" had been laid, but these exploded without much noise and with very little damage, if any. There were flurries and even squalls that rocked the boat for a spell. Why shouldn't there have been, for one may recall that during these years from 1902 there were still the bogies of "evolution," the "higher criticism," and "modernism" to frighten and arouse the orthodox and the watchful guardians of "the faith once delivered to the saints!" I knew that some trouble would start just as soon as the department of Bible and religious education was established. Of course the head of such a department had to be a man of genuine scholarship in this field, and therefore his approach to the subject must be scientific. A fond mother, for instance, would

117

interview a trustee of the college, charging that the faith of her son was being destroyed by the teacher of the Bible at Wofford; or a student or a minister would want me to look into the evolutionary tendencies in the departments of biology and geology; or a letter from a student would say he was withdrawing from college because the instruction in religious education was following the "beer-soaked theology of Heidelberg." Such matters I handled directly myself without ever mentioning them to the instructors attacked for fear their freedom of teaching might thereby be restricted; and while my colleagues in other denominational institutions were in constant turmoil, and enforced resignations from their faculties were not infrequent, Wofford kept an even keel and came through shipshape in this respect. Of all the attempts of the press to summarize my long administration, none gave me more satisfaction than that in the official weekly of the Methodist Church in South Carolina, in which the maintenance of academic freedom at Wofford was among the greatest "accomplishments." Here is an accolade I wear with pride because in a period of fierce controversy the church in an extremely conservative state—conservative to the point of easy explosiveness—permitted the president to conduct an educational institution in a free atmosphere when the church was in a legal position to dictate any terms it chose as to what might be taught and how.

Another thing I had to think about as I went over in mind various angles of the task of being president of a denominational college was the personnel of the faculty with respect to their church affiliations. My colleagues at the time of my appointment were all members of the Methodist Church. Should this be continued as the rule of the college in the selection of new additions to the faculty? I did not think so, for to hold to such a rule would be putting a restriction on scholarly competency. Not to employ a man who had all the qualifications except that one of being a Methodist would be a limitation in choice that might substitute an inferior man for a superior one, and I could not bring myself to do this sort of thing. It would be a betrayal of trust to the students for whom the college existed. Here once again I had to inquire of myself whether the church would allow freedom in this respect. Once more I took the risk, insisting, though, that members of the faculty should be members of some Protestant church and men of impeccably correct habits.

This latter requirement I have never regretted in view of the invasion of blackguardism, open and unashamed, into American speech, oral and written, from which college and university faculties have not escaped. I recalled Thomas Jefferson's statement of the qualities of one of the teachers at William and Mary who had much to do with shaping his life: "A man profound in most of the useful branches of science, with a happy talent for communication, of correct and gentlemanly manners, and of an enlarged and liberal mind." "Correct and gentlemanly manners"—with this estimate of the fundamental qualifications of an instructor I started, and have not yielded to anything less since. I am sure that not a few instructors have carried even into their classrooms no little of the profanities and the indecencies of language that have soiled the speech habits of the American people during the last decades. A few best sellers written by "ladies" give point to this statement, as well as a generous sprinkle of "hells" and "damns" in the serious essays written for our more highbrow monthly magazines. Anyway, not merely because Wofford was a college belonging to a Christian denomination did I in every choice of a member of the faculty demand the qualities here suggested, but also because I thought boys growing into manhood should be taught by scholars who were also gentlemen—a rather old-fashioned conception, to be sure, during the days through which we have but recently passed. I wanted very much to have at Wofford men who would respect the manners and morals of youth as well as their minds.

Besides the danger to these freedoms inherent in the control of an educational institution by a religious denomination, there was another important matter I had to consider. Wofford belonged to the Methodist Church, and this made a difference. This church is essentially missionary in the sense that all its enterprises must be carried into every individual church or "charge," and they were in every nook and corner of South Carolina. Each minister was required under the law of the church to preach on the subject of Christian education at least once a year, bringing to the attention of his congregation the needs and service of any institution set up for this purpose—Wofford College, for instance. I knew therefore that it would be counted among the duties of the position I had accepted to take the message of the Methodist Church to its people in terms of the college. To do this, even but partially, would carry me to all sorts of people living under a variety of conditions, literate and illiterate, for Methodism in South Carolina represented every social stratum—cultured city people, well-to-do and not so well-to-do farmers, underprivileged tenants, mountain folk, in little weather-worn frame churches in the pine woods and steepled houses of worship in the larger places. To these, all of them, I would become a "missionary" of education, a kind of education that put into the intellectual training of youth the spiritual forces represented in the faith of the church.

While I was thinking of this aspect of what might be expected of me as president of Wofford College, a recent experiment came vividly to mind. It was a warm spring night in a little one-room frame schoolhouse twenty-five miles below Spartanburg. It was dimly lighted with but one electric bulb, but crowded with people, plain country folk of all classes and ages, from a dozen crying babies in arms to tottering grandfathers who were out to see what changes the two visiting strangers might be plotting to make in the settled ways of the community. The atmosphere of the crowded little room was reeking with body odors, and the cries of the babies reached choral proportions while the talented young woman from the State Department of Education was pleading for the school district to tax itself for a better school for its children. I tried to do the same thing, moved as I was under a deep sense of human need here in this group of old unadulterated American stock. Their ancestors, not so very far back either, had cleared the wilderness and had fought at King's Mountain and at Gettysburg; and they were living on lands that had been in the family since pre-Revolution days. Yet even as I tried to talk to them in the interest of a better school for their children, I was aware that the shadow of the frontier still rested upon their ways of living and thinking. Stranded out on the fringes of progress, they had missed the currents of civilization. I did the best I could to bring that company of people to a sense of their duty to their children.

When the meeting was over, the young woman who had put her woman's heart and soul into her talk said to me: "My address was a failure. Did you see that fine-looking young man sitting near the front, making faces and scowling, seeming to get madder and madder as I tried to persuade these people to perform their simple duty?"

I hadn't seen him, but as she pointed him out—a tall, well-set-up, sandy-haired, blue-eyed man in the early thirties—I casually approached him, asking how he liked the meeting.

With flashing eyes he replied: "I hate South Carolina, I hate this community, and at times I hate my father. The state, the community, and my parents let me grow up in ignorance and didn't care. But I swear my children shall not be so treated, and I dare any man to say he'll not vote these extra taxes when I go to see him."

"Go to it!" I said as I grabbed his hand.

The implications of this remembered scene, indicting as it did the social failure of a proud and gallant state, came over me, and I said: "Yes, this shall be one of the major duties of the new president of Wofford College in educationally backward South Carolina. For into what more worthy missionary enterprise could I lead my church than that of better schools for these forgotten people of their own flock, the lost sheep

121

of the house of Methodism?" Mixed with this feeling was a deep sense of humiliation and shame, for my church had for nearly one hundred and fifty years been ministering to this people, and had served out to them a highly emotional type of religion, but in the cultural aspects of their lives had left them where it found them. Shades of Wesley and Asbury, you did not intend it should be so. And I did resolve, looking ahead in those summer days of 1902, that I would go to the remotest country circuit with even a greater zeal than to the high-steepled city churches. With immense satisfaction I can say that under the leadership of Wofford College the Methodist Church in South Carolina has been kept "educationally minded"; and no little of the progress in South Carolina in the field of public education in these forty years—and it has been great—has been due to the intelligent activity of this church.

So these were some of the matters I had to face in advance as I entered upon an administrative career exceptional for length of service, if for nothing else. They involved considerations fundamental in my own thinking. I did believe, to repeat, that education and religion should be united, and that they could be. I was eager to make the experiment with Wofford College as my laboratory. Its spirits and standards throughout its history were of high quality academically and ethically. As far as I knew there were none better. But would the rather conservative denomination to which it belonged permit the freedom necessary for success? It did, and Wofford became first of all an educational institution, and yet in the process kept faith with the enduring values in the spiritual aims and practices of the Methodist Church. In 1944, before the historical society of the two conferences in South Carolina, a scholarly minister read a carefully prepared paper on "Wofford College and South Carolina Methodism—Ninety Years of Co-operation."

7

LIGHTS IN DARK PLACES

HAVING SETTLED as far as I could the forces that entered into the creation and maintenance of Wofford through hard years, with its existence threatened at almost every turn in its history —by the Confederate war, reconstruction, social, economic, political chaos, the sense of defeat, poverty beyond the measure of words adequately to assess—I began immediately to study its educational relationships, its place as an educational institution in that scheme of things understood as the South of 1902. In the matter of academic standards I have already indicated that I found at Wofford an atmosphere congenial to the maintenance of the highest standards. I discovered, moreover, that this had always been so from the very beginning of its history when it opened its doors in August, 1854, to seven freshmen and the two sophomores and twenty-seven preparatory students. But these twenty-seven students in the preparatory department were significant in that for most of the years until 1888 the number in this department continued to be greater than those in the college department. In this year in the buildings of a defunct ante-bellum "female college" the Wofford Fitting School w a s established under separate management and faculty, though it was owned by the college and responsible to its board of trustees. Four years later at Bamberg, in the lower part of the state, another Fitting School was established, holding the same relations as a "feeder" to Wofford. Consequently, when in 1895 a group of sixteen southern colleges met in Atlanta, Georgia, under the leadership of the new chancellor of Vanderbilt University, J. H. Kirkland, Wofford was already in a position to meet one of the fundamental requirements of the new Southern Association of Colleges and Secondary Schools—the complete separation of college and preparatory instruction—that grew out of that gathering. I represented Wofford and was its temporary secretary.

This was a history-making group of men that came together in one of the classrooms of the Georgia Institute of Technology on that fifth of November, 1895. As I recall it, speech-making was not in order; the audience was too small for that—only sixteen of us—but we were dead in earnest to protect and preserve the integrity of the four-year college, and to do this meant also the protection and preservation of the integrity of the four-year high school, giving it a chance to live by refusing to accept its students until they were prepared to do the work of the college. A really great story was brought to the discussion table from Vanderbilt University. In 1888, with an exhibition of academic courage unmatched in the South, this institution cut off all preparatory classes and proceeded to throw the weight of its influence to the establishing of private fitting schools. The next year thereafter it registered a decrease of one third of its already none too large student body, and suffered no little from the criticism of its friends and a loss of financial income for what seemed but a quixotic adventure. But it had its reward. In a few years it saw its student body grow in numbers and quality, acquired a new self-respect, and found itself girded about with a circle of high-class preparatory schools that formed the habit of directing their graduates to Vanderbilt and to nowhere else. Some of these graduates I myself had while I was a teaching fellow in Latin there, and I have never taught better-trained men. Of course, these preparatory schools were conducted after the fashion of old southern academies, and their work was confined chiefly to Latin, Greek, mathematics, and English, with a little history thrown in. But it was thoroughly done, and these students I taught could hold their own in any college in America.

124

And so the Southern Association of Colleges and Secondary Schools was modestly launched to become the most potent force in the elevation of standards in college and high school in the southern states, and that under the leadership of one institution, Vanderbilt University. And I venture to assert, with no little pride and satisfaction, that the leadership within this institution came to Vanderbilt by way of Wofford College. W. M. Baskerville had taught at Wofford, as also had J. H. Kirkland and Charles Forster Smith, the last two being graduates of Wofford, and these three were the head and front of Vanderbilt's battle for academic standards at a time when it seemed to be of the nature of a lost cause. How lost the cause seemed was made concrete and vivid by an investigation of educational conditions based on the report of the United States commissioner of education for the year 1901. While the figures given in this report may be far from accurate, yet they can be depended upon to present a picture rather depressing, to say the least.

In the thirteen southern states I found there were *ninety* denominational institutions calling themselves colleges. They were giving instruction to 24,255 students—men, women, boys, and girls, nearly half of them being in preparatory departments. These institutions were, moreover, instructing more than three times as many students as were in the tax-supported colleges, exclusive of the agricultural and mechanical colleges. The income from the total endowments of these ninety institutions of the church was $797,488 as against a total of $980,662 in the state colleges from both endowments and legislative appropriations. However, the denominational colleges, all of them, received from tuition fees $740,288, while the state colleges got only $174,849. It is clear, then, that the three numerically leading denominations—Baptist, Methodist, Presbyterian—of the South, were at least willing to pay for their kind of education, though they could get another kind, which at that time they didn't want, free. Another comment should be made as to the financial resources of these ninety institutions: If we subtract from the totals the endowments of a half dozen colleges, what is left for the remainder is negligible. This is to say that most of the colleges in the South in the year 1902 depended almost entirely on tuition fees and relatively small annual appropriations by the respective churches.

Now I was well aware that this was not a good picture to look at, and educational leaders were not at all satisfied with it but were working heroically to mend conditions. Each of the denominations had a board of education. I was a member of the board of education of the Southern Methodist Church, and like the boards representing the other churches, it strove valiantly to elevate standards, to encourage and direct campaigns for money, to merge institutions, and to assist some in the process of passing out. But their efforts in these directions were distressingly slow in producing results. The forces opposing progress were often too strong—local pride, sentimental attachments, historic roots going back deep into a worthy past, and the leadership of able men with more faith and hope than judgment and educational understanding.

The hardest thing in the world to kill is a college that ought to die and may even be slowly dying, with everything apparently against its surviving. Such an institution seems to find more and abler friends when it is at its last gasp than it ever had in more flourishing days. Of course, some of the leaders—indeed, the majority of them, one might say—were honest men, men of consecration and sacrificial motives, with a sense of martyrdom in their efforts to keep these little struggling institutions alive. They just could not believe that providence would let them die; they felt that somehow an educational miracle would happen if they could only hold on. In a few isolated cases they even saw the miracle happen. There were other leaders, not many though, within my knowledge, who were plain charlatans and quacks who sold shoddy for broadcloth, and knew it was shoddy. But the days of such were numbered, though alas! the numbered days too frequently would stretch into years and for a time these men would be succeeding where others because of their very integrity would fail. Some of them I have met—suave, unctuous, with a persuasive glibness in conversation and public address, seductively clerical in garb and manner. After shaking hands with one of them, an experience I avoided if I could, I wanted to get somewhere at once to wash a soil from my hands, for next to hypocrisy in religion there is none worse than hypocrisy in education, for this represents the corruption and betrayal of youth.

Ninety denominational colleges in the thirteen southern states, an average of seven to each state, with Tennessee and Missouri leading the procession with fifteen each! Looking back on them—and I knew many of them at first hand, their presidents and faculties, the constituencies that supported them, and the kind of young people who attended them—I ask myself if they served in any way a worthy purpose, and I always answer "Yes" when I consider existing conditions. Much good they did in the field of education at a time when theirs was the only road to "higher" education that led beyond the elementary school. I remember the zeal with which the churches propagandized their constituency—no little of it illiterate and semi-illiterate—on the religious duty of educating their children, of building local schools, and of sending their boys and girls to their own institutions; on the necessity of putting religious motives in the processes of education; on the bounden duty of parents as Christian men and women to sacrifice to the last limit to these supremely important ends. Each minister became a crusader in a great cause, an educational missionary seeking to convert his people in behalf of the education of their children. In my own day I have seen ministers bring to Wofford groups of stalwart boys— one, two, and three of them—getting them properly matriculated and settled in their rooms. Then throughout the year these ministers would drop in for counseling and guidance, still looking after their young protégés all through the college course, doing a better job of helping and steadying the boy than college instructor or dean could do. What I am doing is emphasizing the responsibility the denominations in the South felt toward these many little colleges they had set up, and the closeness of the relationship between the church and its college, each with fixed convictions that neither could do without the other and that the society they sought to serve would not long endure if religion were not the guiding motive in education.

Knowing that a kind of religious fervor and purpose was throbbing in these small sectarian colleges and in the homes from which their students came, I could never take to the wailing wall, shedding tears over their existence as did so many of my educational friends when we met together solemnly making plans to raise standards to heights impossible for them, or failing in this to ostracize them from respectable educational society. When the educational technicians were in their most murderous moods toward these institutions, I would be seeing things, so to speak. It was a hot August noon; behind a slow-moving horse in a two-seated topped buggy, we had been grinding through the heavy white sand of the rutted country road. From a little gray frame church, so sheltered from the heat by pines and oaks and hickories as to offer an inviting coolness, came the sounds of an ancient hymn of the Christian church. We got out and went in, as much for rest and escape from the heat as for anything else. The singing had stopped, and the group were kneeling in prayer. A man, gray of hair and beard, was leading. His language was not always of the strictly grammatical kind, but as he warmed to his confession and petition, his voice acquired pitch and resonance, and he began to weave into his speech great purple patches out of the Great Book which he and his kind knew, the King James translation of the Scriptures, and one forgot the lapses of grammar in the sheer beauty and eloquence of this plain man's prayer. Bunyan does no better in *Pilgrim's Progress*.

In the simple, unaffected hospitality of the people of his class, he invited us to dinner. His home was on a sandy ridge, and was shadowed by oaks and pines; the yard was swept clean, and everywhere were evidences of thrift, decency, and order. He wore a cotton suit, washed till it was threadbare and patched or darned in many places. The mother greeted us with a simple dignity—a farm woman she was in all the essentials, and a lady with the natural courtesy that comes from the heart. Four or five children came into the dining room, with freshly washed faces and in their work clothes. It was a bounteous meal, mainly of the products of the farm prepared by the mother and daughters. The stranger must say the "blessing," and there was a chorus of "amens" from the family. The talk was of the "meeting" at the church, of the weather, of the crops, of deaths and illnesses among the neighbors, of the price of cotton—five cents a pound, as I now recall. Altogether I was aware that I was in a plain, ordinary farm home, in the labors of which every member shared, with two people at its head, father and mother, who accepted reverently and as their chief business the bringing up of the children in "the fear and admonition of the Lord."

After dinner we sat on the porch, that is, the father and mother and the two strangers, who felt no longer strangers, but somehow friends; the children had disappeared. It's the father's talk, his philosophy of parenthood, that I do not forget: "I haven't much to leave my children; the farm is too small to divide among them; one will have to stay to keep it in the family and give a place to which they may all return from time to time; the rest will have to scatter and make their living in other ways. Anyway, I don't believe in leaving money and land to children. They mostly waste it, and it don't do them much good. We want to leave to our children something nothing can take from them because it's in them and makes them grow into better men and women. I mean my wife and I feel it's our Christian duty, as the preacher says, to give them an education. That'll stay with them, an education in religion as well as in books." And they did, and with what stinting and saving and sacrificing only God knows. But they had their reward, and their philosophy of duty was justified. They sent the children to the little schools of their church. One of the boys we saw on that day became a bishop in a great church; another the pastor of a large city church and a man of wide influence; another, the dean of a reputable college; and a daughter became a missionary to China.

These were the kinds of things I would be seeing as I listened to the dry hesitant talk of my colleagues trying to set up requirements for the "elevation of standards" as if they were not dealing with human beings and with conditions, economic and social, that made their own institutions seem artificial and remote from most of the people of this section. I couldn't keep my mind from wandering to the porch of a small farmhouse, located on the sloping side of a red clay hill. Two people in their middle seventies were looking wistfully into the far distances, into which "the children" had gone one by one, as they became strong enough to leave the family nest. There were eleven of them, nine boys and two girls. How the little house had even sheltered all of them at one time, I could never guess. But somehow it did. Every one of them had gone to college. How it was done was too much of a problem for me to work out even after they told, in matter-of-fact ways, of the toil, the sacrifice, the prayers, the faith, in which each shared, the older children helping in succession as the younger followed in their steps. And there was not a "black sheep" among them. I knew them all. Fine substantial upstanding citizens they were. As lawyer, doctor, merchant, farmer, they could be depended upon to take their stand for the best things in the communities in which they lived. They had books and magazines in their homes, and could hold their own in any discussion of the current thought of their day—educated men of character, respecting others as well as themselves, loyal to church and school, helping to forward the interests that counted for most in the best life of their friends and neighbors. For them the only kind of college available was the small academically unregulated, unstandardized institution, and yet from this they got a discipline, an urge to go on, worthy aspirations, motives of service, ways of using their minds, and a fidelity to things of honest and of good report. If all this is not "higher education," what is?

And that other man—him, too, I shall never forget! His father had fought under Lee, and he was brought up in the grim, gray, haggard days of reconstruction and thereafter. Everything about him showed that there had been no soft hours for him; his clothes were neat and clean, but worn slick and thin; they were his best because he was at church; his hair was grayer than it should have been for his years; his face was deeply seamed by weather, reddish and leathery, for in summer sun and winter cold he had followed a mule and a plow all the days of his life. He had sent two daughters and two sons to college. I wondered and wondered how he did it, knowing the conditions under which he made a living, such as it was, and so I put the question to him: "How did you do it?"

For answer he held up the biggest pair of hands I ever saw, all calloused and gnarled, and said simply, "With these!" And more than forty years after, those hands have a way of popping up before me, and I think of them as a symbol of the toil that entered into the purpose that his children should have a better chance than he had, of the church to which he belonged that inspired and kept alive this purpose, and of the sacrifices needed to realize it as chief among his religious duties. There's a glory about those big hands as they rise before me. His kind, with a sort of blind faith in education in a day when it was not a social habit to go to highly standardized schools and colleges, quite the reverse being true, followed the gleam in a time of educational, social, and economic confusion and darkness, seeking the best there was in the mysterious magic called "education."

And such instances as I here set down were not exceptional,

131

but were plentiful enough to impregnate the very air that enveloped most of these unregulated citadels of learning as they fought, most of them in vain, for something quite worth fighting for. I used to like to go to them at commencement (with accent always on the last syllable), particularly if I had just made an address at a university—as much less than a university, by the way as these small institutions were less than a college. I would like to breathe a bit of educational fresh air, and be stimulated by a thousand or so plain, simple Americans, most of them countryfolk, who believed whole-heartedly in education and in the conviction that those who were receiving their diplomas had actually acquired them. They came to the campus grounds in huge numbers in every kind of mule- and horse-drawn vehicle, many of them to camp out during the several days of commencement. The politicians from all over the state were there—the governor, a senator maybe, several congressmen, members of, and candidates for, the legislature. It was a happy picnic occasion until the bell rang, and then everybody crowded promptly into auditorium or chapel to hear the next event. Sunday a bishop of the church, not often seen in these parts, preached the sermon, and every-body was still talking about how great it was, some having wept under the spell of it, and a few having shouted. Then there had been some mighty fine speaking, declaiming, done by the boys. "Did you approve the decisions of the judges in awarding the medals? I thought Billy Brown ought to have had it"—and so on.

But the day of days had come. The gray-haired president presided with a dignity that bordered on pompousness. But he knew everybody, and these graduates were in an intimate, personal sense his boys. He knew them by name, had visited in their families, and out of his own pocket had lent them money in a pinch. It didn't matter if it was talked out loud that he sold honorary degrees to his brethren of the ministry at from $25 to $50. For had he not used the money to help worthy boys through his college, especially those who had been called to preach the gospel? That was only one of his many ways of helping those who needed help, and those upon whom the purchased degrees were conferred usually deserved them—so it was said in defense.

Then the president would introduce in glowing, extravagant terms the man who would deliver the "literary address," not "the address to the graduating class" full of sage advice about what they were to do next, nor an address concerning some of the major problems of modern society. Not a few times I have enjoyed the honor of making a literary address on such occasions, and until comparatively recent days, I have tried to do just that. In fact, I have actually attempted a subject from Browning or Tennyson, or more often from Shakespeare. What my audiences thought of my efforts I was never certain, but I do know I would get the best of attention, though it may have been no more than the innate courtesy of the people of the countryside, whom the very presence of their college had trained to give a respectful hearing to those who spoke from its stage on so significant an occasion as commencement.

But the chief interest would center in the speeches from the graduating class. Each member would deliver an oration of his own composition on some phase of humanity's mighty progress to the present time and of the stupendous promise of the future. But there was one exception to this line of subjects. Sitting with these youngsters to receive a diploma was a man about forty years old, a strong, rugged, well-set-up man, clad in his black-suited best, not at all ill at ease in this group of eighteen- and twenty-year-old boys. Instead of borrowed thunder from books and other men's speeches—I mean reflections—in simple, direct impressive words he talked about himself: More than twenty years ago he had completed the third year of this college, but the death of his father, a little farm in a mountain valley, and the lure in a maiden's eyes had drawn him away to live and to make a living. But he was never quite happy in the sense that he had started something he didn't complete. Four boys came into his home, and he couldn't think of their looking on their father as "a quitter." He meant to send them to college, and his failure to stick it out might be a bad example for them. "They and my wife are sitting down in front, and I believe they are happier and prouder than I am at this moment."

And I saw them sitting there on the front bench—the wife and mother with eyes shining through the tears, and four stalwart sons looking up at their father as if they saw a glory about him. The audience fairly held its breath as he recited his story. They were his friends and neighbors, and were there to share in his hour of triumph. When he finished, there were a few brief seconds of tense silence, and then a spontaneous thunder of applause that shook the very rafters. He sat down, bowed his head, and if ever a strong man was justified in shedding a few tears, I knew he was. When he was handed his diploma, again the building trembled with applause, and I knew I had heard a great piece of oratory because what this man said and the way he said it gave that audience release of some of the noblest human emotions—approval of a man who saw his duty and in the face of great odds gallantly met it. My own effort to try to interest these people in some phases of Shakespeare's art under the title, "Pictures from an Old Master," seemed trivial enough as I listened to the natural eloquence of a man telling a heroic story without knowing there was anything heroic in it.

No, this is not an unusual story, the rare romance of one man whose experience brought a new meaning to life and its responsibilities, and who proceeded to make the dream that emerged come true. Such stories gathered about each of these little colleges which academic conspirators were doing their best to discredit and destroy and which the march of educational progress was gradually forcing into the limbo of useless agencies of human service unless by some magic of support one here and there found a way of keeping step with educational progress. But the memory of such stories will still be kept alive in the legendary lore of the countryside, and children and grandchildren will be reminded of how "education was gotten" in days gone by. And if the once small struggling institution has somehow come out of its past much bigger and more prosperous, older alumni will still tell at their gatherings with sentimental approval these ancient romances of heroic endeavor in a great cause, when their college, or university now, was a group of ramshackle buildings on a remote country hillside. And they will be heard with that choking of the heart that is felt when men listen to the story of achievement that has in it courage, faith, self-denial, and high purpose.

Just before the end of the last century, September, 1897, there came into the president's office at Wofford a man of good height, his black hair streaked a little with gray, bearing himself with the assured manner of one who had achieved enough success to ask no special favors of anyone. The president of Wofford thought he had come to discuss the matter of entering his son. But no, not that. He had come to enter, and in the direct and quiet way of a man who knew what he wanted and why, he told this story: "I've been a country doctor for fifteen years up here in the foothills of the mountains and have been successful in financial and other ways. Before going to the medical college, my schooling was had through several years at one-teacher schools at intervals between plowing, planting, and harvesting. Now I have made some discoveries: A doctor must be something more than a healer of the sick. He should be a leader to his people, helping them improve their homes and living conditions, provide better schools and churches. I want to serve them in these ways as well as minister to them when they are sick. And somehow I would be fumbling aimlessly when I tried to handle these important matters, and so I thought I might get help if I came to college. In driving down to Spartanburg several times a year from the mountains, I would see the college towers and hear its bell. I couldn't resist, and here I am."

There were no standardizing agencies in 1897 threatening

the wise old president of Wofford if he dared "to let down the bars," and the standards of Wofford were not low at that time. They never had been. But he swept them aside with an understanding sympathy to tell the doctor that all doors were open wide to him and every instructor would be standing by to assist in the fulfillment of a great purpose.

He came, rented a little house near by, placed his fifteen-year-old son in the Fitting School, and employed a teacher for his wife; here was a case of a whole family going to school. This forty-five-year-old man, pretty wise in the ways of life, took his place by the side of young freshmen, did the required work as well as the best of them, shared in their speaking and debates in the literary societies, looked on and cheered at their sports, and won their respect and admiration—something of a campus hero without suspecting it. After four years, the most interested and interesting student on the campus, he earned his diploma, going back to the high hills of western North Carolina whence he came, affirming with a proud satisfaction that he was now ready to do for his people what he had planned. And he did. For the next twenty-five years he was not only a better physician, I venture to affirm, but also an inspiring, constructive leader of the things that make for progress in backward communities, an evangelist for the privileges that lift the underprivileged from their low estate. The towers and bells of a little college in a small upcountry South Carolina town called him to be this kind of man and gave him his chance, his only chance. When I think of this man, I can never get myself to despise the work of such institutions. They kept the flame of learning alight in many a dark place in the stricken, desolated South after the war, before other and perhaps better institutions had emerged to change the whole educational pattern.

There was another thing about these institutions that was always a source of wonder to me. Among their instructors there were sure to be one or two men of unusual capacity, scholarship, personality, and teaching skill. Why they should be content to remain in one of these out-of-the-way, unknown, unhonored, and unsung colleges, with their light hid under a bushel, so to speak, was just more than I could understand. Wise men they would seem to be, and happy where they were. Maybe they found content in the spirit of Chaucer's clerk: "And gladly wolde he lerne, and gladly teche." Anyway they too became legends; and in the years after their passing there would be men, some of them big men, important men, who would not let them be forgotten, but gratefully, tenderly, would tell one another of the sheer greatness of their "old" teacher and of what they "owed" him. When I became a college president and the Ph.D. rash had broken out all over the face of American higher education and I was finding it more difficult to "educate" a young instructor than a freshman, I was sometimes possessed with a nostalgic covetousness for the men I have been describing. I knew they were becoming increasingly scarce, and education increasingly the poorer for it. Will they come again, or were they the products of conditions that will never return? Was it a way Providence had of compensating society for some things it did not have?

It must be remembered too that these colleges were schools of the people. Planted in country places or in small towns or villages, they drew their patronage mainly from the locality or from a comparatively narrow circle, rarely going beyond state lines. They brought education to those who might not have gone far to seek it. In this sense even a superficial observer will see that they served as social, intellectual, and moral uplifting forces, quite out of proportion to their meager resources and equipment, doing a work that no other kind of institution could have done. It was Lord Bryce, that sane and acute observer of American life, who understood this aspect of their service. This is what he says of them in his *American Commonwealth*:

They set learning in visible form, plain indeed, and humble, but dignified even in her humility, before the eyes of a rustic

137

people, in whom the love of knowledge, naturally strong, might never break from the bud into the flower but for the care of some zealous gardener. They gave the chance of rising into some intellectual walk of life to many a strong and earnest nature who might otherwise have remained an artisan or storekeeper, and perhaps failed in these vocations. They lighted up in many a country town what is at first only a farthing rushlight, but which, when the town swells to a city, or when endowments flow in, or when some able teacher is placed in charge, becomes a lamp of growing flame which may finally throw its rays over the whole state in which it stands.

Most of these educational rushlights flickered and died out, unable to survive in the struggle for existence, but some were to become nationally known institutions. For instance, Duke University, like Trinity College and other institutions, wandered pathetically all over North Carolina before it found a home in Durham; and Emory University emerged from a little college located in a Georgia village called Oxford to settle down in metropolitan Atlanta permanently, and so with other worthy southern institutions not so widely known. But their progress came later when I was well into my presidency. When, however, I began in 1902, my educational world was of the multiplicity of little colleges whose function and service I have been at some pains to appreciate as lights in dark places. They had their day and ceased to be, but to disparage them is to be blind to a significant phase of the South's epic struggle to hold fast to the things that counted in its civilization. They are symbols of the faith of the human spirit in enduring values and of its sacrificial fight to keep the light of such values burning when conditions were darkest.

8

CRUSADERS AND REVIVALISTS

SINCE THE SILENCING of the guns at Appomattox, I wonder if J. L. M. Curry, taking him all in all, has not been really the most potent force in the history of the post-bellum South. Certainly I know of no politician now dead enough to be called a "statesman" whom one might think of in the same breath with him. Born in a little Georgia town, prepared for college at the famous Waddell Academy in South Carolina, from which John C. Calhoun went to the junior class at Yale and the law school at Litchfield, Connecticut, he moved with his family at the age of thirteen to Alabama. He graduated from the University of Georgia with such men as Joseph LeConte the geologist and Ben Hill the statesman, going thence to the Harvard law school, with Rutherford B. Hayes as a classmate, then back to Alabama to practice law. He was a soldier in the Mexican War, a member of the state legislature and the National Congress, a member of the Confederate congress, a colonel of cavalry in the War Between the States, president of Howard College in Birmingham, professor of English in Richmond University, Baptist minister, United States minister to Spain. Here in brief outline is the preparation for a great constructive task such as few men have had placed in their hands to perform.

The young southern law student at Harvard in 1843 heard speeches by Wendell Phillips and William Lloyd Garrison, and one may well guess that the words of the great abolitionists didn't please him much. But he also heard another New England voice, that of Horace Mann, pleading for the rights of childhood in a free democracy; and as he was fighting the

139

same fight forty years later in his impoverished section of still bitter memories, it was at Horace Mann's flame that he confessed his torch had been lighted. Through all the crowded, varied, intervening years Curry never lost the vision inspired by hearing Horace Mann on that New England night in 1843. The most important single person in the audience, on that occasion, was this young Southerner from Alabama who one day was to carry the message of popular education by public taxation where it was more needed than it was in New England even when Horace Mann began his crusade. Throughout the South young men, particularly those in the field of education, felt the contagion of Curry's personality and message, and they too became crusaders in the great cause.

But it was in North Carolina, to a greater extent perhaps than in any other southern state, that the big fires were set burning. This was because North Carolina was really more democratic in its social stratification and political thinking than the rest of the Confederate states. Very early it showed at least a tendency to refuse to let the past continue to keep its dead hand on the present, and it was the first to show gleams of that nationalism that began to brighten, slowly enough, the face of things southern. It accepted the industrialization of southern life more quickly than its other sister states below the Potomac. The important thing here is that it found within its borders an appropriate leadership—men like Walter Hines Page, Edward P. Moses, Edwin A. Alderman, Charles D. McIver, James Y. Joyner, and Charles B. Aycock, who rode into the governorship in 1900 on the platform of this group.

From 1889 through 1891 Alderman and McIver, though very different in appearance and methods of presentation, conducted institutes in every county in North Carolina. These institutes were used not merely as occasions for discussions of ways and means of improving instruction on the part of teachers, but as occasions for stirring communities to a wiser and more liberal support of their schools and the duty of a democracy to educate all the people if it would survive. There is an epic quality about the campaign of these two young men and no little of the power of a religious dedication to holy and enduring service. They plowed deep in the soil of their commonwealth and sowed seeds that later were to bring a mighty harvest in the rebuilding of a great state. Among other things the state set up the North Carolina college for young women at Greensboro in 1892, of which McIver became the first president and put new life into the old university at Chapel Hill. To its presidency Alderman was called in 1896, and Aycock was elected governor in 1900. The crusaders had their reward, but had also prepared the way for the emergence of forces of progress that were to spread their beneficent, creative influence throughout the entire South.

For one thing the churches in North Carolina joined aggressively in the campaign for popular education, putting into it the compulsions of the religious motive, compulsions which had great virtue in the two larger denominations in North Carolina, made up as they were of the great majority of the people of the state that most needed the educational awakening. But fortunately or unfortunately in the long run—my guess is fortunately—a bitter fight was made on the tax-supported institutions, particularly the state university. The churchmen argued that free tuition and scholarships should be abolished, that no legislative appropriations should be made at least until the elementary schools were adequately provided for; even that the state institutions should be supported by voluntary contributions just as the denominational institutions were; that it wasn't just to tax members of the church for state schools while they were giving financial support and paying tuition at their own institutions for their sons and daughters; that if people will risk the religious faith and moral character of their children by sending them to secular institutions, they should pay all expenses as Christian people do at their colleges, and so on and so on.

If one thinks that North Carolina was not having a perfect-

141

ly gorgeous fight from 1890 until well over into the next century, one has never seen thoroughly aroused ecclesiastics in action when they think they are divinely called to defend or destroy what they consider life-and-death issues—and the issues suggested above were to most of the Baptist and Methodist ministers life-and-death issues. Their ablest men took part in the controversy. J. W. Bailey, now senior Senator from North Carolina, Charles E. Taylor, president of Wake Forest College, and John E. White, secretary of the Baptist State Convention, having won the Lord to their side through prayer and meditation, could hold their own with any other group in the state, political or educational. Whoever entered into a debate with these men knew he would need all his resources. There was no mincing of words, and bitter, violent language was used, even to the extent of virulent namecalling. During these years the people of the Old North State were having the time of their lives, for this semireligious-educational controversy was the kind of public talk they liked.

But if they thought the discussions were a bit overheated at times, they were to find out that the debaters hadn't even warmed up until Dr. John C. Kilgo came from Wofford in South Carolina to accept the presidency of little moribund Trinity College at Durham. This fiery protagonist of Christian education really put on the heat. He literally turned himself loose, going up and down the state from the mountains to the sea, speaking to more people than any other man had ever spoken to in North Carolina. Great crowds thronged to hear him wherever and whenever he spoke or preached, and within three years he became to many people the most famous man in the state, and to many the most infamous. He had everything it takes to make a popular orator: convictions, courage, humor, biting wit, rare skill in illustrative storytelling, pathos, moving eloquence, mimicry, the actor's power of dramatizing a situation, an extravagant use of vituperative language, and an extraordinary way of labeling an opponent with a belittling phrase. And he was frugal with none of his gifts. The new recruit from South Carolina proved a more effective fighter than the native veterans.

In 1897 Walter Hines Page came down from the editorial desk of the *Forum* in New York to make an address at the recently established North Carolina Normal and Industrial College for Women at Greensboro. Into the midst of the educational battle then raging he threw a high-explosive shell labeled "The Forgotten Man." Page had tried to edit a paper in his native state, but his views had been too modernistic, too caustically disrespectful of the prevailing folkways, and his verbal efforts to release the present from the "dead hand" of the mummies of the past had been too violent. With such views he couldn't make much headway in the Old North State, and so he had gone to New York to find a congenial atmosphere for the free expression of his great talents. He was looked upon already as a Yankeeized expatriate Southerner, who was bent on capitalizing to his own advantage his unfriendly attitude to the traditions of his section. In forthright English he packed into "The Forgotten Man" all his pent-up resentment toward the forces that had held in bondage from the beginning of its history the educational and economic potentialities of the plain everyday people of the southern states—men and women of unadulterated Anglo-Saxon stock, held back and kept down by basically wrong conceptions of life. He did not spare the aristocratic conception, still lingering in decay but kept alive by "professional" Southerners, nor the exploitation by politicians of these plain people, the failure of the churches, the playing up of the glories of the past by the Confederate veterans associations to the obscuring of the needs of the present and the promise of the future. Even the hillbillies, the crackers, the sandlappers had found a champion outside of politics for the first time, in Page's white-heated belligerency in their behalf. That address was perhaps the most important word spoken in the South since 1865. Its reverberations could not be confined within the boundaries of North Carolina, and its repercussions so shook the whole section that the yelping barks of the dogs of reaction and obscurantism followed Page for years thereafter. But anybody with even a tiny flame of real understanding in his brain knew that here was the truth and the only road to progress—the right of every child born in the commonwealth to the free education of mind, body, and hand—and that for the sake of society itself the forgotten man must at last become the remembered man.

In the other southern states the forgotten man was being discovered by the politicians like "Pitchfork" Ben Tillman, but educationally in a much less stormy way. The leadership of these states was reasonably busy through the 1890's working toward a free school system for all, but with an exasperatingly slow degree of success. The old aristocratic attitude of each man's taking care of his own was still strong in spite of educational conditions generally and, specifically, of the dark shadow of white illiteracy that hung like a blight over the entire South. But the politicians were mightily in action discovering the forgotten man for their own uses by exploiting his low economic estate and his latent social antagonisms to the old aristocratic order. Jeff Davis, James K. Vardaman, Tom Watson, and "Pitchfork" Ben Tillman rode roughshod into positions of political power, not only interrupting the ancient tradition that none but gentlemen should hold office, but even destroying this tradition beyond survival in some states.

For example, in his violent way Ben Tillman assumed he was the voice of the forgotten man, not, however, in the failure of the state to provide free elementary and high-school education for its children but in not providing appropriate colleges. He attacked throughout his campaigns the old order for its many sins and especially for the nature of the two institutions of higher learning to which its sons went—the South Carolina college at Columbia and the Citadel, the state military college at Charleston, both deeply entrenched in their affection. He came near closing both, calling the latter a "damned dude factory" and the former a "pleasant loafing place for the sons of aristocrats." But they survived his assaults when he turned his

144

interest to the establishment of two new institutions—Clemson Agricultural and Mechanical College for men and the Winthrop Normal and Industrial College for women. He won his way easily for them by asserting in his most vehement manner that they were for the "poor" boys and girls of the state, offering as they did the kind of education they needed for the improvement of their economic situation. In this of course he was right, and he started the "cult" of the poor boy and girl in South Carolina, and the cult still has vitality, for even yet a boy applying for entrance into college may claim assistance on the ground that he is "just the son of a poor farmer." Alas! The forgotten man makes one wish at times he were still forgotten, and that high-headed upholder of that other tradition in the South, even in his slovenly decay, were more in evidence. At least he would not be apt to ask favors because he was poor. In fact, in his pride he would always be making a pathetic struggle to hide his poverty. This would be a part of that heritage of the code of the gentleman along with his memories of Lee, and Jackson, and Wade Hampton, and Stuart, and of that old home whose walls were lined with ancestral portraits. From such homes men might emerge in the morning in frayed, slick clothes of an ancient vintage; walking stick gracefully in hand, heads high, they would take the air in the manner of those to whom the world still belonged, heroic figures even if they suggested an order of life that was in process of a death being hastened by more or less violent assaults from within and without, and by social, political, economic, and educational forces, from which there was no escape.

Also to be counted among these forces of change was the sugary, melting oratory of Henry W. Grady with its note of commercialism and nationalism. "The South of secession and slavery is dead!" To be sure, Mr. Grady, but that moving picture you drew, in that appealing way of yours, of the ancient white mansion with its stately columns and of the return of the Confederate soldier after the epic struggle in which he gained enough glory to cover almost all his losses, nearly made us forget that New South of nationalism and commercialism for which you were pleading. Walter Hines Page stirred our hot wrath with his forgotten man; but Henry Grady, without indicting us for high crimes and misdemeanors for which history, and not we, was responsible, warmed our hearts with an affectionate reverence for our past, stirred a faith in ourselves, and gave us new hopes for the future. The youth of the section memorized his speeches, and without sensing the full implication of their meaning realized that their South was on the march toward a finer and richer progress. He is therefore to be counted among those who disturbed us out of the traditionalisms of the Lost Cause conception of things and a narrow embittered sectionalism. He too was a part of a movement of liberation in the South, a pioneer a little ahead of Page and Alderman not only in point of time, but also in mood and method of approach to the softening process that was necessary to the breaking down of the hampering traditionalism of this section. He had his day of glory but also of great service in this direction—and a great day of national acclaim it was, though all too brief, but yet long enough to set the entire nation thinking about this orphan child of the republic with its immense potentials of natural and human wealth.

Now these men—all of them I knew, and some with more or less intimacy—whom I have been trying to lift out of the significant last decade of the nineteenth century for a fresh appreciation of their leadership at a vital moment in the history of the South, have been often described as "crusaders" in the cause of popular education. To be sure, in their fervor of spirit, their sense of human need, and their dedication of mind and soul, they were crusaders, but they were also forerunners of other crusaders who, though fired with the same zeal and purpose, would make more definite the aims of these earlier crusaders, taking the latter along with them as they proceeded to assist in "the rebuilding of old commonwealths" by unifying the forces engaged in offering better educational facilities for all the children of the South. I am here referring, of course, to

146

the movement begun by the so-called "Conference for Education in the South" that finally led to the organization of the General Education Board in the early days of 1902.

When I consider what has happened to American life in these recent years, even before the great war—its passing under a variety of alphabetic controls subsidized out of federal taxes and directed from Washington, tending always toward the debilitation of the self-reliant, self-helping element in American character—even the memory of a movement so thoroughly charged with that old-fashioned Americanism that built the republic and made it great serves as an exhilarating tonic as one thinks back on the spirit, aims, methods of organization, and steps in the processes that finally resulted in the most beneficent influence in the rebuilding of the South and in the formation of the most far-reaching and the most wisely administered philanthropy in the records of mankind. In the summers of 1898 and 1899 a group of American citizens met at Capon Springs, West Virginia. There were no politicians among them, no "experts" of any kind, nobody expecting any subsidy from the government. They were just patriotic American citizens who had ideas as to how to serve their country at that moment in its history.

The South was in the midst of an industrial renaissance and was moving forward at such a rate as to arrest the interest and attention of the nation. But this group at Capon Springs thought of other aspects of southern life, which in the long future would determine whether this commercial progress would become not so good because it was leaving out of consideration another kind of progress even more important, education, particularly the education of the colored people and the mountain whites. As they thought and talked together, their view widened until it took in the education of all the people of the South. As Americans they couldn't leave anybody out, and they dreamed great dreams of the salvation of the whole South by means of a revival of popular education. Many other highminded, liberal, understanding men and women, north and south, were drawn into the conferences; and the educational revival fire spread, taking on no little of the inspired emotionalism of a religious movement.

Its leader, Robert Curtis Ogden, a greatly successful New York merchant, conducted for a dozen years annual campaigns throughout the South, stopping for several days at various important centers for a series of public sessions in which some of the best minds of the nation took part. Without exception they too caught the contagion of his own consecrated zeal. He used with extraordinary effectiveness the merchant's art of advertising his wares, the psychological insight of the religious evangelist in stirring the imagination and emotions of people, and the wisdom to know not only how to make the iron hot but also when and by whom to strike when it was hot. Anyone who knows the South, its sensitiveness, its prejudices, its suspicions of outsiders, its traditions, must feel that Ogden was a man called of God for just the service he rendered at that particular moment in the history of his country. Any other kind of man, north or south, could have made the movement a ghastly failure, halting progress for a decade and at the same time retarding indefinitely the growth of a wholesome trend toward nationalism throughout the South by an acute revival of the bitterness of a then waning sectionalism.

I was privileged to attend the fifth meeting of the Conference for Education at Athens, Georgia, April 24-26, 1902. President Carlisle of Wofford, the dean of southern educators, had been invited to deliver an address on "The Denominational College and Popular Education." But President Carlisle was of that anomalous type of stay-at-home-on-the-job college president. In fact, I always had the suspicion that he did not believe much in big meetings of any kind, assessing them largely as vaporous talk and little else. So when calls came to him to share in such gatherings, he would appoint a member of the faculty to represent the college and bring back a report of the proceedings. I am sure that his main interest was that of educating members of the faculty rather than of promoting any large educational enterprises. Anyway, he sent me on this occasion, and the meeting produced in me, who was to succeed him as president of Wofford within a few months, profound and lasting impressions and resolves.

The truth is, I can conceive of no better preparation for the duties of the presidency of a small denominational college in the South in 1902 than the thoughts and emotions inspired during those three April days in middle Georgia, and the opportunity of coming to know a kind of educational leadership, both lay and professional, that created a new faith in the rich future of the South through the sympathetic understanding and co-operation of men of good will from all sections of the nation. I believe I was born again educationally, and I know that I came from that meeting a kind of dedicated soul. This attitude was of the very atmosphere of each day's proceedings. Nobody could well escape it because it somehow glowed in all the addresses—addresses by Edwin Alderman, of Tulane; Governor Aycock, of North Carolina; Walter Hines Page, now editor of the *World's Work;* Albert Shaw, of the *Review of Reviews;* Senator Hoke Smith, of Georgia; Hamilton Wright Mabie, editor of the *Outlook;* Felix Adler; Dean James Russell, of Teacher's College; John Graham Brooks; U. S. Commissioner of Education W. T. Harris; President David Houston, of Texas; W. H. Farham, of Yale; Judge Emory Speer, of Georgia; and others. They represented an array of important Americans whose utterances were alive with the sincere warmth of a kind of consecrated service and a prophetic sense that the meeting was the beginning of great things for the South and the nation. Even the formal reports dealing with facts and figures were not cold and dry but revealed so much progress and promise of more progress that they, too, seemed to have a gleam and a glow in them.

The atmosphere couldn't have been otherwise under the presiding genius of R. C. Ogden. He possessed all the arts of a popular evangelist in the field of religion: skill in frictionless

149

organization; a flair for advertising and propaganda; a manner of speaking that was irresistible in its appeal, tact, understanding; a winning passion to convert people to his way of thinking; and the conviction that he was carrying on a redemptive educational process. He brought to his undertaking those deep religious motives that made him a great churchman and philanthropist. Nobody could for a moment make any mistake about his integrity, sincerity, and disinterested devotion. It was as if he were set apart for the very business he was in, and he drew us all to him and it. Who else could say things of this kind, and not wake at least a suspicion of an overly unctuous type of piety?

"The clarion call of patriotism summons this assembly and rings out the keynote for its utterances, altruism pure and simple gives it vitality, human brotherhood is the tie that binds it together. If this be true, pessimism can find no foothold here and selfishness no standing ground. This Conference is a Band of Hope." "Band of Hope"—a phrase that leaped out of the days when he was teaching youth in Sunday-school classes in New York and Philadelphia to flavor with religious values the civic privileges of what he was advocating. His versatility and words stirred us then, and they stir me now as I recall them after more than forty years.

It was well that this fifth session of the Conference for Education in the South met in Athens, Georgia. It had something that neither Atlanta nor Birmingham could have. These two, the *nouveaux riches* among southern cities, had too much of the raw crudeness of the hustling, bustling New South, but Athens was a beautiful type of the Old. It had been a college town for more than a hundred years, and had the unmistakable qualities that go with such centers. Many old homes there were white-columned, sitting back from the streets and resting peacefully under the shadows of ancient trees. One who knew his South was aware that within their wide and hospitable doors were gracious and gentle living and all the charm of the arts that old culture gives. In one of these homes I was a fellow guest with Mr. William H. Baldwin, Jr., who at one time had been president of the Southern Railway System, and was the president of the newly organized General Education Board. "Here we are," he said one evening, "planning with all our hearts for the educational uplift of the poor whites and Negroes of the South, and rightly so. It is a glorious task. But what can be done to preserve the people and culture of such homes as this one in which we are guests? They represent a rich asset of the nation, and shouldn't be lost. Can anything be done?"

"No," I had to reply, "it cannot be kept, as gracious and beautiful as it is. It is the product of a special kind of economic and social system, the plantation system based on human slavery, and that is gone forever. The beauty and charm of the old order, its courtesy, courage, sense of honor, simple dignity, are already becoming a memory. Of course there will always be a day when the novelist will discover over and over again the romance, the gentle and gracious culture of these ever-receding days, and so tell the story as to remind the nation of the worth of the only genuine aristocracy that ever flourished under the flag of American democracy, and yet an aristocracy more fiercely, more individualistically democratic at times than that that existed in any other section of the country." So regretfully we both felt we could do nothing about it except bewail the loss of such a civilization as one of the tragedies of American history.

This presence of the past of the South could not escape the thoughts of all in attendance at this Athens meeting. One felt it in the atmosphere of these old homes in which we were guests, and of the university whose influence was everywhere. The sessions were held in the university chapel, in the State Normal School for Women, and the chapel of the Lucy Cobb Institute for Girls. It was to this last institution that the daughters of the Old South had been going for a long, long time to learn their music, French, dancing, and the manners and graces of a "lady," and they were still going. The coming together

151

of these two worlds, the world of a vanishing yesterday and the world of tomorrow's progress, was brought to a moving climax by that fine gesture on the part of the newly formed General Education Board, when through its secretary, Dr. Wallace Buttrick, the board added $7,500 to a scholarship fund provided by the women of Georgia for worthy girls at the State Normal School, and $6,000 toward the Winnie Davis Memorial Hall on the campus of the same institution. No words could have been more sympathetic, more understanding, more inspiring than this: "The gift to the Winnie Davis Memorial Hall is made in recognition of the fact that this is Memorial Day, and that this is a supremely appropriate contribution to the Daughters of the Confederacy. It is to the young women who are entering upon one of the noblest inheritances of the world that we crave the privilege of making these gifts. We ask that we may have a little part in the great work which has been inaugurated by the people of the South, and in which the women of Georgia are bearing so honorable and noble a part." No more fitting words could have been spoken. They warmed the hearts of every Southerner who heard them, and we girded ourselves all the stronger for the tasks of the new era really because we were permitted to carry into it the memories of the old.

I have already commented on the deeply religious mood of this meeting. Its presence was unmistakable, for, though that derogatory label "the Bible belt" had not yet been plastered on the South in ridicule of what certain of the intelligentsia considered its narrow, antiquated religious beliefs and practices, in 1902 the South was essentially the Bible belt of the nation, and in not a bad sense. After the Confederate war Southerners had only faith left to sustain them—faith in themselves, faith in the values worth preserving in their shattered civilization, and faith in God. As the old saying goes, they still read Scott's novels, studied the Bible, worshiped God Almighty, spoke one language with the same accents, had social customs that needed no changing anywhere south of the Potomac, married one woman for life, and voted the Democratic ticket. In these things it was the Solid South, and they found their hearts strangely warmed when the Ogden group in no way flouted their familiar *mores*, but seemed even to approve them. They melted under such an influence as if they were in attendance upon a great revival meeting.

Mr. Ogden himself, as I have said, had the ways of the evangelist; Edgar Gardner Murphy, the executive secretary of the Southern Education Board, was an Episcopal clergyman; Frederick T. Gates, the controlling spirit in the two-months-old General Education Board, brought a lifetime of service in the various activities of the Baptist Church to this crusade for better educational conditions in the South; and Wallace Buttrick was also a Baptist minister who had worked with Dr. Gates in missionary efforts of this church among the Negroes, of the South. Under such leadership the flavor, the color, the emotional mood of this epoch-making enterprise to lift the South upward and forward had to be religious in its essential characteristics, and this is why this section was so profoundly influenced into a co-operation amazingly complete when the normal prejudices of the South, very much alive in 1902 in other directions, are considered. And so I think that a better name for the Ogden group, or party, going even as far back as J. L. M. Curry and including those later pioneers that broke the first post-bellum trails into the educational wilderness, would have been "evangelists," the revivalists of popular education, rather than "crusaders," the name by which they became known, and in which they themselves seemed to have a sort of pride.

This mood of revivalism was warmly present in the first session of that remarkable gathering called the "Summer School of the South," held at the University of Tennessee in the summer following the meeting of the Southern Conference for Education in the South at Athens. If this Athens meeting widened the horizons, clarified the understanding, and deepened the convictions as to the educational needs of the South of a young professor of English, who, without being aware of it, was within two months to be called to the presidency of a small southern college, the Summer School of the South furnished just the sort of experience needed to vitalize his aims and purposes, and make him feel that, however small his college, the opportunity of sharing in a great forward movement would create a real bigness in the position he had just accepted.

This great enterprise, the Summer School of the South, was originated, organized, and carried through in the genuine American way. We knew no other in those far-off horse-and-buggy days. No subsidy came from anybody's taxes, and consequently there were no bureaus of any kind to lay down regulations and demand reports "in triplicate." The University of Tennessee merely offered the use of its grounds, buildings, equipment, and its very capable president, Charles W. Dabney. He associated with himself P. P. Claxton, who was later to be United States commissioner of education, Wickliffe Rose, afterward successor to Wallace Buttrick as chairman of the General Education Board, and Edgar Gardner Murphy, secretary of the Southern Education Board. The financial resources needed came from private donors and from the two boards. These men brought together from all over the country a faculty of ninety-five, offering fifteen courses of study related to all ranks and grades of education in the South, and lecturers of national importance in almost every field of human interests. Conference discussions were held upon those matters, both special and general, that had to do with the whole problem of southern education. In a word, a great school of more than two thousand students and eight hundred registered visitors, the largest summer school ever held in the United States, was carried on for six stirring, blistering summer weeks. But the torrid heat of Knoxville in no wise reduced the zeal and energy of either instructors or students. To the very end the school was a combination of the campaign mood of the early crusaders of popular education, of the patriotic fervor of the Ogden movement, of a passion to know conditions and improve them, and of the close application of men and women who desired earnestly to add to their knowledge, learn better methods of teaching, and come to a clearer understanding of the subject matter of their profession. I doubt whether there will ever again be such a combination of high and noble human emotions as those that fused into an enthusiastic unity that miscellaneous group of nearly three thousand people, coming as they did from thirty-four American states, *90 per cent* of them from the southern states.

It was well for me that, before I entered upon the active duties of the presidency of Wofford College, I was among the faculty of this great American enterprise, offering a course in southern literature with more than three hundred hearers each day. I had the opportunity to know the teachers of the South, the men and women in every kind of school as well as those in college and university, and, in particular, to get acquainted with every type of leadership in the field of southern education. As a new college president I was in process of being educated, as it were, and of getting what was to prove to be an indispensable background for the job that was to be mine for the next forty years. Of course I discovered very early at Knoxville that I had a fight to keep my head in order to preserve the soberer and less highly colored aspects of that phase of education represented by an institution like Wofford. Educational zealots for this, that, or the other were clamorous on the Knoxville campus even as far back as the summer of 1902, and one had just to smile at them and let them have their brief hour of noisy glory. This early learning to assess them at their real worth, or worthlessness, then, has given me a sort of immunity to them ever since. But my Knoxville summer gave me the best possible start for my new duties and a few weeks to think very hard about them.

9

FIRST YEARS

I COUNT the three weeks spent at the Summer School of the South, coming as they did so close upon the session of the Conference for Education in the South at Athens, Georgia, and following immediately my acceptance of the presidency of Wofford, as a most valuable experience. At one time or another most of the southern college presidents took a look-in to see what was going on, or to take part in the many and various discussions that were held daily. Superintendents and principals of schools, particularly those who had pioneered into some new ground, were there. Also one had the opportunity to take the measure of the men who were teaching in the collegs and universities of the South, as a rather selected group of them were offering courses in their specialties. Then important lecturers could be heard at the noon hour in the Thomas Jefferson pavillion—men like Richard T. Ely, the economist, and Stanley Hall, the psychologist. Altogether I was getting firsthand, so to speak, a vivid picture of the educational world in which I was to work, and with all its limitations the picture was an inspiring one, constituting a call to patriotic service as the major element in my duties as a college president. I very much doubt whether later college presidents can know the joy of putting all one's soul into the task of redemption of the South through every phase of education. That great day is gone except in the memory of the very few left who actually took part in it.

Besides, I do not believe I ever got more satisfaction out of anything than I did from the course of lectures on the literature of the South which I delivered daily for three weeks.

Some three hundred listeners sat on plain wood benches, an eager, deeply sympathetic group. They were mostly young women, daughters of the Old South who in its sheer poverty found teaching their only self-respecting way of making a living, who were not yet ready to go into offices, stores, and other commercial enterprises. What they may have lacked in special preparation for teaching in either technical training or knowledge of the subject matter, they made up for in intelligence, character, consecration, charm, and the social graces that were as instinctive with them as breathing. If the children of the forgotten men, as they were doing in increasing numbers, sat in schoolrooms presided over by such young women as listened day by day while I tried to interpret through literature the civilization of their section, these children of the masses could not fail to get something more valuable than they received from textbooks and formal recitation. It wouldn't do for me to make the statement given out publicly by Dr. G. Stanley Hall concerning these qualities of the southern "schoolmarm" so engagingly in evidence at this Knoxville summer school. This is part of what he said in giving his impressions of the school: "The most important impression made on me, next to the number, is the social quality of the students. You have the advantage over us in the North by far, in the high character, socially, of the ladies especially, who are teachers in the schools. Most of our teachers are from the lower walks of life while yours are from the best." And they were from the best, and this is the significant thing one sensed in the student teachers at Knoxville, and later at all summer schools for teachers in the South.

I felt the educational revival that was spreading throughout this section, as far as the elementary schools were concerned, was in good hands in those aspects of education that had to do with the important matters of character and manners and the outward amenities of civilized living. The Old South was still very much alive in the schoolroom by the presence of its daughters. And well was it for the schools that they drew their teachers from this class, as the mood and purpose of the educational revival became organized into normal schools and summer schools in every southern state for training teachers. It was they who thronged the classrooms—intelligent, eager, patriotic, and passionately dedicated to their high task. It should be added that they not only filled the classrooms in the schools of their home state, but also began to attend the advanced educational institutions in the North and West in increasing numbers. Through them important new methods and principles found expression in the schools of the South. They represent that gallant army which for low salaries, in primitive rural communities, in dilapidated schoolhouses, and with inadequate equipment, fought to overcome ignorance in the states they loved. While we shall always be calling the names of the significant leaders in the movement that transformed educational conditions in the South from 1900 on, these young women carried out the orders and made progress possible. No part of my experiences at the Summer School of the South remains more vividly with me than this impression of the superior native and cultural qualities of the teachers of the South and of their service to their section.

Another phase of the three torrid weeks spent at Knoxville that sticks with me as a sort of symbol of the South of 1902 was the dilapidation and the inadequacy of the physical plant and equipment of the University of Tennessee. Perched on a high bluegrass-covered hill for a campus, the university could hardly be surpassed in sheer natural beauty of surroundings by any other southern institution. But its buildings were old and in a distressing state of disrepair, and students of today would not live in its dormitories or eat in its dining rooms. However, as I recall it, my colleagues and I did not comment on what seems to me now, after the lapse of forty years, such desperately poverty-sticken conditions. We probably did not do so because the institutions from which we came were in no better state, and we therefore felt at home in our temporary University of Tennessee surroundings. Nashville, Memphis,

Chattanooga, and Knoxville itself might be booming forward under the impulse of the new industrialism; but here at the apex of the state's educational system—its more than a century-old university—there was no evidence of any "boom." It stood there as the stark sign of a great state's poverty of taxable resources or of its indicting failure to recognize the nature of the service its university might render if generously supported. Probably the sign pointed both ways—to the state's poverty and to its failure to understand the relation of its university to its own progress. At any rate, there the university stood, stripped down to the bare meager necessities of existence, the tragic symbol of higher education throughout the entire South, where every institution was struggling heroically to make bricks without straw, and doing not a bad job in spite of staggering limitations.

With an understanding and tact little short of miraculous, the General Education Board moved into this lean land of educational backwardness. It placed high-school inspectors as professors of secondary education in each of the southern state universities and turned them loose; it attached rural school men and women to the state departments of education under the direction of the state boards of education; it quietly made factual surveys of educational conditions and needs with no display of criticism and condescension; and it even made health investigations, particularly in the matter of hookworm and pellagra, without offending a proud, sensitive, individualistic, self-reliant people. Knowing the South as I do, I still wonder how the General Education Board managed to direct so wisely the whole course of the progress of education in the South, so recognizing characteristic moods, attitudes, and sensibilities as to work with them without stirring up the usual "hornet's nest" of resentment and opposition on the part of the southern people. The fact is that even most of the politicians did not fight the efforts of the board. My conviction is that the crusade or revival might have disappeared as a sort of nebulous mist as most emotionalized revivals do, had it not been for the board's more or less scientific study of southern conditions and their singularly wise co-operation with southern leaders.

And the significant thing is that their study and co-operation did not stop with elementary and secondary education. The board took in the whole range of southern education, accepting as a fundamental fact that education to be far-reaching and permanent in its results must be considered as a unit, beginning with the primary school and going all the way through college, university, and professional schools. Moreover, sympathetic attention was given to every type of institution—private, denominational, tax-supported, state boards of education, and standardizing agencies. Whoever worked out the board's plan of stirring the constituencies of colleges by conditional gifts from the board after study of the worth of the institution and its potential service, if its resources were increased, evolved a method of advancing higher education that produced results of the first magnitude, results that salvaged those colleges that ought to be saved and assisted in the demise of those whose usefulness as colleges was over.

As soon as the board's plans got noised abroad—and the "noise" was soon a rather loud noise, raising immense hopes in the minds of most college presidents—I too, like the others, sat down to do some hard thinking about the present and future needs of Wofford. First, there was the student patronage. Would it grow, and could it be made to grow? But a growing student body would necessitate an increase in the faculty personnel. This brought up the questions of adding other departments in which Wofford was weak and under-manned—the political sciences, chemistry, and biology, for instance. Then I knew that to do its work effectively Wofford must have two buildings—a library building and a science building. But several additional instructors and two buildings would cost money, and a good deal of it from the standpoint of the rather lean days in South Carolina in 1902. At first, it didn't occur to me that it was my business as president to raise the needed funds. It had not been the business of any of my predecessors. They had been chosen specifically to conduct the educational aspects of the college. Scholars themselves, they were almost full-time instructors, and the fund raising had always been in the hands of an official called the "financial agent," and a succession of very able men had filled this important position. Even in the midst of the Confederate war as much as $60,000 was added to the endowment of the institution by one of them. This and other funds are today the possession of the college in the form of Confederate bonds and securities—historic reminders of southern patriotism and of how far the tragedy of the Lost Cause went in its disruptive, retarding influences.

Of course, I could have followed in the footsteps of the other presidents of Wofford as well as the presidents of most small denominational colleges, accepting the historic *status quo*. But somehow I couldn't. It may be that I could not because of temperament. Seeing needs, I just could not sit down and do nothing about them. In a word, without surrendering one whit of the strictly educational responsibilities—that I have never done—I became absorbed in this other duty of finding funds for pressing educational needs. So calculating how much money it would take to put Wofford on its feet financially, I estimated it could be done for $150,000—$25,000 for each of the two buildings and $100,000 for the endowment. Thinking of the costs of college buildings and the value of endowment funds in today's terms, $150,000 seems a pitifully meager sum; and yet when I shared with the trustees of the college and other friends my purpose to go after a sum so huge, they wondered at my daring and gave me a smile of doubt rather than a pat of encouragement. But I was young and ignorant; and with the courage that goes with youth and ignorance I laid my plans to attempt even the impossible.

Providence gave the new president a good start. Through the influence of his predecessor and the professor of the natural sciences, an alumnus, a classmate of the latter, was easily

161

persuaded to furnish the science building. It was ready for use in 1904—a sturdy, impressive structure, classical in its architecture, and exceptionally well-equipped as to laboratory facilities for physics, chemistry, biology, and mineralogy. There was none better in the state for a college the size of Wofford. But when the building was completed, the science department would have to have another full professor and an assistant instructor. The rub was to get the income needed to make the addition of these men to the teaching force when the science building would be ready for use, and this had to be done quickly. It was done almost at once. The Methodist Church in South Carolina doubled its annual appropriation, that is, increased it from $1,500 to $3,000, and there was my professor provided for! Then, with the help of the extraordinary services of the professor of mathematics, I went out after students, the only other source of immediate income. They too came. In two years, that is, when the science hall was opened in September, 1904, the student body had grown from 182 to 220, an increase quite sufficient to pay for the instruction in science with something left over for other uses.

The library had to wait, but that addition of $100,000 to the endowment couldn't wait. So I called to my aid a Methodist minister, Dr. R. A. Child, giving him the usual title of "financial agent." But I had worked out plans different from those that other agents had used. For more than thirty years they had gone up and down South Carolina, preaching in the churches and taking collections for the college, and the best they could show for their labors—and they were "labors" in South Carolina from 1870 to 1902—was an endowment fund of hardly $60,000. It must be remembered, though, that poverty, grim and dire, stalked the land during the days of their service; memories of an unhappy past still filled the minds of the people; and economic, social, and political unrest kept the state boiling and fermenting in the bitterness of strife among its citizenship, culminating in the eruption of the Tillman movement. The wonder is that as much as $60,000 was raised under such conditions.

I felt a new plan must be tried, and it was this: I would go into the churches, two each Sunday and sometimes three, addressing the congregations on what the college might do to assist the church in the field of Christian education and the church's responsibility to support its college. I did not mention money explicitly or even that a campaign was on. Dr. Child would remain through the week, soliciting pledges from individuals in the form of notes, payable in five annual installments. The plan was successful beyond our expectations. By the end of the year we had subscriptions to the amount of $103,000, and the cash was coming in fast, faster than it had ever before come into the treasury of Wofford College. At the beginning of our campaign our prospects were brightened by a conditional gift of $25,000 from the General Education Board if we should raise the $100,000, and no little of our success was due to this. At that time $25,000 seemed to be an extraordinary amount of money for anybody to offer a Southern college. Four years later when collections on pledges were naturally slowing down and it looked as if $85,000 was about all we would realize in cash on our many small subscriptions, a windfall dropped suddenly, unexpectedly into the lap of Wofford, a miracle out of the blue in the shape of a legacy of $10,000 for a library from the daughter of the first professor of English literature at Wofford. He was appointed to this chair, as was not infrequently done in southern colleges, on his retirement from the active work of the ministry. There was half of my dream come true. But where was the other half to come from? I had already scraped the bottom of the financial barrel in South Carolina as far as I could see.

So I turned to Andrew Carnegie, thinking this was an ideal situation for him to share in, inasmuch as he was tossing money around rather freely for libraries. I probably made the mistake of telling him what we were doing in the way of raising money for the endowment of the institution. His reply was strange and disconcerting. He didn't even refer to the library, but "noted" that we were working toward increasing the endowment, and he would therefore donate $20,000 for this purpose as soon as our collections amounted to $90,000 "in cash or the equivalent." I was bothered by the word "equivalent." We had collected about $80,000 in cash, and the General Education Board's *pro rata* and $23,000 in unpaid notes would be more than the "equivalent" of $10,000. But by correspondence I seemed unable to make his secretary see it this way. So I asked for a conference on the matter in New York, and got it. Promptly on the appointed minute I was in his outer office. I sent my card in, was told he would see me at once, and was ushered toward his office. He met me at the door with: "What did you come here for? Why couldn't you conduct this business by correspondence?" He was a short, squat man, as I recall, with sandy hair and a reddish moustache of considerable proportions. His voice and manner showed much irritation, and his reception seemed to me almost of the nature of an insult. "Mr. Secretary," I replied, "I am here on your own appointment, but any words between us with reference to Mr. Carnegie's conditional gift will have to be by correspondence."

I turned my back and walked out, and through all the years I can still see him standing in that doorway, wondering why any college president should so walk out with $20,000 of his master's money at stake. By the time I reached Spartanburg, I had cooled off a little, thinking, if he had lost something of the civilities of life, I shouldn't have done so. Anyway, I wrote back a cool, brief business letter concerning the "equivalent" —precisely what I had done before, though with fewer words —and received in reply a most courteous letter, enclosing a check for $20,000! Was he apologizing, or was he heaping coals of fire on the back of a college president from the "hick" lands of the Bible belt? He got a very, very appreciative letter in return, for I guessed he had been having a bad day before he saw me. Anyway, I wrote no more letters to Mr. Carnegie to assist Wofford College, preferring not to risk the breaking of the peace apparently now established between his secretary and me.

But that library legacy and the $10,000 needed to proceed with the building of the library! How and where to get $10,-000 for this purpose obsessed all my waking thoughts and went to bed with me at night to become a part of my dreams. Raising $145,000 for the endowment seemed to have exhausted all my resources, requiring the draining of the last small "strippings" to accomplish it. Of course, more than forty years later to raise $10,000 is an easy financial effort. But in 1906 it was a huge sum, and to get it under the circumstances of those times was all but impossible.

So I was mulling over the matter one morning, trying to persuade myself to be patient and trust to providence. Maybe something would turn up. And something did. It was a murky, muggy, at times drippy, early spring day, unseasonably warm —the kind of day that took the zest out of life and slowed down to next to nothing all one's energies, creating a rather jaundiced view of the universe. A telephone call came from a friend to come by to see him if I happened to be downtown. I went. The "office" was a soiled, untidy helter-skelter little room in what was no better than a clapboard shack by the railroad tracks. This friend was almost a state-wide character. He had no reticences of thought and speech. What entered his mind he spoke out in sharp, biting, picturesque words. He had two related obsessions. One was that the poverty of farmers was due to laziness and ignorance—that they didn't work hard enough and were too unenlightened to understand the business of farming. He constituted himself a voluntary propagandist, going from point to point in the county, lecturing his fellow farmers on their shortcomings in terms that must have blistered, or, as he would say, "got under their hides." He used to take me with him in his rickety, two-seated buggy, drawn by an ancient slowgoing horse, or occasionally by a mule with less speed, to present the educational side of life—his other obsession. I wondered that they didn't resent the roughness of his speech, his belittling of their trust in politicians, and his indictment of their fumbling, bungling, stupid ways of farming. They put up with him because they, with all who knew him, had faith in him, in his disinterestedness, his rugged stubborn integrity of character, and his success on his own farm. Out of experience he talked of real accomplishment. He had taken two hundred acres of red earth and by hard, unremitting labor had made a fortune out of it. His farm was more eloquent in its speech than any appeals he made in words.

As we rode along the rough country roads to one of his meetings, he would tell me about himself in a loud rasping voice, as if addressing a group of farmers, for emphasis flicking flies from the horse with his buggy whip. He grew up in the war days when he could hear cries from every home as he walked down the main street of the village of Spartanburg on the day of the posting of the casualties after one of the Virginia battles. Then the days that followed after Lee's surrender were worse, he would say—the people were stunned under the sense of defeat and dazed as to what to do next. Their civilization was destroyed, their economic structure in ruins. There was the dark shadow of the menace of slaves freed but yesterday, who, not knowing what to do with their freedom so suddenly and violently acquired, were misled by the presence of Federal bayonets and the leadership of white carpetbaggers and scalawags.

This was the world of Ed Archer's college days from 1867 to 1871. But there was no bitterness in his talk as we jolted along over rutted roads. He saved a caustic bitterness for those farmers, whose places he would point out, calling by name who had no gardens, whose stock was scrawny and starved, whose lands were being washed away for lack of terracing—men who failed to support church and school, but spent their time on the street corners of Spartanburg, discussing politics, telling how many Yankees they had killed in the Virginia battles. "Their eyes are in the back of their heads," he would say, "and they blame their plight on everything and everybody except themselves and their own stupidity and laziness."

As Ed Archer thought of such people in connection with his own more than thirty years of toil upward from nothing to a comfortable competency and a man's approving sense of knowing he has done a good job with a sizable piece of mother earth, he was not especially tolerant of those who had not done likewise. As I moved about through South Carolina from 1902 to 1910, I was to find many like him in every section of the state—not like him, to be sure, in a fierce evangelistic zeal to convert others to his way of thinking and doing, but plain, substantial, hard-working men who, probably without being aware of it, were the real builders of a new commonwealth on the ruins of the old. They accomplished their creative tasks in the midst of forces uncongenial to constructive economic and social enterprise. When the state lifted itself by violent and fraudulent ways from the yoke inflicted by that terrifying crime called "reconstruction," beginning in the late 1880's and moving far into the 1900's, there followed a stormy political and social upheaval that divided the state into warring factions, out of which grew Tillmanism and Bleasism in South Carolina; Vardamanism in Mississippi, Jeff Davisism in Arkansas, Huey Longism in Louisiana, Talmadgeism in Georgia, and every sort of ism in Texas. As I considered the atmosphere, the surroundings, under which Ed Archer and men like him did their work, I gave them a kind of reverence as among the real heroes of the South's economic and social recovery. This is why I am telling Archer's story—he is one among an army of unsung soldiers of the common good. Without his kind, many of them, the great movements toward the general progress from 1890 on would have been much slower in producing results.

One spring day, jogging along, Ed Archer lifted the curtain upon the mystery of his intense, uncompromising, evangelistic zeal for improving the conditions of his fellow men. "You know," he said in quieter tones than he usually used, "the Lord called me to preach while I was in college. Unmistakably I believed he called me to preach a kind of gospel the people I knew needed, the gospel, not against drunkenness, adultery, lying, stealing—the people guilty of such sins were not worth bothering about—but the gospel against loafing, misuse of God's earth, failure to support churches and schools, disloyalty to the family, no thrift or saving for a rainy day. These are the sins I was called to preach against. So I entered the conference and was appointed to a country circuit—just what I wanted. But by the end of the year my throat went bad on me, and the doctor told me my preaching days were over. On my knees I entered into a hot argument with the Lord. If he called me to preach, why didn't he give me a throat to preach with? Plainly he said to me: 'Now Ed, cool down. You've got the gift of making money. Let your money preach for you by the good you can do with it, and you will increase the power of the kind of gospel you wanted to preach in other and better ways.' And I said, 'Yes, Lord, your will, not mine,' and for these thirty years I have been making money, and putting it where I thought it would be preaching my kind of religion."

And this was the man in whose dingy makeshift of an office I sat on that wet spring morning, wanting to hear why he had called me. I knew it would be something unusual, and it was. "My wife and I were talking about you and Wofford College last night, and we decided that Wofford was the best-managed enterprise, financially, in Spartanburg county, doing more good with its money than any other business we knew of. I want to do a little of my preaching through it. Would $5,000 help you?" Would it? I saw my library in process of rising on its foundations, and I gave him a real man's handshake. "Now don't go on so about this matter; we feel better than you do about it." This was his response in words and manner, to my expression of appreciation. The little office was no longer drab and dingy, and as I see it even yet there is a light that gave, and gives, it that touch of the spirit that does something significantly memorable to common things.

The next morning there was another call for me to come down to what had become a very bright little office. And this time he was to say that he and his wife had been thinking once again of the service of Wofford; and if I thought $5,000 more would help to increase that service, they wanted to add that amount, making it $10,000. Of course, it would increase the service of Wofford! I then told what I had been trying to do these past seven years—add $145,000 to the endowment to make the future of the college safe, build the Cleveland Science Hall, and erect a library. With what he had done, I could begin at once with the erection of the library and thus expand the usefulness of Wofford to the 266 students then on the campus, making of Wofford an ideal small college. He shared enthusiastically in my own enthusiasm over an important piece of educational work successfully accomplished.

Those were brave stirring days for the new college president. He had brought to them the revivalistic fervor of the Conference for Education in the South held at Athens, Georgia, in the spring of 1902, and the experiences of the Knoxville summer school that same year. To carry the moods and attitudes of these experiences with him as he went up and down the little state of his adoption gave exhilaration and driving power to his efforts to realize his dreams of a Wofford better prepared in every way to do its appointed work as a liberal arts college belonging to a Christian denomination and therefore dedicated to keeping religion and education in indissoluble wedlock. I learned to know at first hand the state and its people from where Caesar's Head looks down from its more than three thousand feet of mountain height upon the rolling red hills of the upcountry to where the sandy point of Hilton's Head is beaten upon by the waves of the Atlantic. And all between—the Ridge Country from the Savannah River through Columbia to the Catawba; and then the coastal plain where the level flat lands of the true cotton belt, seamed with slow-flowing black-water rivers, apparently endless dark swamps, shadowed in the gloom of cypress and pine, draped in solemn grayness by masses of Spanish moss. And the names the rivers bore—Seneca, Keowee, Saluda, Enoree, Congaree, Wateree, Edisto, Santee, Catawba, Combahee! Having read my South Carolina history and Gilmore Simm's novels, I found not only sheer poetry in the music of these names but history and romance all along their banks.

Then too the people themselves, whose generous, beautiful hospitality and gracious manners opened hearts and homes to me, and whose sympathetic understanding of what I was trying to do for their college—its history being so intimately a part of their church—I learned to know well enough to distinguish from their speech the sections of the state from which they came, whether from the hill country, with their sharp mountain accent, or from the low country with their soft mushy drawl. But their manners were nearly the same—simple, direct, natural, courteous, considerate, particularly to one in their homes. However, as I got closer to the coast in the tidewater regions, where the blacks outnumbered the whites twenty to one, I would feel that nowhere in the world were there finer-mannered folk, white and black. Here were those graces and amenities that confer upon human relationships that certain charm and beauty and dignity of gentle and kindly intercourse. I used to say half facetiously, recalling historic forces behind ways of living in the Deep South even in 1902, that it took about twenty Negroes to make one white gentleman, for where more of the former were, there were more also of the latter. Some of these days somebody is going to write an understanding book on what these two races really owe to each other.

A few years ago when they first came out, I read William Alexander Percy's *Lanterns on the Levee*, and Wilbur Cash's *Mind of the South*. The former was a poetic picture, with beautifully phrased interpretative comment on the aristocratic

South of sentiment and romance. The roses and magnolias were all there, as were the stately homes and a gallant procession of fair women and brave men, enveloped in a nostalgic haze of sad regrets. Cash's book was not so friendly to this side of the picture of southern life, but he did pay a kind of left-handed tribute to the vitality of Percy's South in reproducing itself in even out-of-the-way places below Mason and Dixon's line. Acutely and truly, I think, he explains the presence of such homes, duplicating precisely the architecture of the low countries, perched grandly atop upcountry hills—not many, but enough to show that the civilization of the coast was flowing out of its boundaries up into the backcountry, which only yesterday was frontier, the tragedy of 1860 halting a distinct social trend. When the Scotch-Irish and the Germans came from Pennsylvania, Virginia, and Maryland, with them there moved out from the coast the restless, the adventurous, bitten by the land hunger of pioneer days—they who sprinkled themselves all through the unwasted red lands of what is now known as the upcountry. But a few hundred acres were settled and cleared at first; and then for the enterprising, the thrifty, the ambitious, these small holdings became a thousand, three thousand acres, worked and acquired by the labors of many sons and daughters. But a day came when there were three slaves to help, after a while six, a dozen, twenty-five; and then there had to be the big house and ways of living that repeated the mores of a civilization already in its full bloom, for better or worse, in South Carolina below Columbia.

As I read these two books, thirty years after my travels throughout the state, they brought vividly to mind these two aspects of the South—an aristocratic South of large plantations and generous living, of a folk rich in the virtues of courage, honor, and courtesy; and that far more numerous South, of plain, substantial, conservative, hard-working, God-fearing, liberty-loving people, whose social habits, with the frontier still not far away, had acquired the flavor and no little of the charm of those who owned broad acres and many slaves. Not a few of these upcountry men would create for their families the same sort of world. I acquired the conviction, moreover, before I read the books of Percy and Cash that, after one has said his worst about slavery, there developed throughout the South a civilization that might have made a rich contribution to the varied life of the nation, had human slavery been peaceably and progressively abolished without the tragedy of a fratricidal war.

True or not, something like this remains with me as I recall those distant adventurous days when in trying to build a college, or at least give it a security it did not have before, I had the chance to know with more or less intimacy South Carolina—a typical state of the Old South, shall I say?

Now I would not have it understood that I did not see with a poignant sense of tragedy that other side of South Carolina life—that class that made up the big illiteracy percentage, to the shame of the state. There would be a cabin by the roadside, a pine tree at one corner, a spreading oak at the other, maybe a stunted rose bush or two giving a splash of color to the little porch. The mother would be sitting there in a straight-backed, homemade chair; the father plowing in a near-by field—a field not his own; four or five children playing together in the shade of the clean-swept white sandy yard; a "good morning" from the strangers in the buggy, a courteous but shy "how're ye," in response, and "Won't you-all alight and come in?" from the mother on the porch. The playing group of children would be from the sixteen-year-old daughter down to the three-year-old baby. A few carefully tactful questions would reveal that neither the mother nor any of the children had ever seen the inside of a schoolhouse. "It was too far away, and it takes more money than we got to buy books and clothes, and we gets along better than most that goes." And yet these were of the oldest American stock, with ancient English names. Their ancestors had cleared the wilderness, fought the Indians, and may have been among

those who, clad in buckskin and coonskin caps, had saluted
General Washington under the historic elm at Cambridge,
Massachusetts, with "We come from the right bank of the
Potomac, suh!" With their rifles and courage they helped
build a republic whose opportunities somehow were denied
their descendants. They were still living in the shadow of
the frontier, in the first decade of the twentieth century with
currents of civilization flowing around them without seeming
to touch them—and this, too, in one of the oldest original
American states.

Then, too, to deepen the sense of tragedy, letters like this
would come to my office: "Please send us a teacher, married
man preferred. We can pay him forty-five dollars a month
for five months. He can get up a subscription school for another three months, and rent a little land to do some farming
on." And that southern social exclusiveness would be satisfied by the "select" few of the subscription school. Or another letter would read like this "We want a teacher. Send
us a man who can whip the big boys, some of their fathers,
and even members of the board of trustees."

Here was an educational situation requiring great care in
making the right selection of a teacher. After studying the
matter, I called in the biggest man, physically, in the senior
class—a tall, broad-shouldered, stalwart man from one of the
less favored sections of the state, and laid the letter before
before him. With a dry smile he looked up from it to say in
his slow soft drawl: "Yes, suh, I'll take it. I know schools
and folks like that."

Years afterward, when he was a successful country doctor,
I ran into him casually, and that scene in my office at once
leaped into my mind. "What about that school? I see you
survived it."

With the same slow smile and soft drawl, the middle-aged
doctor made his report: "Yes, suh, I had literally to do it
all—whip the big boys, a father or two, one of the trustees,
and one day as I was walking down the big road toward my

173

boardinghouse, a woman drove up, the mother of one of the boys to whom I had given a good thrashing. Without saying a word she got out of the buggy, bringing the whip with her, coming toward me with fire in her eyes. I backed off a little, trying to put a fire in my eyes which really wasn't there, saying with all the challenge I could muster in my voice: 'Madam, I have never whipped a woman before in my life, but if you hit with me that whip, I'll take it from you and lay it on your back.' She quickly turned, got into the buggy, giving the horse the licks she meant for me."

"And, doctor, would you have done what you said you would do?"

"No, suh, had she called my bluff, I would have run like a rabbit."

Then he added with evident satisfaction, "But I turned over to my successors a better school and an easier time."

Were this man's methods one method of progress toward better educational conditions? Yes, in the sense they picture the sheer backwardness of those at the time in control of the ways and means of educating the children of the state, constituting a challenge of an inspiring nature to all who were working with the forces of progress in process of release. Certainly, as I caught the darker side of the pattern of South Carolina life, the pattern was not depressing but constituted a call to make Wofford College and the Methodist Church more wisely and more deeply dedicated to the whole business of education in the state from top to bottom. And here again the new president was being educated for his own job, and he was also seeing his money raising in terms of placing his college in a better position to serve the state. Yes, it was more than increasing the endowment and adding two important buildings to the plant. It was helping to lift a state to higher levels of living; and to be engaged in this was a brave, creative adventure.

10

STORMS OVER DIXIE

About 1905 the Pittsburgh Ironmaster, Andrew Carnegie, exploded into the world of higher education with what seemed the answer: the Carnegie pension system for the "lowest paid of all public servants of the first rank"—college and university professors. Under his plan they could, or—if college trustees desired—*must*, retire at the age of sixty-five. The proposal was so beautifully worded as to warm the cockles of the hearts of this overworked group that had not yet heard the phrases "social security" or "retiring allowances," or, indeed, thought themselves worthy of such generous consideration for the service they were rendering human society. By and large they were a modest class. No association of university professors had yet come along to make them acutely class conscious as to "tenure" of office, nor had standardizing agencies laid down minimum salary scales for membership. For a while the Carnegie proposal was the happiest piece of explosiveness ever tossed into the quiet humdrum of academic shades. To college presidents it was the answer to a prayer for new blood in their faculties and for relief from the conservative pressure of the older men by retiring them into honorable desuetude without expense and without friction. To the professors it was a generous pat on the back for recognized service and a vision of a comfortable old age with even their widows provided for in case anything should happen to them.

Those were really exciting days on college and university campuses. The presidents proceeded at once to find how their institutions might "qualify"; and the sixty-five-year-oldsters, who but yesterday were boasting they were as young as they

175

were at twenty-five, were already packing their trunks for winters in California or Florida and summers in the Adirondacks. Certain not so creditable phases of the Carnegie pension system soon developed. With the professors it was the haste with which they were willing to throw over their jobs for a life of ease, though some met this reproach with the opportunity the retirement would give for doing that piece of important research or writing that big book. A considerable group of presidents found their institutions blocked out of the benefits of the system by the sectarian prohibition in it, that is, the boards of trustees must be self-perpetuating and the college independent of any denominational control. There was plenty of legal and ethical casuistry on the part of some to part company with historic relationships for the sake of what turned out in the end to be but a mess of financial pottage. It is not a pretty story, this trying to face both ways so that it was said of some institutions that they were quite independent when they looked toward a Carnegie pension, and quite dependent on the church when they faced the need of students and certain annual appropriations. Alas! by somebody's large miscalculation, the sum set up by Mr. Carnegie proved quite inadequate to meet the generosity of his intentions. The original pension system, after conferring its benefits upon relatively few institutions, passed into an annuity scheme, no better, but a little cheaper, than what was offered by the regular insurance companies.

However, a great stir of discussion did develop out of Mr. Carnegie's proposal, and this stir became a veritable storm around certain southern denominational colleges when it seemed they were more anxious to be pensioners on "infidel" money than they were to keep faith with religion. On such an issue the Bible belt always girds itself for battle. But the very name "Carnegie" was an upsetting word in education. The Carnegie Foundation, under the leadership of President Henry S. Pretchett—a very able man who interpreted the meaning of educational forces in a large, states-

manlike way—continued to disturb the whole field of secondary and higher education during the first two decades of the
twentieth century, and no college president could compla-
cently accept administrative life as it was. There was that
devastating report on the state of medical training in the
United States, with more than hints as to the low estates to
which other kinds of professional education had fallen. Not
a few of the medical schools either demoted themselves to
two-year institutions or folded up to go quite out of business, while all of them underwent a drastic process of self-ex-
amination and lifting of standards. All this, of course, affected
college administrations. Medical schools had been reaching into the colleges to take students from the freshman and sophomore classes, but the better sort of medical schools began
to demand for entrance a bachelor's degree which included
the fundamentals of at least three sciences and one foreign
language. Certainly, every self-respecting college would gladly co-operate in such an elevation of standards. The results
were soon apparent, chiefly in that the abler, more intellectual type of student no longer turned to law but to medicine.
The truth is that there has been a steady deterioration in the
quality of prospective law students and an equally steady
rise in the quality of those electing medicine. This feature of
the Carnegie crusade is both good and bad for human society
in the United States.

Having thus been in a position to observe what has happened
in the raising of standards of professional education in these
last forty years, I venture to remark that something important has been lost when that required "loafing around," if
one must put it that way, in the office of an "old doctor" for
a year or two preliminary to a diploma, was left out of the
training of students. For observing the ways of a skilled prac-
titioner as he goes about his healing the sick, all the ceremonies,
white gowns and masks, rubber gloves, sterilized implements,
becapped and berobed nurses, are no adequate substitute.
These latter can be no better than the ghostly, liturgical ac-

177

companiments of modern scientific magic, more impressive in creating atmosphere than in curing the ill. The "old doctor" had none of these things with which to conceal his ignorance and hide his mistakes. Barehanded, as it were, he wrote the epic story of great achievements in the school of experience where character, personality, and hard-won understanding count when life is racked with pain and its forces are at their lowest ebb. For his aspiring successor to share with him such experiences is to learn something without which his patients are the losers.

However, this exposé of the shocking state of medical education published in 1910 under the auspices of the Carnegie Foundation, written by Abraham Flexner and based on his own firsthand investigations, constituted a historical document of the first importance. As far as the South was concerned, what was said in it once again reflected general conditions in this section—its conservatism, its lack of funds, and even its sheer ignorance of what the training of a doctor should be. After the first shock of Flexner's ugly picture of how bad conditions really were and of their effects upon the health of the entire South was somewhat subdued, and the physicians teaching in the medical colleges had spluttered forth their indignant resentments, the Carnegie Foundation singled out Vanderbilt University as the most promising of the medical schools of the South with the gift of $1,000,000. And once again the Ironmaster's money upset old educational practices in a special field and started the use of new methods and standards that have since transformed completely the procedure in the training of physicians. In the processes of accomplishing results there were, of course, heartbreaks and bitter disappointments as old institutions found they must either conform or die, and they didn't want to do either. The worthy ones conformed, and today there is not a medical school in the South that does not adjust itself to approved standards.

A few years after this gift of $1,000,000 to the medical school of Vanderbilt, that is, about 1916 or 1917, Dr. Wallace

Buttrick was a guest in my home. During his active service as secretary and chairman of the General Education Board, I might get a telegram at almost any time saying he would be in Spartanburg on a certain date. There would be lunch or dinner with me and hours of talk over the coffee and cigars. He would want to know about this or that institution, its president, the quality of its faculty and work, its future, its constituency, its standards. After such a séance with him, I could well understand the nature of the knowledge, both exact and general, the General Education Board had of educational institutions and conditions in the South. Its executive officers did not rely wholly upon its field men for such knowledge. They themselves also went after it. At least Wallace Buttrick did, and Wickliffe Rose.

On this particular occasion, after we had discussed a number of miscellaneous matters as usual, he suddenly said: "Of course, you've read Flexner's piece on the medical colleges."

"I have," I told him. "A pretty bitter dose for the doctors to take, but there are wholesome curative elements in it that must in the end work for educational health in the medical field."

"And," he went on, "there must be, for the sake of the future of the South, a really first-class medical college located somewhere between Johns Hopkins and Tulane. Geographically, Nashville seems the place. It ought to be related to an institution whose academic standards are high and courageously maintained, and whose president would have the courage and educational idealism to transfer the standards of his liberal arts department to the medical school with even more exacting scientific methods and spirit. It seems to me that Vanderbilt is the institution, and Chancellor Kirkland the man."

A few years later, 1919, the General Education Board startled the whole South with its initial gift of $4,000,000. The Carnegie Foundation followed with large gifts, and by their joint gifts there now stands on the campus at Nashville a medical college equal to the best in America, whose buildings repre-

179

sent an investment of $5,000,000 and whose endowment is $14,000,000.

I have always thought of this Vanderbilt Medical School as the symbol of the end of an era, perhaps the last expression of at least one phase of what we have been vaguely calling "the American way of life," to maintain which we went into World War II. Giant men, using the opportunities and natural resources of the country to build up colossal fortunes, applied the ruthless individualism of the frontier in the epic process. There are Cornelius Vanderbilt, James J. Hill, E. H. Harriman, C. P. Huntington, and Leland Stanford with the railroads; Andrew Carnegie with steel; John D. Rockefeller with oil; Andrew W. Mellon with aluminum and other interests; the Dukes with tobacco; and J. P. Morgan in banking. They were typical products, on an immense scale, of the American way in their march toward the accumulation of fabulous fortunes. Then, again in the American way, they turned the major portions of these fortunes into the hands of independent, self-perpetuating boards of trustees of exceptionally able men of the highest character to minister to the service of their country, particularly in the southern section where it was most needed. These trustees on their part placed in the hands of other men like themselves, trustees of institutions of higher learning, great sums of money for the beneficent uses of human society, spiritual and intellectual.

Question as one may the motives of the original donors, call these gifts sinister in purpose or so much salve applied to uneasy consciences, or the subtle purchase of some sort of political immunity, there they stand, Vanderbilt and Duke, beacons of liberal, independent service in a politics-ridden section, whose tax-supported institutions can hardly draw a free breath. Witness only what has happened in Louisiana, Mississippi, Georgia, and Texas, and can happen again anywhere. Not from the president's office on the campus, nor by the conclusions arrived at after serious discussions in faculty and trustee meetings with the educational service of the institution chiefly in mind, are policies and plans evolved that concern the very destinies of these tax-supported institutions, but by legislative committees made up of men who, however well-meaning, though they are not always that, have not even the natural ability nor the educational understanding to direct the affairs of a state university or its agricultural and mechanical college, not to mention the professional schools of law and medicine.

As one considers these great philanthropies and the men who first administered them, statesmanlike in their conception of service, one wonders if their successors, fallen into the hands of the researchers, are not frittering away their resources in a multitudinous array of special projects, spectacular in a way, but in the long run—and anything that has to do with education must be considered from the long-run view—not accomplishing much that can be described as genuinely creative or broadly patriotic in its potential service to the nation. For instance, why not make Emory University in Atlanta an indicting antidote and a saving influence when the poisonous politics of a Talmadge threatens the intellectual health of the entire system of the tax-supported institutions of the state? Or why not go into Louisiana and make Tulane so powerful in its influence and leadership as to force even the politicians, though they be led by a Huey Long, at least to keep their soiling paws off the youth of the state? Then these great boards might go to Texas, select one of the best independent institutions, make a great university of it, so great that that bubbling pot of political chicanery called the University of Texas dare not stay what it is because the people of Texas, with a real, free university to measure by, wouldn't let it. Besides, these boards would be further building constructively, if they should go further by seeing to it that in each southern state there were one or two independent liberal arts colleges equal to the best anywhere, which would be a standing rebuke to the shoddy stuff dished out by institutions in the name of "serving the practical needs of the people of the whole state"—educational hypocrisy for the securing of legislative good will and appropriations. And alas! those who use such phrases know it, but they forget that the education that counts, whatever kind it be, can be built only on the bedrock of sincerity. Here are suggested projects which would have no immediate returns but which, in the long future, would create more researchers and call forth more worth-while research projects than much that is now subsidized under the name of "research."

But all this seems a long diversion from the excitement created in the educational world, particularly in the South, my world, in the fifteen years after nineteen hundred. The magazines of the day had made muckraking popular, and President Roosevelt—"Teddy," I mean—had put the "big-stick" method of reform into everybody's hand as he belabored "the malefactors of great wealth" and, indeed, anybody else not of his way of thinking. So when the Carnegie Board—that is, whoever made its reports and wrote its bulletins—went into action, it was in the strenuous manner of the big stick in the sheer gusto of the indictment. One could not escape the feeling that whoever wrote the bulletin on secondary education and gathered the factual material had quite an enjoyable time in exposing "the malefactors" in the fields of secondary and college education. (Perhaps I ought to say on the secondary and college "levels.") The colleges were taking students into their freshman classes from the first, second, and third years of whatever high schools there were; and superintendents were complaining it was impossible to organize a fourth year for this reason. Of course, there were other reasons: They didn't have the taxes to do it with, and some of the principals wouldn't have known how if they had had the money. At any rate, the Carnegie Foundation made life interesting for both colleges and secondary schools, and no college president could feel at ease in his educational Zion. The curtain was lifted on the whole ugly situation—in a manner very different from the methods of the Southern Association of Colleges and Secondary Schools. This organization issued no such propaganda, but simply made an institution uncomfortable because "it didn't belong"; and so many didn't belong that a college felt itself, if not in good company, at least in a large company.

But the Carnegie Foundation did something very much more than just hit resounding blows with the big stick. It went in for definitions, and thus laid the foundation for permanent and significant reform by inventing, so to speak, the "Carnegie unit," and by defining how many could be satisfactorily completed for each of the four years of the high school, a "unit" being a subject pursued for one year of thirty-six weeks, five periods a week, forty-five minutes in length. A new era was born, setting once and for all the metes and bounds of secondary and college education.

It is clear enough that these two boards, the General Education Board and the Carnegie Foundation, together with the initial Duke benefactions to Trinity College at Durham, N. C., and the Candler millions to Emory in Atlanta, started reforms destined to change the whole face of southern education and to affect permanently the entire structure of southern life, if education possesses the potent force attributed to it. They were donating, however, "tainted" money, and few institutions were permitted to accept any of it without at least a flurry, and sometimes a storm of protest. Wasn't old Andrew Carnegie a foreign atheist, and because of this fact, didn't he exclude from his pension system all institutions at all religious in character?

On the campus of a small liberal arts college in South Carolina, there is—or used to be—a little building called Carnegie Hall, incongruously dedicated to technological instruction. One of the former presidents, a young minister, was going to Europe one summer. Walking the deck at night after dinner, he happened to run into no less a personage than Mr. Carnegie, on his way to Skibo Castle. They fell into conversation, which somehow got into the theological channels—the divinity of Christ, the virgin birth, the miracles. In the midst of the discussion, a lady came up. "Listen, Mary," said the Ironmaster, "at

183

the fairy tales this young man is telling your husband." "Fairy tales" got the "young man" a week's stay as a guest at Skibo, and a $60,000 building in which to teach things at his little college not strictly of a liberal arts quality. But the young president had to defend its acceptance against the charges not only that it was out of place but also that it was "infidel" money.

The conditions of the pensions and the sudden discovery by not a few college presidents and boards of trustees that, though their colleges had been supported by the church for a hundred years, they did not really belong to it, and the efforts of some even to change their charters in order to "qualify" made the churches extremely sensitive in regard to Carnegie money; and there was a tightening of legal and moral bonds in the matter of ownership and control.

John C. Kilgo, the new president of Trinity College in 1894, was the guest of stalwart old Washington Duke, that ex-Confederate who came back out of a Federal prison to take up life on a little farm some half dozen miles out of Durham. To help him he had a twelve-year-old daughter and two boys in their teens—B. N. and J. B. Together they built the great tobacco empire. He met the new president with: "My home has always been the home of Methodist preachers. As you are a preacher, it is yours, too, but I ain't going to give nary nother cent to Trinity College. You're welcome as a Methodist preacher." But somehow, for each of the next three years he was giving $100,000 to this little college. The storm broke. Organized church bodies uttered clamorous protests against receiving the money. Were not cigarettes undermining the health of young boys (not girls yet), weakening their minds, and corrupting their morals? The metal arch over the gateway to the campus bore in iron letters this legend as the ancient motto of the institution: *Eruditio et Religio*. In the heated discussions over receiving "tainted" cigarette money the motto acquired two additional words, becoming: *Eruditio et Religio et Tobacco et Kilgo,* and Tobacco and Kilgo managed to weather the storm to give more power to both Learning and Religion.

But the issue was not so simple as using for education funds acquired from the sale of a noxious drug that was undermining the health and corrupting the morals of the youth of the land. No, not by a good deal, and everybody in North Carolina with even a small modicum of understanding knew it. Kilgo's heated advocacy of Christian education and his violent assaults upon tax-supported higher education had created a host of enemies, and here was their chance to arouse the leaders of his own church against him.

Then, too, North Carolina politics were sizzling and boiling just right. There were Populism, fusionism, Bryanism, Republicanism, agrarianism, Negroism, bimetallism, "goldbugism," traditionalism, and each found rather able leaders. It was the noisy day of the "have-nots" in North Carolina, as it was everywhere in the South; and Wall Street, the trusts, the railroads were responsible for their ills, which after all were very real. The politicians thrived on conditions seemingly made to order for getting them into office. With the Duke family—in the beginning the father, Washington Duke, or "Old Wash" as he was familiarly called, and the younger brother, B.N.— dropping their largesse into the lap of the struggling little college, Trinity and its president became the target of every known kind of vicious assault as the recipient of the bounty of all the trusts, and of the recently organized American Tobacco Company. But President Kilgo met his attackers more than halfway with his fiery, violent sort of eloquence. It was now the college they were trying to destroy, and this went deeper than their efforts to run him out of the state. If it was wrong to use tobacco, he would say, it was even more wrong to raise it on their farms, which the rank and file of those critical, self-righteous Methodists, Baptists, and Presbyterians were doing. As for the trusts, they were beneficent organizations, natural, necessary outgrowths of the American spirit of industrial progress, and should be fostered and encouraged; they

185

were great civilizing, nationalizing forces; by increasing wealth they contributed to the economic and social advance of backward sections; and crossing all state lines, they were agencies making for the destruction of sectionalism and the creation of national unity. In sermons, speeches, and pamphlets he became the most aggressive protagonist that big business had yet found in America.

I knew Kilgo intimately. The friendship formed at Wofford continued warm and deep to the end, though there were always polarities of difference in temperament and experience. I think I knew his inner motives and purposes as well as anyone, and I am sure he believed most profoundly in the rightness of even his most extreme views. He told me once that, when politics in North Carolina was at its worst and when it seemed those pioneer industrialists, whose work was finally to make this state one of the richest and most progressive in the union, might actually be run out of the state to transplant their commercial genius elsewhere, he saw Mr. J. B. Duke, the younger brother, in his office in New York. "Mr. Duke," he said, "do you see what's going on in your state? That the politicians are threatening the life of every business enterprise you have in it; that they will tax your business there out of existence or even burn your factories down?" Mr. Duke did understand the situation with all its threatening economic possibilities. "Then," continued the college president, "there is only one antidote to the poison that now menaces the health of North Carolina, and that is a free, independent college of the highest grade equal to the best anywhere. That's the only cure to what afflicts North Carolina now."

Dr. Kilgo always believed that this conversation was the occasion of the sowing of the seed whose fruitage was the university that bears the name of one of the nation's greatest builders of industrial enterprises. Who knows? At any rate, J. B. Duke, who had heretofore been a bit cold toward Trinity College, leaving its support to his father and brother, now began to show his interest with the gift of a noble library building and $10,000 to stock it with books. Was he thinking of the "antidote" suggested by President Kilgo? And, in the long run, may not Duke University, mellowed by time, finding itself for what its real mission is, turn out to be just the antidote needed in the unfolding life of the South?

And this president, John Carlisle Kilgo, labeled by some as the "stormy petrel" of southern education from 1894 to 1910, never had a quiet moment in all the sixteen years of his administration. He was accused by his enemies of high crimes and misdemeanors, of accepting annuities from the Dukes. His expulsion from his position was sought by one of the leading members of his own board of trustees, a man of great ability and influence in the state. He was haled into court by a traveling seller of Bibles in the two Carolinas, who brought back from South Carolina bits of mean gossip that float around even among ministers. For six years he was subject to exposure in the glare of a court trial, every act of his life investigated, true and false—he was everything that no minister of the gospel or college president ought to be. Yet he gave not one inch of ground in any fight; and, supported by his friends, his trustees, faculty, and students, he never lost one. He had that power, given to but few men, of inspiring and keeping the—shall I say?—blind loyalty of all who knew him intimately and worked with him officially.

The real testing time came in 1903 when the suit against him was in the very middle of its worst stages. Dr. John S. Bassett published in October of that year in the *South Atlantic Quarterly*, a periodical sponsored by the college, an article entitled "Stirring Up the Fires of Race Antipathy." Dr. Bassett was professor of history at Trinity and a productive scholar of high rank in his field. But if he intended to put out fires of "race antipathy" with his article, he reckoned disastrously. What he did was to start a conflagration that enveloped the entire state and, indeed, the whole South. The central offending thought in the article was that Booker T. Washington was, with the exception of Robert E. Lee, the greatest man the

South had produced in one hundred years. All the pent-up racial prejudices were let loose; and the enemies of Kilgo had at last in their hands the weapon with which to rid the state, the church, the college, of him. He was a Republican; a preacher with the low practices of a ward politician, subsidized with the soiled money of a hated trust that was impoverishing the farmers and choking the economic life of the state, using "tainted" money that came from the sale of a weed that corrupted the youth of the land; a marplot; a disturber of the peace of the commonwealth; a criminal whom the courts had virtually convicted of attempted bribery and of destroying the small business of an innocent preacher. But now at last we have him revealed in his true colors—"a nigger lover," seeking to break down all the barriers that have been set up to protect from social and political destruction the fairest and noblest civilization yet known on this planet!

The Bourbon South called at least for the expulsion of Bassett from the faculty, though its guns were really aimed at Kilgo. All the latent greatness in Kilgo came forth in this fight, and he kept the issue clear—not the right or wrong in what Bassett wrote, but his right as a member of the faculty of a free college in a free democracy to say what he thought. President Kilgo, disagreeing starkly with the views of his professor, kept the issue sharp and clear—that of academic freedom—and this little North Carolina college became the center of national interest. Around it surged some of the ugliest forces of southern life; and, stated bluntly, the cries hurled at the authorities of Trinity College were, "Lynch him! Lynch him!" President Kilgo himself told me that, when the controversy was at its bitterest, Mr. J. B. Duke said to him: "This man Bassett maybe has played the fool and oughtn't to be on any faculty, but he must not be lynched. There are more ways of lynching a man than by tying a hempen rope around his neck and throwing it over the limb of a tree. Public opinion can lynch a man, and this is what North Carolina is trying to do to Bassett now. Don't allow it. You'll never get over it if you do." When he said this, the tobacco tycoon was greater than he knew and was also standing in the breach when intellectual freedom on a college campus was at stake.

But the victory was complete and resounding. The president, the college, the trustees, the faculty, and a host of the choicest spirits in North Carolina stood firm; and the state, in spite of itself, was saved from the stigma of shame. The entire South, always admiring courage, even in the causes it disapproved, felt the tonic of the North Carolina battle, and knew one more step forward had been taken in the intellectual progress of the section. President Kilgo himself, valiant champion of perhaps the noblest cause for which he had ever fought, had more quiet days thereafter, and was able to shape Trinity into the most distinguished college in the Southeast, and next to Vanderbilt in its standing. Its financial resources grew during the next half dozen years; its faculty grew also not only in numbers but in quality; new buildings were added; the roll of its students increased fast, coming from a wider geographical range than that of any other small southern college; and the fighting president had his reward. In 1910, seven years after the great battle for "a free college in a free democracy," his church, the Southern Methodist, elected him as one of its bishops, and the days of storm and stress were over for him, the constitutional duties of this office hemming him in to inescapable routine. For this reason I think, though, that his later days were not his happiest. His combative spirit must have chafed under the restrictions of his great office, and he even longed for battle when the bugles sounded.

Now for obvious reasons there were hardly more than a few breezy eddies, no storm, when the Coca-Cola millions began to flow into the coffers of little Emory at Oxford, later Emory University in Atlanta. Asa Candler, the founder of this king of all the soft drinks, was an ardent Methodist churchman, a leader in Methodist councils, as was also his brother Judge John Candler, while his other brother, Warren Candler, was the most conservative of all the bishops of the Southern

Methodist Church. The Candler brothers could do no wrong, at least in Methodist circles in Georgia. Besides, hadn't the chemist shown in certain court proceedings that a glass of Coca-Cola was no worse than a cup of hotel coffee? If the pious wanted a defense of its growing consumption, wasn't it really becoming a wholesome substitute for that arch enemy alcohol? Still there were those throughout Dixie who hung their heads in shame at the thought that its youth were being educated with Coca-Cola and cigarette money! At least, though, Coca-Cola was no trust as yet, and its headquarters were not in Wall street but in Atlanta, the very heart of the South. So Dixie was not able to lash itself into a storm of heated emotionalism over a college's being supported by that home-manufactured harmless drink, "the pause that refreshes."

But things were not so quiet at Nashville. The big winds were beginning to blow around another Methodist institution, Vanderbilt, founded in 1875 by Yankee money, but entrusted to the Methodist Church to administer for the benefit of the whole South. The editor of the *Christian Advocate*, a Methodist minister with a rare, forthright gift of clear, forcible expression that always carried a punch, got excited over such trivial matters as athletics and student dances. He took off his gloves and was at his linguistic best, or worst. He had been a professor in the theological faculty of the university, and no doubt carried attitudes into the editorial chair acquired in the normal controversies of a university faculty, attitudes not always brotherly even in memory. He was a very able man, of intense feelings and deep prejudices, and an ecclesiastic whose loyalty to what he conceived his duty to his church and its interests could blind him to every other consideration. Once convinced that the honor, the rights, the mission of his church were involved, or rather at stake, he became a fighter who gave and asked no quarter. Now behind this initial assault upon the social life of college boys, assaults powerful enough to be directed against mightier evils, there lurked other more significant dissatisfactions with the administration

190

of Chancellor Kirkland. It was suspected, whispered, talked about that he was engaged in an insidious undercover effort to de-Methodize the university—in a word, to take it away from the church that "founded it," and "owned it in law." Propaganda like this was spread through the entire church, and leaders who had never shown any interest in Vanderbilt came to life with an unexpected, sudden affection for the institution, and wanted to save its soul as a Methodist university.

While attacks of this nature were superficially on things that didn't count, they served to fill the mind of Southern Methodism with accumulating suspicions that sinister forces were at work "to steal" the University from its rightful owner, the church. All this came to a head officially at the meeting of the board of trust in 1904, when the board virtually failed to approve the nomination of the dean of the academic department on the ground that he was not a Methodist but a Baptist. Now here was an issue which a man of Chancellor Kirkland's temperament and views could not avoid—his unwritten prerogative to name the faculty and officers of the institution. So he let it be known that he would resign if the board were of this mind, and called a special meeting to decide the issue. The board evidently came to an understanding of the significance of the issue raised, and unanimously made the unwritten law its written law—the right of a university president to name those who are to serve with him.

On the surface it looked as if there might be a period of peace for Vanderbilt. The chancellor, unyielding as to the issue involved, was conciliatory, and sincerely so, in his attitude toward the relationship between the university and the church. But no, there was yet no peace for Vanderbilt and its chancellor, but a ten years' war, with that bitterness that comes when able men somehow get convinced that the God of Hosts has called them to war. In 1905 the charter of the university was amended to get rid of certain impossible ex officio memberships, which ran counter to the laws of the state of Tennessee. But these ex officio memberships happened to be

191

the bishops of the Southern Methodist Church, who in addition, as an extrajudicial group, had visitorial and veto powers over all acts of the board. Here is another power, not that of the chancellor to name his own official helpers, or that of the board of trust itself to manage unhampered the affairs of the institution, but the power of the College of Bishops, a sort of superpower, to control and interpose their will at any time when any action of the board didn't suit them. Was ever an institution doing such excellent work, steadily expanding its beneficent service, throughout the South and nation, growing in reputation as the institution of highest academic rank and standards this side of the Potomac, drawing a select patronage from all parts of the country, the center of such a conflict and of such continuous attacks from the accepted leadership of a great religious denomination? It must have had within it a sheer virtue of survival, and a wisdom, a courage, an unwavering purpose on the part of its chancellor and the majority of its trustees actually to save it from its would-be saviors. Everything seemed to increase the inflammatory attitudes and propaganda of those who would make it no better than a narrow sectarian college. When Andrew Carnegie gave a million to the medical school and wrote a letter expressing his well-known views of denominational education, he added fuel to the flames, earning for himself throughout the South the title of "that agnostic steelmonger," who with the Standard Oil Company (Rockefeller boards) was leading in the conspiracy to take from the Methodist Church by trickery, by subtle, hidden methods, by money, the choicest jewel in its educational crown.

There is no use in going into the details that led to the decision of the Supreme Court of Tennessee in March, 1914. It is not a pretty story. I took an active part in it, being a member of the three general conferences, 1906, 1910, 1914, that handled the Vanderbilt question, and also a member of the committee by which the issues were considered. I knew all the principals in the drama that ran its course to a climax in a courtroom; and my relations with most of them, on both sides, were friendly and even intimate. I learned the perils inherent in astute leadership in positions of guaranteed constitutional power when men choose to exercise it in causes that seem theirs by providential ordering. They need not be wicked men—none of these men were who fought with their great ability to salvage Vanderbilt University from the evils they thought threatened it. However, I would be amazed at their methods, their intellectual refusal to discriminate between the narrowly sectarian and the broadly Christian in the service of an educational institution; and more than anything else I would be shocked at the kind of men, both lay and ministerial, they chose to carry out their campaign to control the university—men who, understanding not at all the significance of the issues involved, did not hesitate to use the adroit ways of politicians in the affairs of a great religious denomination.

On March 21, 1914, the Supreme Court handed down its decision in that *cause célèbre*—the Vanderbilt case. It affirmed that under the original charter and the laws of Tennessee the board of trust was a self-perpetuating body, with its nominations, however, subject to confirmation by the general conference of the church. In the decision was an unhappily worded *obiter dictum*, in which was a singularly affronting word. Here is the offending word in its legal setting: "If the General Conference should *contumaciously* refuse to confirm members elected, . . . the Board of Trust could proceed independently of the General Conference to the election of members to fill vacancies in its own body." This word "contumacious" sent Methodist leaders and people to the dictionary, already excited as they were over the long controversy to discover that, if they were "hardheaded," "willful," or "disobedient" to the wishes of the board in confirming nominations, the board could, under the law, go on without them, and no doubt would. I doubt whether any single word ever contributed so much to the final settlement of so great an issue. It was as if the court went out of its way to put a "clincher" on its decision, implying that in the long run the last word was with the board of trust.

When the general conference met in Oklahoma City in the following May, its members had been worked up to such a pitch that it was ready to wash its hands completely and promptly of Vanderbilt University. At the first meeting of the specially appointed Vanderbilt committee, of which I was a member, the chairman announced that the church had made up its mind and that in fifteen minutes the committee could pass a resolution declaring all relations severed between the church and Vanderbilt. But it was not so easy as that, for some of us fought for two weeks in the committee for a minority report accepting the decision of the court and starting anew in helpful and friendly co-operation—but to no avail. After many a stormy session of the committee, two reports were brought to the floor of the conference. There the debates were as heated as any of the political debates to which we had grown accustomed in the South in the last twenty years, and the parliamentary tactics as full of tricks as those used in our political conventions.

I was not particularly proud of the way my church conducted itself in the handling of so momentous a matter. But I had to remember that Asa Candler of the Coca-Cola fortune was offering an initial million to establish in Atlanta a real Methodist university after the heart of the most conservative bishop, preacher, or layman; little Trinity was having growing pains in the direction of being the big Methodist institution in the Southeast; while out in Dallas, Texas, a genuinely dyed-in-the-wool Methodist university was in the making, and it had the right name—Southern Methodist University. So in Oklahoma City, the Vanderbilt issue, stripped bare of extraneous influences, was not permitted to be considered on its merits. As always, these outside influences seeped in to confuse and disturb even the thoughtful. When the vote was finally taken, 150 to 140, Methodism had tossed away in a fever of blinding emotionalism the richest opportunity for educational service ever given to an ecclesiastical body in the South. I closed the debate against the majority report, with mixed words of prophecy and appeal, and I find great satisfaction in recalling them now. "We (as a church) owe a duty to the biggest educational opportunity in the South today. It may be that in the process of the years, when 'the tumult and the shouting dies,' when the personalities and passions of this short, heated day have gone into the coolness of the past, in that long day of time we shall wake up to the fact that we have gladly here kept faith with this great opportunity." But we didn't keep faith there; and Vanderbilt University, with the storms that for so long had beaten upon it blown over, entered into its era of greatest usefulness, and nobody whose opinion is worth anything would now affirm otherwise. It won its fight for freedom from external domination of any kind, and has in no wise lost the spirit of Christian service under which it was founded.

On my way back to Spartanburg, I stopped in Nashville for a day. I wanted to go out to the Vanderbilt campus, where I had spent seven happy, fruitful years, just to roam about a little, sentimentalizing over past and present experiences. Of course, I must see Kirkland. He was at home in bed convalescing from a minor operation. As I went into the room, I saw he had been ill. Raising himself up, he held out his hand without speaking for a time, with a display of feeling I had never seen in him; then he said: "I shall never forget the fight you made for the university and me. It's tragic you failed. But the forces were all organized against you, and even then you came near succeeding. I don't know what the next steps will be. But the university is greater than any person, and will go on."

"Yes, Mr. Chancellor," I replied, "the university has its greatest days ahead, and you can lead it and us unhampered by prejudice, misunderstandings, and the efforts of unwise men to divert it from its purpose."

He wasn't sure yet. We talked for a while of the beauty of spring on the campus and the dear friends we had in common in our Vanderbilt yesterdays. From 1914 on, in his hands Vanderbilt expanded in resources and influence even beyond his dreams, I imagine.

Both James Hampton Kirkland and James Carlisle Kilgo held Wofford diplomas. They were sons of Methodist preachers, each of old South Carolina stock—Kirkland of the gentle low country Huguenot strain, Kilgo of the dour Scotch-Irish upcountry blood. The one was "called" to preach, as he would say, but allowed himself to be diverted into the field of education to build great a small college in North Carolina; the other, Kirkland, was called by his genius to scholarship, but permitted himself to deviate into the administration of a growing university. But they, in spite of all differences in ancestry, rearing, training, and purposes in life, became one in spirit when freedom and truth were threatened from without, and they fought in the defense of both. Every educational institution in the South is intellectually and spiritually richer and stronger for them. What did this little college called Wofford have that nourished both of them in those grim days of the seventies and eighties? Something, yes, for it has always produced men of their kind; for when James B. Duke in 1924 dedicated his millions to the service of higher education on a national scale, it was William Preston Few, another Wofford man, who was called to be the first president of Duke University and to lay its foundations in wisdom, and with a prophetic understanding of its future.

11

EXTRACURRICULAR ACTIVITIES

THEY HAD BEEN college friends, nursed on the selfsame academic hill, fraternity mates. He was passing through, and thought it might be a proper gesture to drop in on his friend of the dear dead days, now the president of a distinguished American university. By the time he had been ushered through a series of preliminary offices, he had reached the boiling point, and had to explode with: "Brown, what's come over you? Where are your janizaries and mamelukes? You're as hard to get at as the Sultan of Turkey!" What he saw was not what he expected—the young, eager, aspiring comrade of their college and graduate days—but a man past middle age whose dress and manner made him appear like the president of a big bank or of a large industrial organization. The cordial friend, the scholar, the teacher, the more lovable dean, the educator, had been lost somewhere along the way, and through some magic change there sat before him a perfect example of what the fellows of the baser sort used to call "stuffed shirts," when they saw the kings of finance toppled in humiliating, bewildered confusion from pedestals of authority under the blows of the great depression.

A new type of college and university president has been evolving in the last decade. Men who started their presidential careers as educators concerned chiefly with the strictly educational aspects of their duties, regarding the administrative aspects as "extracurricular activities," have come at last to the point where the latter are their main business, the side show having swallowed the circus. A great western university called a successful city manager to be its president. Around me in

the South I can count four lawyers, one physician, and a retired rear admiral as college and university heads, appointed not
for their understanding of educational principles and policies,
but for administrative skills and expert devices for extracting
appropriations from state legislatures. It's a joy by contrast
to read the annual reports of the presidents of Yale, Harvard,
Princeton, and Columbia and find in them not merely a mild
flavor of educational concern but discussions that have to do
with the whole big business of higher education. It is consoling,
too, to know that in the South the three strong institutions
whose influence is not localized within state lines but is spread
through the entire section have as presidents men who, themselves trained and experienced, whatever their administrative
virtues may be, still count their main business to be that of con-
ducting an educational enterprise. Such men are at Vanderbilt,
Emory, and Duke, anyway. When they discuss "education"
in public or before a more or less specialized group, they do
not need a ghost writer or a moldy manuscript of their own
written when they were really thinking about education.

Just to see how far we had come in the matter of the change
of emphasis in the activities of the American college president,
I read a report of the first president of Wofford College to
his board of trustees in 1855. I note, first, that it was not the
report of the president but the report of the faculty to the
board. The president signed it "by order of and in behalf of the
faculty," and recommendations and comments in it were always those of the faculty—concerning the conduct, the health,
and the quality of work of the students, gifts to the library,
and the request for the appointment of an agent to collect
funds not only for the college generally but also specifically
"for the purchase of apparatus for the department of Natural
Philosophy" and books for the library. Though the president
was an eloquent minister and as a pastor of leading churches
had been accustomed to collecting money from his people
and also had served as financial agent for another institution,
he was the director of a college, an enterprise dedicated to

198

the education of youth, and not the manager of a business organization. My own immediate predecessor at Wofford followed precisely the same lines, reading the report to the faculty for final comment and suggestions because it was their report he was making. However, I was the first of Wofford's presidents to break this precedent, going directly to the trustees without even consulting the faculty. I changed the custom because I found that it had passed into disuse at other institutions and because the trustees required me to break another precedent by sitting with them in all meetings, taking part in discussions, without, however, the right to vote. I quickly sensed, moreover, that they were placing all responsibility for the direction of the affairs of the college in my hands, not in the hands of a more or less abstract group called the "faculty." But this does not mean that I abdicated one whit of my responsibility for the strictly educational purpose of the institution but, if anything, rather increased it. Never for a moment did I let a growing concern—which naturally developed from the discussions in the board—for other interests of the college obscure the dominating fact that I was still chairman of a group committed to the business of education. The truth is that when in the process of time the extracurricular activities multiplied and multiplied, I can say in all honesty that I remained an educator—a good or a bad one, but still an educator. During all the forty years, I taught one or more classes, if only to keep "my hand in" and not to lose touch with the processes of education.

Even the raising of money remained for me but an extracurricular activity, as fascinating and, at times, as exhilarating as it was. During the forty years of my administration there came into the coffers of Wofford College by wills, voluntary donations, and solicitation, $1,500,000—not much to be sure when measured by what colleges in other sections of the country received, but a quite considerable amount when it is remembered that South Carolina is far from being a rich state and potential sources of financial support that Wofford might assume to tap were relatively few. Nevertheless, this amount, $1,500,000, seemed sufficient to minister to the needs of a student body that grew from 180 in 1902 to 460 in 1942; to hold academic standards high, enabling the college to meet the requirements of all the academic approving agencies, sectional and national, and finally in 1941 to win the accolade of a chapter of Phi Beta Kappa on the sheer quality of its work and the extraordinary record of its alumni. I know only that I was never a beggar, having too much respect for the college to be that. A friend, after a little conversation on certain immediate needs of the institution, ordered his secretary to write a check for a considerable amount and mark it "a charity." I declined it, saying that, if he did not believe he was contributing to the intellectual and spiritual progress of the community, the college had no use for his money. A new check was written, with "investment," not "charity," as the label directing it on his books. Really what I tried to do was "to sow by all waters," trusting to the gathering of the harvest at the proper season. Of course, I had a campaign every now and then, particularly in Spartanburg for $100,000 or even as much as $150,000, but I never employed any of the high-priced, high-pressure agencies. They cost too much, and their methods always seemed to me a sort of artificial galvanizing of an interest that might leave a bad taste in the mouth when the time for collecting pledges came. The Wofford campaigns were conducted by friends of the college in their own way, and ended in a mood of high fellowship, making collections easy because the effort was wholly a community affair.

I closed my money-raising extracurriculars with agreeable memories. Hardly at any time have I been made to feel that I was an offending intruder in my approaches. An occasional secretary, especially if he was a man, might abruptly close the doors, figuratively, not permitting a crack wide enough for one to get his toe in. I recall on one occasion, when Wofford was needing $100,000 to meet a generous condition from the General Education Board, that I wrote to a friendly acquaintance stating the nature of the need and the General Education Board's conditional offer. A brief, curt letter came back from Mr. Secretary, saying my friend had quit giving to colleges and was not well enough to be bothered with business matters anyway. The letter looked suspiciously like a bit of "protective coloration," and I discussed it with a mutual friend of the prospective donor. He suggested that I wait a month or two and write a totally different letter, not even hinting in it that I had written before. I took the suggestion, and there came back as beautifully a written letter as ever accompanied a gift of $100,000 to a hungry college president.

As I think back on a multitude of other extracurricular activities that draw the president of even a small denominational college from the main business of his position, "kaleidoscopic" is the only word that can describe the number and variety of images as they come and go. The wonder is that, as I recall the number of meetings I felt conscientiously bound to attend, I had time for any continuous home life, not to speak of time to attend to my official duties in an office inhabited most of the time only by the ghost of a far-wandering college president. I knew all the railroad schedules better than the man who sold me my tickets and the best hotels in the towns and cities and their rates. In these vagrant habits I was not alone, for I was sure to meet all my colleagues in these many gatherings, and if I missed a meeting every now and then, I would be rebuked by them for a sort of failure in my presidential duties. Not infrequently when far from home, hearing the rhythmic rattle of the wheels of the train or suffering under a nostalgic depression in the lonesome sleeplessness of a hotel, I would question myself as to whether my predecessors at Wofford were not wiser and more faithful to their real responsibilities than those of us who came after them. They stayed at home, training the leadership of a state and section without having to make and listen to endless talks about the problems of higher education in "our world which is constantly changing, demanding real adjustments of a most

201

vital nature." This would be the theme, though called by many names. The futility of the whole business of conventions and conferences, educational and religious, would all but overwhelm me, and I would swear to myself a mighty oath to cut some of them, most of them, off my calendar, especially since on my almost every return I would find acculmulations of troubles of one kind and another that might not have happened had the president of the college been in his office and on his job. But alas! the quiet voice of the secretary would remind me of my next appointment—it might be as far away as Texas—and the "oath" weakened under the pressure of an acquired habit of sheer wandering.

Did I really go to all these conferences with a fair degree of regularity, and was I president of some of them or member of their executive committees, requiring considerable ad interim time and labor, or did I read papers and make addresses? Here they are: the American Association of Colleges, with its regional meetings, the Southern Association of Colleges and Secondary Schools, the Southern University Conference, the Association of Church-affiliated Colleges (it, too, having regional meetings), the South Carolina Education Association, the Association of South Carolina Colleges, the Christian Education Association of the Methodist Church, the district annual and quadrennial conferences of the Methodist Church. In addition to these were various boards and commissions, whose meetings often went into weeks on a stretch: the State Board of Education of South Carolina, the Board of Education of the Methodist Church, the Historical Commission of the State of South Carolina, the Commission on Ritual of the Methodist Church, the Commission on Revision of the Hymnal, and for twenty years the commission on the unification of the long-sundered branches of Methodism. On all of these there would be other college presidents, and some of them, in fact, might be called meetings of college presidents. This presents the pattern not of one man's life but of a whole group, whose tasks if they remained at home would be difficult and absorbing enough. But the American college president is not permitted to stay at home but is expected to cover the earth in his peregrinations and activities, so much so that it might seem a marvel that so many of them could build great educational institutions in spite of their extracurriculars. I say this because I have heard the charge against not a few of them that they really "do not know what is going on on their campuses"; that is, while they are reforming the big world with an address before an educational conference, the little world of their college is badly in need of reforming. Maybe so—I don't know. But I do believe no abler group of men is working harder in the service of the nation than the men who are its college presidents. They have been worth knowing, and I would justify the apparent futility of many conferences and conventions by a grateful feeling of a stimulating comradeship with them.

As president of a denominational college, I was naturally drawn into important movements, in some cases historic in their far-reaching results to the church to which Wofford belonged, the Methodist Episcopal Church, South, with a membership of two and a quarter million people and affiliated connections of more than five millions. For instance, immediately following World War I, 1919-21, the Southern Methodist Church sensed the need of a revival of its concept of Christian education and the need of its educational institutions for a larger financial support in order to carry out this conception, and inaugurated what it called the "Christian Education Movement." As its associate director for nearly two years, I saw the South at first hand from Virginia to Texas and from Missouri to Florida—its people; its leaders within the church; and once again its sheer unity in racial stocks, in social habits and customs, in speech, in political allegiances, in religious thinking and practice; its prejudices so easily aroused to stormy expression under certain stimuli; its fighting spirit, aggressively stirred when the older American ideals of individual freedom seemed menaced; its

203

sensitiveness to foreign influences—communism, socialism—all the more threatening because they were not understood.

I came to the end of this particular extracurricular activity with the conviction that in the states below Mason and Dixon's line was a potential human wealth not surpassed by any other section under the flag. After twenty-five years my conviction in this respect has been strengthened. These people didn't pick up overnight a queer brand of Americanism, diluted and streaked with strange, alien thinking, but theirs is an Americanism as natural to them as the air they breathe—an Americanism deeply rooted in all their historic memories. They did not need the artificial voices of overly wise radio commentators to explain the "four freedoms." For these their ancestors had fought, and they knew it. When the dastardly assault at Pearl Harbor came, for them there was only one thing to do, and they did it—rush to arms and get at their enemy wherever he could be found. There were no camps for "conscientious objectors" or "militant pacifists," for there were none of these except a few pathetic, neurotic intellectuals whose reading perhaps had perverted the Southernism to which they had been born. I wonder sometimes when I think of what goes on in Boston, New York, Pittsburgh, Cleveland, Detroit, Chicago, San Francisco, Los Angeles, Hollywood—and all I know is "what I read in the papers," to quote a familiar phrase of a great southern philosopher—I wonder if a day may not come in the history of the republic when this southern section, such a fertile field for missionary enterprise of one sort and another, so probed and picked at by many varieties of reformers; so soundly lectured for its ignorance, its prejudices, its provincialism, its loyalty to a rather simple type of religious faith, may not turn out to be a saving remnant in a land federalized, socialized out of that free independence, that self-reliant individualism that gave character and greatness to the nation. Maybe, though, the pressure of centralization will be too strong for the South itself in the irresistible force of depending for resources of satisfactory living on everything except self-help. Who knows? Some twenty years ago Hamlin Garland delivered a lecture in the Wofford chapel. To the three hundred Wofford students who heard him that night were added two hundred young women from a near-by woman's college. After the lecture we came over to my study for cigars and talk. As we sat down, he said: "I failed tonight outrageously. My mind wouldn't stay on my subject because of the memories stirred by those young people. I've been living in New York for many years where real American voices and faces are scarce and I have become used to the foreignness of it all, on the streets, on the subways, and in the stores and hotels. But to see the genuine American faces of those young people in your chapel once again, and to experience their gentle courtesy, and to hear the soft lilt of the warm American South as they came up to speak to me after the lecture—well, I was back again in my old Middle Border with others of their kind, and a surge of emotion almost choked my utterance at times in the thought of a lost America refound here in the chapel of this little college."

"Yes, Mr. Garland, in the long ago, out of Virginia, South Carolina, Tennessee, Kentucky, their kind went into your Middle Border—Ohio, Indiana, Illinois—because they didn't want to live under the blighting un-American shadow of slavery, and set up homes very like those they had left in the South. Later on some of them kept their political loyalties and were called 'Copperheads.' However, to this day their great-grandchildren proudly tell of their southern geographic and ancestral connections, and one can almost imagine that even now he hears a note in their voices that is not of your Middle Border. But don't be unduly alarmed. They are not a remnant of a lost tribe of Americans—these young people you met tonight—but they represent a million or so of their kind south of the Potomac and the Ohio, an exceedingly rich human resource in the future life of the nation."

Another extracurricular would give yet another approach

to the life and thought of the South and the nation. While there were two large branches of the Methodist Church in the United States, still sharply divided sectionally by historic causes, in 1905 they began using a common hymnal. Thus at least in song Methodism was a united church. I was appointed to the hymnal commission in 1902, and again twenty-five years later when the third important branch of this church, the Methodist Protestant Church, joined in the preparation of a revised hymnal for all. I count among my most enriching experiences the work on these commissions. It involved a general study of the religious lyric, of the historic hymns common to all Christendom, including the early Latin hymns of the Catholic Church and their use in translation by Protestant denominations, of the hymns sung by all Protestantism, of those peculiar to the Methodist churches, of those especially popular in sections of each, and of the hymns preferred by city folk and country folk. One discovered from another viewpoint the social and intellectual variety in American life and how it was expressed in religious songs. So a book acceptable to all had to take into consideration these social and intellectual differences, and yet at the same time interpret in the lyric mood religious aspirations, thought, and practices common to all the people called Methodists everywhere. This was not an easy thing to do, but the discussions about it and the test by the singing of each hymn aimed at just this—hymns that would not seem strange to Methodists anywhere. So I was given yet another chance to study what this America is from its religious songs; for I investigated, as a member of the Committee on New Hymns, the hymn books of all the Protestant churches in America with the view of finding those hymns common to all—and that number was surprisingly large—and with the further view of selecting some that might go into the Methodist book—and the number of such hymns was also surprisingly large. In addition new hymns were sought from fresh lyrics floating around in religious periodicals and even in so-called secular magazines.

In sheer beauty of expression, in sincerity of thought and emotion, and in singable quality some of these suffered nothing by being on the next page of the hymnbook to one of the great ancient hymns of the Christian Church. And so in making a hymnbook used in one denomination, one gets the conviction of the essential unity of spirit in American Protestantism that may be prophetic of a closer union of future practical co-operation in common causes. Then, too, the discovery of hymns of rare poignancy of appeal calling to the very depths of man's religious nature in the midst of the "jazz age" witnessed the vitality of his faith and hope.

One meeting of the commission was held in Washington during the administration of President Theodore Roosevelt. He heard about it, and sent word he would be delighted to meet the members of the commission on a certain hour the next day. After introductions and handshakings, we sat down and were greeted in his usual vigorous, energetic, forthright manner: "Gentlemen, if I had to change churches, I believe I'd become a Methodist. You are still a singing church. The church that quits singing today is doomed tomorrow. A singing church is a conquering church. Then I like your system. It plants churches everywhere. When the immigrant leaves Ellis Island and starts across the continent, wherever he stops he finds a Methodist church and a Methodist preacher. I like your church, too, because it is a church under orders. You have bishops, who tell people where to go and what to do, and they follow orders."

Then someone let it be known that two of the group were lineal descendants of two of his frontier heroes: Bishop E. E. Hoss stemmed from John Sevier and I from James Robertson. Then he seemed concerned with just the two of us and launched at once into Tennessee history, soon to be involved in warm argument with the bishop, who also knew his history. Then it became a debate between just the two of them, and it was worth listening to. But the appointed time limit came, and we rose to leave, the president going to the door with the bishop in an unbroken stream of argument. Finally he queried: "Bishop, how did you come to know so much about Tennessee history?"

Promptly the bishop came back: "I've read *The Winning of the West*, Mr. President."

And with equal promptness the president said, "A diplomat as well as a bishop."

Of all my extracurricular activities none gave me more satisfaction than membership on the commission for the unification of American Methodism, which began its work in 1914, consummating it at Kansas City, Missouri, in May, 1939, exactly twenty-five years later, with the organic union of the three branches of the church under the name of The Methodist Church: the Methodist Episcopal Church (Northern branch), the Methodist Episcopal Church, South, and the Methodist Protestant Church (nonsectional). The merging of these long-separated religious bodies constituted the largest and most significant union of ecclesiastical groups in the history of the Christian Church. In view of the supreme importance of the task in hand the commissioners were selected with the utmost care, and they represented the ablest leadership, lay and clerical, in the three churches. In fact, I do not hesitate to say that, taken all in all, they were the ablest company of men with whom I have ever been associated. They sensed from the beginning the magnitude of their task, the difficulties involved, the historic forces with which they had to contend and somehow reconcile; and they knew also that they were making history that would affect the world-wide service of a great religious denomination, one of the greatest in point of numbers.

In 1830 Jacksonian democracy was in the saddle and riding high, and not even the churches could escape the leveling forces released by it. In fact, there was a small group of Methodists, secessionists, that called themselves "The Republican [*sic*] Methodist Church." But the major protest on the part of the laity was against their exclusion from the councils and conferences of the church, and that on the part of the ministry was against the power of the bishops and presiding elders, whose constitutional controls were, if not autocratic, certainly undemocratic. The Jacksonian democrats didn't mind a dictatorship provided the dictator was of their own choosing and they could depose him at the next election. So the Methodist Protestant Church was born in 1830. An aggressively vital political mood of the hour gave the seceding laymen the right of sharing equally with the ministers in all affairs of the church, and to the latter a church free of the autocratic appointive powers of bishops and district superintendents. So for more than a hundred years the Methodist Protestant Church maintained what it believed to be true democratic practices under a democratic flag.

But American Methodism couldn't escape the social and political forces of history that beat upon it and into it from yet another direction in the name of democracy. The abolition movement got itself identified with religious principles and motives in the North, and its uncompromising propaganda served to justify human slavery with religious principles and motives in the South. Could such apparently irreconcilable contradictions exist in a group bound together by the ties of a common faith and by sixty years of common achievements which had established Methodism among the leading Protestant denominations of America? They did, and these differences grew to a head when a Georgia Methodist bishop by marriage and inheritance found himself the owner of a few slaves, whom under the laws of Georgia he could not set free. Methodists north of the Potomac would not accept his services. The issue of slavery or no slavery was sharply, concretely drawn, and the dividing forces of sectionalism on this issue created at Louisville, Kentucky, in 1844, two Methodisms, South and North—a tragedy poignantly prophetic of what was to happen sixteen years later, the tragedy of civil war.

The story that followed through the period of war and of reconstruction is not a pretty one to consider. Men have a way of displaying their most uncompromising prejudices and bitterness when they believe they have God and religion on their side, and the long-continued display of hostile human motives on the part of each made no contribution to good will and peace and the renationalizing of a divided country. I merely hint at these matters to record what I regard as the miraculous achievement of a continued company of men of very great ability, who patiently, sympathetically, with an ever-increasing understanding sustained and guided by the highest religious motives, brought together these long-sundered branches of American Methodism in a triumphant ceremony in Kansas City in 1939. As I go through this quarter of a century's association and service with them, I find myself thinking of what such a group might do in planning for the long future of this shattered world. I know they would bring into their planning a singular clarity of intelligence, a dedication to the welfare of mankind, deep sympathies, a patient, generous tolerance of the views of others, a sensitiveness to the rights and privileges of even the weakest of minorities, a solid firmness against the assaults of selfish pressure groups, and no taint of self-seeking for themselves or for any party to which they might belong. The next elections would mean nothing to them. It is good to think that I was associated with them, and that there are many, many others like them everywhere in this America; else we should not have an America worth fighting for.

However, when association with a superior group like the men composing the unification commission is recalled, it is not always the important debates and discussions that leave the most vivid memories, but certain incidents, dramatic in character, that unexpectedly explode, so to speak, out of the discussions. Two Negro men represented on the commission the 300,000 colored members of the Methodist Episcopal (northern) Church. Legally and superficially at least this branch of the church drew no "color line." The colored friends of these two Negro members in New York, Pittsburgh, and Washington kept things warm for them by charging that the whole scheme of unification was just an underhand, adroit method either of getting them out of the church altogether, or of "Jim Crowing" them into a separate organization. Every now and then one or both of them got a bit overheated under the pressure being applied from the outside, and his temper revealed it in unwarranted imputations. A northern Methodist bishop, a great man from every standpoint, who had grown gray and wise in the service of his church and country, moving over in front of the two colored members, forgetting that anyone else was present but him and them, calling each by his first name, deeply stirred all hearts with these words: "In the days of my youth I placed this body in front of Confederate bullets that you might be free and sit with us this day in high council for the advancement of the Kingdom of God, and I bear scars yet. Now you listen to evil voices that would continue the strifes of the past, forgetting the friends who have loved you and suffered and sacrificed for you." And there was silence for a time and some tears, not alone from the eyes of the two colored men.

The bishop was as white as any man present, and had all the best that was open in education and culture to the men of his race. In his voice were the rich appealing tones that seem to make so many Negroes natural musicians and orators: "I'm a Negro by choice, and I don't have to remain one, as you can see. Time and again under slights and slurs and injustices which you, my white brothers, understand as well as I do, I have been tempted to 'cross the line' and be white in order to be treated 'white.' When I go back to the town in my native southern state where I was born, I don't know who are gladder to see me or are prouder of what they think I have done, my white kin or my colored. When I got ready to choose my wife, the woman who was to be the mother of my children, I chose the blackest young woman I could find and love, because I did not want my children to suffer as

211

I had suffered in this land of my slave fathers." A more moving statement I had never heard, and the pathos of it will haunt me to the end of my days. In these two brief speeches throb the piercing tragedy of one phase of American life, and one must know that "you cannot escape history," two hundred and fifty years of it, in one brief day of time in spite of the clamors of all the impatient reformers who know it all on the basis of very limited objective understanding.

In 1917, just as we were entering World War I, I received a long-distance request from Governor Richard I. Manning to accept appointment as a member of the state board of education. Having had friends on this board, I knew something of the nature of the duties involved, exacting and time-consuming. However, the governor was urgent, especially on the grounds that a state textbook adoption was coming on, and that he wanted a board not only competent professionally to give the schools of the state the best kind of books but also quite above suspicions of favoritism in its awards. I accepted on the condition that I might resign immediately after the adoption without any protest or misunderstanding on his part. But I didn't resign—on the contrary, I became so absorbed in the responsibilities of this new extracurricular activity as to remain on the board for twenty-four years, serving under the administrations of seven governors.

The board as appointed by Governor Manning was made up of an exceptionally competent group of men and women, school superintendents and principals, a college president or two, a college professor, and a lawyer to keep the board straight in matters of law. The governor was ex officio chairman of the board, and the state superintendent of education was an ex officio member and its secretary. Whatever the political ways and means of these seven governors in other directions, all of them without exception displayed a disinterestedly patriotic concern in the educational welfare of the state and in their appointments to membership on the board in spite of heavy pressure at each vacancy to recognize some

212

thoroughly incompetent political henchman for services rendered. I was thus able to get a close-up insight into political conditions in the state, especially a sort of understanding of the men who practiced politics as a business, even the tricks of the trade, hidden and open, scrupulous and not so scrupulous, the result being that I lived in a constant state of wonderment at how democracy did as well as it did in its processes of self-government. When Hitler wrote of representative government as carried on by "parliamentary bedbugs," I just couldn't help calling names if I ventured to speak out loud. On the other hand, learning day by day what was going on in educational progress in South Carolina, entering into comradeship with the men and women who were making this progress possible, sharing with them officially in the work of directing it, were an antidote to the political poisons seeping into even the state's efforts to give its children and youth the best education possible.

When Governor Tillman (Pitchfork Ben) was promoted to the Senate, where his violences of language and manner and his real ability were exploited from a national platform, he left behind him at least three enterprises in which he took great pride: the Clemson Agricultural and Mechanical College for the "poor" boys of the state, and the Winthrop Normal and Industrial College for its "poor" girls (incidentally both filled up very rapidly with the sons and daughters of the well-to-do from the cities), and the State Dispensary for the state control of the sale of alcoholic liquors, a "noble experiment," as it was called by its promoters. But more than this—he left a swarm of political imitators who sought and got political offices, from governor to coroner, by aping his violent methods, a peewee crowd they were, without his genuine passion for economic and social reform. They boasted of being among the "original" Tillmanites, and didn't even resent being called his "coattail swingers."

For a dozen years this sort of thing went on in South Carolina until at last the people of the state seemed to grow tired

213

of the bickering, the strife, and the fighting, and elected in 1903 Duncan Clinch Heyward to the governorship. He was the last of the great low-country rice planters. The first Heyward in direct line backward owned seventeen plantations and 2,400 slaves. So was the Tillman purge of the old aristocracy at an end and was South Carolina entering upon an era of good feeling? A farmer friend, whom I knew had been an ardent Tillmanite, and who had "whooped 'em up" as noisily for Old Ben as anybody, said to me with satisfaction: "Heyward doesn't seem to have much sense, but we got again a gentleman in the Governor's mansion and the state house." The tradition of the "gentleman" in high places dies hard in South Carolina. Heyward was followed by a mild-mannered, conciliatory, good-natured lawyer from the up-country, and it looked as if political peace would continue in South Carolina. But alas! it was broken by a comparatively young man called Coleman Livingston Blease, who for the next dozen years was to keep his South Carolina in a riotous state of turmoil by arraying once more class against class, and drawing to himself in a strange sort of loyalty the worst elements in the commonwealth, with many not so bad. In addition to being young he was a gallant figure to look at, with an uncanny power of popular appeal, particularly to the rag, tag, and bobtail of every community in town and country. To them he was "Coly," their man—and he was, for they made him twice governor and sent him to the United States Senate with "To hell with the Constitution" on his lips.

Yet, while Blease was running for the Senate, this same South Carolina in 1915 elected to the governor's chair Richard I. Manning, the perfect represensative of the old aristocracy of the state. Moreover, since 1802, the blood of five other governors was in his veins. His grandmother, born a Richardson, was the niece of one governor, J. P. Richardson, 1802; the wife of another, Richard I. Manning, 1824; the sister of J. P. Richardson, 1840; the mother of J. L. Manning, 1842; the aunt of another governor Richardson in 1856. I doubt whether

214

there was anything just like this in the history of any other American state—the governorship being so much a family affair. But South Carolina was in trouble in 1915, and knew it. Blease was storming up and down the state sowing seeds of dissension once more; the State Dispensary was a filthy source of state-wide corruption; that inherent, but at times, latent, self-respect of its citizenship was ashamed and humiliated because of the little men that sat in the high places of control; and, then, the war in Europe was having a sobering effect. South Carolinians, like the rest of the country, sensed the impending entrance of the United States into the gigantic conflict. So in a crisis in its history it turned to the old order, with its dependable qualities, for leadership. Richard I. Manning had come up the hard way during the grim, bitter days of reconstruction. Under the oak trees on the lawn of his plantation home was born the Red Shirt plan for the political redemption of the state. With "free" Negro labor and white tenants he succeeded in farming, laying the basis of a sizable fortune out of the soil. When he was elected governor, to his farming interests he had added banking and other capitalistic ventures. For South Carolina he was a rich man, but above all to South Carolinians he was a Manning-Richardson, and they knew what to expect—not brilliancy, not selfish plotting for political advancement, something they had become shamefully used to in these recent years, but a practical competency, a disinterested love of his state, and an instinctive sense of *noblesse oblige* to the standards of his class: honor, honesty, courtesy, and courage. When the war broke, from the governor's mansion went six sons to France, one to give his life in battle. Nobody in the state was surprised at that. That was the Richardson-Manning way. It always had been.

Now, there was in office as state superintendent of education when Richard Manning assumed the governorship, John E. Swearingen, an able enough man, who in spite of the handicap of blindness had graduated from the state university with a distinguished record. In respect to his unfailing mem-

215

ory of details in ordered sequence and proper relationships, and a quick grasp of all that was going on around him, he was a constant source of amazement in his management of the affairs of his office. He was a nephew of Senator Tillman; he looked not unlike his uncle; he had the same penetrating, rasping voice, and something of his abrupt, aggressive, picturesque skill of phrasing. But more than this, he was a Tillman in temperament, prejudices, hates, and in his instinctive, impulsive ways of letting them out. Now I could never see these two men, Richard I. Manning and John E. Swearingen, when they faced each other at meetings of the board, as merely two conflicting personalities, but rather as symbols, living symbols to be sure, of two antagonistic, historic, always hard-to-reconcile forces in South Carolina and indeed in the entire Deep South. In the one was the great plantation system, based on large slaveholdings, and the aristocratic social group produced by it with their virtues and weaknesses. In the other was that undercurrent of protest, suspicion, jealousy, even hate, ever ready to break forth into turbulent violence when a leader like Ben Tillman comes along to release it. So at every meeting of the board, there stood these two men, showing, even in trivial matters, what sort of history had been made in South Carolina, a history that still goes on with a vitality that can explode the state into political divisions more bitter that if there were a two-pary system in South Carolina.

I have said I taught in my classes at Wofford three of these seven governors under whom I served as a member of the state board of education: Thomas G. McLeod, '92, governor 1923-27; Ibra C. Blackwood, '98, governor 1931-35; Olin D. Johnston, '21, governor 1935-39, and again in 1943 to serve until he defeated Senator E. D. Smith in 1944.

McLeod was of an old upper middleclass South Carolina family of low-country planters, with a few Methodist preachers mixed in to leaven the lump. He was a cousin of "Cotton" Ed Smith—Elly, as he was known in the family. Mc-

Leod was a roly-poly type of fat boy in college, but quick in his physical movements and very alert in mind. He was much given to debate and oratory in his literary society, with a smooth, easy flow of really good English, though to the disinterested listener it didn't seem to mean much. The legend on the campus is that he used to tell his intimates the steps in his future career: first the lawyer, then after practicing awhile, a state legislator and senator, the governor, and finally the United States Senator. He mounted all the steps except the last, ill health and death soon after leaving the governor's chair halting this step. He was almost an able governor, certainly a patriotic one. But I saw his best efforts to serve his state frustrated by politicians, who, doubtless knowing his ambitions toward the seat in the senate, brought to nought his plans for the betterment of the state. That I found was their way, and only a man of Tillman's extraordinary ability and driving force could bend their ways to his, keeping them so frightened as to be mere followers of his, if they wanted office in South Carolina.

Not so long ago I was riding toward the mountains. Very near the North Carolina line and in the first lift of the foothills of the Blue Ridge, I stopped to look at a humble house by the side of the road. It was winter and the leaves were gone from the stunted oak trees, which furnished a rather bleak setting for a cottage from which time and the weather had washed all paint if it had ever had any. There were no signs that it had. From this home, more than fifty years ago, a black-haired, black-eyed, smiling boy came to Wofford College—eager, interested always, but never a student. He was too busy with campus politics, and there was plenty and to spare in his day, when Ben Tillman, the "farmer from Edgefield," was riding roughshod over the old regime of the state and changing its history forever. But this boy, Ibra Blackwood, brought no bitterness into his campus political activities, but a rare gift of storytelling that made him always the center of a laughing group of fellow students, an engaging quality of

217

charm that few men have, and an appealing voice and graceful manner that gave him a suave, facile kind of oratory, without his having to go to the trouble of putting much thought
into his speeches. Probably he couldn't if he had tried. These
qualities he capitalized thoroughly until he became one among
the most popular men in the state and in 1931, and for four
years thereafter, he collected dividends in terms of the governorship of his state—from cabin to the mansion. His smile,
his suavity, his contagious good humor and sheer kindliness
of temperament, his charm, the appeal of his oratory served
to brighten no little of the gloom of the great depression days
in South Carolina. He really served a special purpose for that
hour beyond the reach of a far abler man. It was as if he were
called by destiny for just the service he rendered.

Another black-haired, black-eyed boy sat on the opposite
side of my desk on a September morning in 1916. He was
tall and angular, dead in earnest, no smile on his face. He
had found him a job, reading proof at night in the office of
the daily newspaper. To get started in college he wanted to
borrow as much as $100 from the college loan funds. He was
a boy, a "lint-head," from a cotton mill in Anderson County,
and meant to have a college education. I liked his looks, a certain definiteness of purpose, and that quality of assurance
that even young men have when they have made up their
minds and know what they are doing. He got his loan, and
for the next two years he proved to be a serious student, but
not above the average, majoring in political science and history. At the call of war in 1917 he promptly volunteered for
service, going to France with the famed Rainbow Division.
He made a good soldier, though not a conspicuous one,
bringing back no medals on his breast. He again took his
place in the classroom with the same quiet seriousness as if
he had not been to war. After graduation at Wofford he
entered the law school of the University of South Carolina,
getting himself elected to the legislature while he was yet a
student. From then on it was just one political office after

another until he reached the governor's chair and finally the United States Senate as representative of a state that had been represented by John C. Calhoun, George McDuffie, Robert Y. Hayne, Wade Hampton, and others of their class.

Here is a success story of the true American type—from nobody to somebody, a cotton mill boy with poverty for a background, with no family of distinction to start him with prestige in a state where "family" really counts. With an uncanny political sagacity as his chief quality, he worked his way through college, served his country as a soldier, became a struggling lawyer. He never lost touch with the common people of whom he was one—the cotton mill folk, the tenant and small farmer. To them he was always "Olin," and the doors of the mansion and of the spacious office in the state capitol were always open to them. He was not a good public speaker. There was no great depth of passion in his manner, and in no public utterance of his can one discover much real insight and understanding of the important issues of the hour. And there he sits in Washington, a member of the "most august deliberative body in the world," as one of its members once described it.

Cooper, Harvey, McLeod, Richards, Blackwood, Johnston— it was the violent destruction of the ancient order of things in South Carolina by Benjamin Ryan Tillman in 1890 that gave men like these their chance. Or, rather, was it Appomattox in 1865 that really started the revolution that only found its leadership in Tillman? Richard I. Manning walks with me when I think of the men thrown up out of the political storms of the last fifty years in South Carolina. The conditions producing his kind are gone except as memories, and one may hope that out of the newer conditions will come a freer democracy that one day will create a broader culture from which will emerge a better-trained, a wiser leadership for the service of the commonwealth. But it hasn't come yet, and, alas! it seems a long way off except in the field of industry. The leadership here comes from the old order or its fringes, and some of the leaders may one day turn to politics to serve their state.

12

SPEAKING AND SPEAKERS

THERE HAVE BEEN times when I have felt more like "chucking rocks," as we say in South Carolina, at an audience than tossing words at them. The futility of so much speaking on the part of the president of a small college, intimately related as Wofford was to its constituency, would even shame me into hiding for a while, and I would refuse all invitations until the pressure would be too great, and I would be going the rounds once more with addresses, lectures, papers, lay sermons. And I was never particularly flattered by the variety or, at times, seeming importance of the calls that came to me, nor have I ever been aware of any sort of vanity in the matter of public speaking, though I have spent my life in a state of chronic preparation for some sort of an address—addresses that took me before church congregations or larger official gatherings of the church; to educational conferences of many kinds; to high school, college, and university commencements (I was no respecter of institutions); to summer sessions and convocations; to meetings of chapters of the Wofford alumni and even of those of other institutions; to social and civic clubs. All this involved much travel and becoming acquainted with the people who made up the various strata of the life of this country. Doubtless if those who listened to the wandering college president got little, he got much in the way of an understanding of the people for whom education was intended and a close-up view of those who were carrying on its processes.

But commencement occasions had important compensations. They gave the college president the chance of seeing other institutions in their best "bib and tucker," on dress parade, so

220

to speak, performing an ancient academic rite with the dignity it preserved, with the graduating class the chief actors in the drama and parents and friends as spectators—a drama that to me never went stale by its frequency but remained always fresh and inspiring because it was youth's great day of hope and promise before the realities had begun to hammer them on the hard anvil of experience. With an almost oppressive sense of obligation to the significance of the occasion of a commencement at high school or college or university, or anywhere else for that matter, when youth and their future were the chief interests, there was to me never that sense of a tawdry exhibitionism that at times tried to creep into the exercises to soil the fairness of the occasion.

The truth is, I have never felt that there was anything quite like the American college commencement. Here are fused to create an atmosphere some of the noblest human emotions: the presence in the very air of sacrifice on the part of both parents and students; the glow of satisfaction at the reward for it received at last; the hope, the faith in the future as the result of what these degrees and diplomas represent; then that feeling that comes from the breaking of the ties of comradeship; and also the presence of groups of alumni of varying ages, sometimes noisy in their handshaking and backslapping, critical of any changes made since their day, lapsing back into an exaggerated replica of their college days—all these but hint at the imponderable presence that make commencements unique in behavior and meaning.

This atmosphere came over me with great impressiveness when I was called to Vanderbilt in 1934 during the very blackest days of the historic great depression. It had been thirty-five years since I had been on the campus at commencement—since 1898 when I made the alumni address, or "oration" as it was called. Much had happened since 1898—the Spanish-American war, the strenuous life and the trust busting of Theodore Roosevelt, World War I, the great idealizing phrases of Woodrow Wilson concerning "making the world safe for democ-

221

racy" and "a war to end wars," the "back to normalcy" of hideous memory, the jazz age, the cynical post-mortems on western civilization by the intellectuals, the wild madness of inflation, the mighty crash that shook the world, the New Deal, the bank closings, and finally the alphabetic salvation of the country by every other method than the familiar American method of inner resourcefulness and individual self-reliance. Here was a world in which not even a college commencement could follow the familiar paths or throw about the exercises the accustomed atmosphere. I walked beside Chancellor Kirkland, whose teaching fellow in Latin I had been from 1887 to 1890 when he was Professor Kirkland, who taught me the meaning of scholarship—a meaning to which I have never been disloyal, though I may have betrayed it in practice under the stress of activities that pull a college president here, there, and yonder. In the procession were only three men who were with me in the college days: James Robins, who was in the Latin department; J. T. McGill, retired professor of organic chemistry; and Edwin Mims, head of the department of English, who not so long before had published two stirring, stimulating books, *The Advancing South* and *Adventurous America.* There were also in the procession Walter Clyde Curry, a brilliant scholar in the field of medieval English, one of my own students from Wofford, and Dean Tillett of the school of religion. New buildings towered all around us as we proceeded to the auditorium, but the same Tennessee sky was above us, the soft June airs still whispered in the maples, the first green of the bluegrass had not changed. Otherwise I was in another world, and the ghosts of yesterday, the men who taught in the classrooms and the comrades with whom I had played, walked by my side. Being an incurable sentimentalist, I began to fear that the memories of yesterday would choke out the address I had so carefully prepared for the present, and it would end by being a recital of the slushy reminiscences of an old graduate. I had seen this very thing happen at Wofford.

But once within the building and seated on the rostrum,

with the faculty in the robes and hoods of academic state and some hundred and fifty senoirs down below with eager faces awaiting the accolade of their various degrees that marked the end of an important step in their careers—relatives and friends behind them, each group selecting one person in the graduating class for whom alone all the honor and glory of that proud hour existed—the four walls shut out the whole big outside world, and I was again at home at an American college commencement with its uniqueness of meaning. I had already made up my mind that that outer world of post-bellum cynicism, with its brutal "debunking" of the heroic in life and history, its defeatism, its disillusionment, its farewell to the idealistic, and its ruthless enthroning of the realistic, should not now intrude. Not from me should come any words concerning the problems of the world they were facing. What I had prepared to say might be conceived as if that world did not exist. Not this time would their speaker take any of the joy and inspiration out of this their crowning hour. Rather the address written had to do with the things that were valid in any kind of world, the enduring qualities of the mind and the spirit, the qualities that give worth and dignity to human personality—love and pursuit of wisdom, goodness, truth, beauty, justice, and the courage to live by and for them and if necessary to die for them. From song and story, from the books they had studied and read, from newspaper and magazine, and from what they had really seen for themselves, I drew illustrations and, as vividly as I could, tried to present a panorama of the ancient virtues of the race. Anyway, the doxology and the alma mater song that followed seemed to come naturally out of the theme of the address. They too solved no big problems, but did something to strengthen loyalties to the things that are forever lovely, honest, and true, and of good report.

And what of those gray-haired, bespectacled matrons and those oldsters with shining hairless domes that came crowding upon the rostrum? There were "arms around," handclasps that were slow to break, and maybe a misty dimness in eyes

223

that looked younger than the count of the years; and it was Mary, and Mattie, and Mannie, and Bill, and Ed, and Jim once again—and there was something good to remember to the end of one's days.

Now all this about one commencement must not be taken as the reminiscent sentimentalism of a man returning in triumph to the scenes of his youth. Rather what has been here written has been an attempt to draw the pattern of American college commencements so typically as to suggest them all in their essential features and their abiding, unique value in the scheme of American higher education. They shall not pass in spite of the strivings of the "deans within deans" to reduce the whole business of commencement to a hard, swift-moving, mechanical precision, and to boast how they got through it all in record-breaking time without a "hitch." Alas and alack! Dear Deans, efficiency and speed are not always the marks of a successful commencement, but quite the reverse, if what a great dean of Harvard, LeBaron Briggs, says about a college course is true. If you haven't heard of him, it might help you to look him up. Anyway, in answer to a question he himself raised as to what it is all for, four years in college, he writes:

It's for the friendship that makes life sweeter, the knowledge that makes life richer, training for the task that is high and hard, for the vision that lights the pathway as a pillar of cloud by day and a pillar of fire by night, for the wisdom that suffers and is triumphant, and for the truth that maketh free.

No, Mr. Dean, you may shove them through the mill with machine-like rapidity, but so long as youth is youth, friendship is friendship, parents are parents, and there are a few great professors, even a few on the college faculty who are scholars and teachers, you cannot mechanize out of college commencements what Dean Briggs, after forty years of experience, affirms is in the college itself. Yes, I know many books and magazine articles are being written these recent days about the liberal college, its curriculum, its need for adjustment to catastrophic conditions, its perilous future, if it has any. But after putting what is written into simple, understandable language, if it can be done, do any of the experts say any more than, or as much as, Dean Briggs says in one short paragraph?

Things, surprising things, do happen at college commencements. It was in Auburn, Alabama, at the closing exercises of the Alabama Polytechnic Institute, a vocational, training-for-a-job institution, and a good one. There were some two hundred black-coated seniors receiving diplomas, which guaranteed each a lucrative position upon graduation, but it was still the "great gloom," and it was WPA or nothing. As one stalwart lad was handed his symbol of immediate employment, he got a mighty round of applause, chiefly from his fellow students. I asked the president sitting by me if the boy so honored was the star fullback of the football team. No, he was the only member of the class who had been offered a job before graduation, that of veterinarian to a large dairy herd! Happy boy! the depression had missed him!

In my address to this group I got around to making the point that in normal, routine times it was not easy to tell the difference between a "thoroughbred" and a "scrub," but when crises, emergencies, came, the scrub went down as he always had and would do now in the present emergency, but the thoroughbred would master the emergency and rise to the top as he had always done. While trying to push home this point with an illustration or two, I saw the seniors on the front row were giving their attention to the ferns and palms massed around the rostrum; and there, crawling out of the bank of greenness and making straight toward them, was a green snake, possibly three feet long. For this ancient enemy of womankind, a serpent, in a commencement paradise to get underneath the benches on which they sat would produce a tragedy, accompanied by lifted dresses and screams—the tragedy of a commencement address shattered beyond repair. At the explosive split second of the impending catastrophe a front-row senior, stooping down, quickly caught the reptile just back of the

225

head with one hand and in the middle of the body with the other and, bending low as if to conceal his act, went out a near-by open side door, returning, however, in a minute to his seat to look the speaker in the face to catch the thread of his discourse. The speaker called attention to the dramatic illustration of the thoroughbred meeting an emergency, not only saving an occasion from disaster, but also adding, as if providentially ordered, a shining emphasis of his conception of what it takes to win in times like these! The morning newspapers headlined "Commencement Orator Raises Snakes," when it should have been "A Thoroughbred Saves the Day!"

But it was not all commencement addresses with the president of Wofford. Other kinds of academic calls came, particularly in the summer. One kind was to lecture for several evenings not only at the conventional summer schools for teachers but at the universities, which began to make their summer schools into summer sessions and then summer quarters, with the work and requirements no different from those of any other quarter. The University of Chicago under the leadreship of President William Rainey Harper was, I believe, the first institution of major rank to make the summer quarter of equal importance with any other quarter. Frederick Gates was making educational history on the grand scale when he persuaded Harper to leave his professorship at Yale to go to Chicago, and John D. Rockefeller to back the new president with his millions. If ever a section of the nation needed a great independent university, it was the teeming valley of the Middle West, the very heart of America, and the city of Chicago was as if made to order for the home of such an institution. The president of what might really be called the new university began at once to rob the faculties of the eastern universities, nearly wrecking Johns Hopkins. Almost overnight he drew around him a company of productive scholars that equaled in quality and rank those found in any other American university, and they caught Harper's own enthusiastic idealism and his purpose to found in the great valley, the heart of

America, a university whose standards and accomplishments could not be questioned anywhere in the world. It was as if the mighty spirit of the West were harnessed to higher education in the most progressive sense. Young aspiring scholars from everywhere, but especially from the South and West, found the summer session an answer to prayer. They didn't have to take time out from their positions in college and university to proceed toward their master's or doctor's degrees, but could use their vacations for this purpose, assisted by the newly inaugurated correspondence courses, with university and college credit.

It was as if another Johns Hopkins had come into being, but with a beautiful group of limestone collegiate Gothic buildings to house its spirit, and more money to keep it going and bring to its service the brightest stars in the academic firmament. To be sure, the new University of Chicago was built on the foundations of a not-too-reputable denominational college with a pretentious name, but its past seemed in no way to hamper this new unfolding of power and influence under the contagious energy and the high idealism of Harper. Yet when one looked at that stately cathedral at the center of things, its spires towering above all other buildings, or when one entered the almost twilight dimness of that little chapel, always open, softly, quietly calling to worship without words, one felt that the roots of all this newness went back, like most American institutions of higher learning, deep and far into religious motives that were still present in spite of all transformations.

But nevertheless, it was the exhilarating atmosphere of something big and growing bigger, quite of this day and maybe more of tomorrow, that I sensed when I began a two-weeks series of lectures on southern literature in the torrid midsummer of 1911. As I faced my auditors for the first lecture in a room seating not more than two hundred and fifty, the seats arranged in circular tiers so that the lecturer felt not only that he was looking straight into the eyes of each auditor, but that each was so close that he need not raise his voice above a conversational tone, I sensed that here in this little room was the University of Chicago as it had evolved in but a few short years. There were Chinese and Japanese in the group and a fair sprinkling of Negroes, men and women, and I guessed that a dozen American states were represented. They were all eager, attentive, apparently dead in earnest, not a few of them assiduously taking notes, something unusual with a semi-popular course, though some of my Negro hearers had a way of looking out the windows or whispering among themselves when I would be interpreting "Uncle Remus" or "Marse Chan" by trying to talk like them. If they had known how much I wanted them to tell me what their thoughts were when this man from the Deep South was putting his heart into an effort to help them and the rest of his auditors understand what a rich contribution their ancestors had made to the life and literature of his and their South, I believe they would have come up after the lecture for a little chat that might have been helpful to both. But they didn't.

Toward the end of the course of lectures the southern colony of the university gave a sort of informal reception to the visiting instructors in the university. Once again I felt that inescapable presence of stimulating educational forces at this latest entry into the field of university instruction. It was evident in the promising quality of the young scholars in the making, some with their doctor's hoods only days old. As I now recall, there was Royster, who was one day to head the English department at the University of North Carolina; Frank Clyde Brown, who spent nine summers for his doctorate to be rewarded with a professorship at Duke and to become one of its vice-presidents; John M. Steadman, Jr., a philologist of national distinction, and professor of English at Emory University; and Matthew Lyle Spencer, who, after wandering about a little, went from the department of journalism at the University of Washington to its presidency. Sprinkled all through that cordial group on that summer night were men of this sort, attracted to Chicago by the men who taught there and the fame of its standards of graduate scholarship. It was good to be at the University of Chicago in those days more than a quarter of a century ago and to chat with such youngsters as these. But would it be the same now? I doubt it. I can imagine that, when young Robert M. Hutchins went from Yale to take over the presidency, he found just another conventionalized American university, the magic and glow of Harper's University of Chicago gone out, and in his disappointment he thought that any sort of change would be for the better, even the effort to adjust the methods and ideals of medieval universities to modern conditions. Anyway, whatever the reason, the southern students are again facing east for graduate instruction, to Harvard, Yale, Columbia, Princeton.

From Chicago I went to Chautauqua assembly on the lake. I had been even more interested in this experience than in lecturing at the university, having expected just another group of summer session students, though, as a matter of fact, I did find something more than that in the quality of the students themselves, in the widely dispersed sections of the country from which they came, in the improved opportunities offered by the quarter system, and in a certain tonic element in the atmosphere. But Chautauqua was something different, though the forces that created the assembly there and caused others like it to be repeated all over the country at lakeside, seashore, or mountaintop were familiarly American—the expression of that impulse which affirms that what is good enough for anybody is not too good for everybody, and something ought to be done about letting everybody have it. So I found at the lake middle-class America in quest of "culture" combined with the vacationing disease that seized the nation in the early 1900's. The latent, but always easily aroused, puritanism in middle-class Americans played its part in creating this and other similar enterprises by furnishing more than a merely religious flavor to the standards that controlled them. Hadn't we seen the "wickedness" of the average summer resort, certainly no safe place morally for "our children and young people," the intellectual tone being lower even than its moral (immoral) practices? Can't we, the best people, do something about it? And something was done. A Methodist bishop and a well-to-do Methodist layman gave them just what they wanted, and Chautauqua became a national institution, with a sort of biological power of reproducing itself in every section of the country, offering beauty of surroundings, opportunity for rest, recreation, study, lectures by important men in every field of thought—all under wholesome conditions.

By arriving from Chicago Sunday afternoon, I found myself halted on the opposite side of the lake from the assembly grounds under a regulation that one might not enter on Sunday—an acute illustration of what middle-class America meant by the pursuit of culture under wholesome conditions. Thus I learned in advance what might be expected of even the lecturer who came to make a modest contribution to this pursuit of culture. That vast open-air pavilion, seating perhaps 5,000 people, with its speakers' platform itself vast enough to reduce the speaker and his desk to pygmy dimensions—was this a sort of symbol of democracy's dream of sharing all good things with everybody, regardless of race, creed, or color, or social standing? I felt some of the thrill of this symbolism as I faced my audience for the first time, perhaps five hundred of them, a large enough audience for any lecturer to talk to, though they did seem but a few as they were sprinkled throughout the great spaces of the auditorium. For five days they listened to lectures on "Its Literary Effort as Interpreting the Mind and Spirit of the South" attentively enough, I guess, in spite of the many ladies who never once looked up from their knitting or sewing. There was a little clatter of applause at the beginning and end of each lecture. The *Daily Chautauqua* gave good reports of the lectures, saying they were heard with great interest. However, none of my hearers stopped long enough after the lectures to say so, but after each lecture chatted together in groups and filed out, presumably discussing what the speaker had said. My last lecture was on Sidney Lanier, and I was at pains to tell as effectively as I could the moving story of his life and to place him in the front rank of American poets and to assess his poetry as a rich artistic and spiritual national heritage. I noticed on the front row an elderly man and two ladies, his wife and daughter perhaps. Throughout the lecture they not only were attentive but at times showed no little emotion. They waited at the foot of the steps leading from the rostrum, and literally received me with tears and embraces— the poet's elder brother Clifford Lanier, his wife and daughter. This brother was with him at Oglethorpe College in Georgia and a soldier comrade in the Confederate army. To this day I cherish the feeling that some mystic force must have directed me on that day to do the best I could to present the best in the life and poetry of the Sir Galahad of American letters. Still, this group would have remained behind just to greet the lecturer anyway, because they were from our Deep South. That's their way.

The next summer I was at Monteagle, located on a high plateau in the mountains of Middle Tennessee. It was the first of the Chautauqua centers in the southern states and drew its visitors and cottagers from the farthest South, from lower Alabama, Mississippi, Louisiana, and Texas, chiefly. They came up in mid-June and remained until the first cool days of September and the call of the schools turned them homeward. I spoke to them on the reflection in literature of the social and industrial movements of the first half of the nineteenth century —on George Eliot, Kingsley, Thackeray, Carlyle, and Ruskin. After each lecture the audience made a social event of the occasion with the lecturer as the guest of honor. But more than this: There was hardly a day when either this lecturer or others were not guests in the homes of the cottagers at teas and dinners, and the lectures were the subjects of conversation.

Why these differences between the two Chautauquas? The people of each were of the same American middle class, the best group under the flag, actuated by the same motives and expressing in their standards of conduct the strain of puri-

231

tanism that runs deep and broad in American life. There was also no dancing or card playing at Monteagle—and not even a swimming pool—and Sunday was a very solemn day with the auditorium packed with worshipers.

Perhaps I might add here another illustration for the student of social differences in the United States when he answers the question, "Why these differences?" My professor of Greek at Vanderbilt went to the University of Wisconsin as head of the classical department. At the time of his retirement on a Carnegie pension he was the leading authority on Thucydides in the United States and perhaps in the whole scholarly world. February winds and snows always drove him to his native South Carolina. But when buds began to swell in March and a shimmer of new green spread over the grass, he would turn toward his home by the lake in Madison. I went to the station with him the occasion of his last visit. I instinctively picked up his two suitcases, carrying them into the car as a matter of course. As we walked along the station and into the coach, I heard him chuckling, laughing out loud at times. So as he was seated, I asked, "What in the world are you laughing about?"

"Laughing, yes," he said, "the president of a college carrying the luggage of a retired professor. Well, it is funny. For the president of the University of Wisconsin to do such a thing is unthinkable. It wouldn't even occur to him." And then, holding my hand tight in his, looking into my eyes, he spoke the last words I ever heard from him: "Snyder, that's the difference between two civilizations!"

What is the difference? Is it important—this difference? I turn the answer over to the regionalists and also to those who study the broader aspects of American life. As for me, whatever the historic causes that account for the difference, I believe the glory of this America lies in the variety in the midst of its essential unity. It wouldn't be America if there were uniformity everywhere.

That presidential wanderings in the discovery of America in terms of the kind of folk of varying social and intellectual strata he faced were not confined to academic circles or to those places dedicated to middle-class America in search of culture—a search both pathetic and inspiring—came, a little while after the war broke on us, in a letter from a training camp in Texas. It was from a young major, whom I taught at Wofford. He had just received his "alert" orders and his A.P.O. number. The letter began with: "Don't you remember an address you made at Murrell's Inlet fifteen years ago?" No, Major, I had forgotten the address really; but the occasion of it, the setting, the people who were in the little church that night, and some trivial accompaniments of it—these I had not forgotten. I was the guest of a friend in a small South Carolina city not so far from the seashore. "Suppose we go over to my 'shack' at the Inlet for an oyster roast, and at night you make a talk to the fisher folk in the little church there," he proposed. We went, and after the roast had been disposed of, we sat in the late warm October afternoon, watching the waning sunlight touch with a golden glory the somber green of the live oaks and cypress and the gray of the low-hanging Spanish moss. Twilight came on, and timid lights showed through the windows of the little church, and very ancient the church was. Sea winds and many rains had washed away what paint it once had, leaving only splotches under the protection of the eaves. We took our places behind a very simple suggestion of a pulpit. A single kerosene lamp hung from the ceiling. Perhaps fifty fisherfolk with their families sat on straight-backed, handmade pine benches. These people earned their living crabbing, oystering, shrimping, and casting nets in the surf, whose muffled roarings could be heard. As the speaker began, the babies also opened up in solos and choruses. A lean, gaunt, yellow-and-black hound dog ambled down the aisle, stood for a moment looking up at the stranger, turned leisurely around two or three times, dropped to the floor to rub his nose with his forepaws, then got up again to saunter out into the darkness, but only to return in a few minutes with two friends to give me a "lookover" before lying down to sleep through the noises made

233

by the speaker and the babies. And here also was America.

Yes, Major, this is what I remembered, but you went on in your letter to ask if I remembered the address with a subject like "Living High," to which you as a fifteen-year-old country boy listened, but which you didn't quite understand, and because you didn't, you resolved to go to college where the speaker was, to see if there you might find out what he was talking about. You did go to college by dint of much hard work and saving of pennies, and you found out there what the address meant, and as you have orders to fight for your country on some distant battle front, you know not where, you wanted your college president and teacher to know how grateful you are that you were in the little church on the October night! Did I say that at times I was depressed with the futility of all public speaking, wanting to toss stones at audiences rather than words? I did, but maybe words, like stones tossed into a crowd, might hit somebody, a fifteen-year-old boy, an American boy, who in the American way of self-reliance and self-help, will find the thing he wants, and in an hour of crisis will be leading others to defend the principles and spirit that give them and his kind their freest chance. And shall I not repeat, as a sort of refrain, "This also is America."

New England of the days of Emerson, Thoreau, Bronson Alcott, Margaret Fuller had no monopoly of the lecture circuit, the lyceum, as a means of spreading knowledge and inspiration and adding needed funds to scant exchequers. The lyceum became a national institution—one other expression of America's search after culture and a show of intellectual interest. Wofford had what it called its lyceum course for more than fifty years, set down in its annual catalogue as a part of its offerings. From its foundation its faculty and others would deliver evening lectures at regular intervals to the students and townspeople. To do this was a naturally accepted part of its mission as a college. So if its president for forty years had no disturbing compunctions of conscience for long and frequent absences from college duty, he saw himself in company with a considerable group of itinerating college presidents. For instance, to the Wofford lyceum course there came George Edgar Vincent of Chicago, James H. Penniman of Pennsylvania, Woodrow Wilson of Princeton, Edwin A. Alderman of Virginia, and others of less fame. From the quality of their addresses, the subject matter drawn from their specialties when they were college professors, the dignity and ease of their bearing, and their social adaptability, they added distinction to the office of the American college and university president. I have heard not a few of their later successors, and I cannot say this of them. Perhaps they made up in administrative efficiency for any lack of the qualities of the men I have named—qualities that made them somehow the embodiment of the great institutions they represented and, indeed, of that culture and understanding which such institutions are supposed to contribute to the life of a nation in peril of losing its soul in its search for the great possessions that perish in the using—or in a panic.

But again this Wofford lyceum. In the course of his four years at college, a student might see and hear and even shake hands with ten or twelve men who, for one thing or another, were "largely in the public eye," so to speak, not only because they could lecture well but mainly because they had done something significant. The Wofford lyceum thus called to its platform from many fields of activity the men who were making history, present history. Angelo Heilprin told of the Mont Pelée disaster when the tragedy of it was fresh. George Washington Carver, the Negro botanist, explained to a southern audience the potential wealth in the lowly sweet potato, and they were proud of him as one of their own. Mrs. Sidney Lanier read from her husband's letters and poems and made comments which could come only from the wise heart of love. Lyman Abbott, editor of the *Outlook* when it was the most influential weekly in America, brought his long hair and beard and, still a preacher, the prophetic manner and message of the pulpit he had left. George Kennan told about Russia, and Sir Wilfred T. Grenfell about Labrador. Hamilton Wright Mabie made literature a very sweet and charming influence and a life of culture one of the most attractive goals in the world— followed by Vachel Lindsay and Carl Sandburg who were to prove that literature itself was a terrifying tragic business and life in America, robust and promising as it was, sad and raw and a long way from the sweetness and light of culture. Then Henry van Dyke came down from Princeton and in the skilled, sauve manner he had learned in the pulpit read and interpreted his own writings, almost persuading that there was something to Mabie after all. The politicians (statesmen now, having gone to their rest) were not overlooked—the elder LaFollette, with his gray pompadour and fierce intensity of voice and gesture, appeared to think he was still in Wisconsin as he tried to convince his individualistic, conservative, solidly democratic southern audience that only his semisocialistic theories would save the nation. But when William Jennings Bryan, Champ Clark, and John Sharp Williams came along, the Wofford audience, students and townsfolk, needed no interpreter—they heard thoughts they had always held, spoken in a language that had little strangeness in it.

Now as I recall that procession of American "great" who came to Wofford for the commencement occasion to preach the sermon and make the address, I must feel a sense of satisfaction over the quality and standing of the men who delivered what were called "messages" on these occasions. As was the case with the lyceum, they were selected because they had done or said important things. While most of them were, of course, drawn from the South, sectional lines were no barrier. National figures came to honor and make memorable commencements at Wofford, a little college in a little town of the Deep South; and they spoke without any visible restraint in an atmosphere of liberality and tolerance, though their audience might be far from agreement with their utterances. Moreover, all who came to Wofford for either lyceum or commencement occasions were guests in homes on the campus, chiefly of course in the president's home—that is, before the

236

great depression, which did something to us that went deeper than merely "freezing our fluid assets." They are not now our "guest" speakers—and apparently they no longer wish to be. The speaker now comes the morning of the address to be hidden for a few hours in a hotel room, to be brought to chapel in cap and gown, to "say his piece," to disappear out the back door before the exercises are over to catch the first train away, remembering only that it was a hot day and he nearly smothered in that academic costume. No, in those older days he would spend two or three days on the campus, being dined and supped and "teaed," coming into friendly relationships with the people he would address, catching, if he were at all sensitive, the atmosphere, the *feel* of things, with the result that there would be a warm note of understanding in his sermon or address.

Walter Hines Page came to Wofford in June, 1908, for the commencement address. Since leaving the South, he had taken over in succession the pallid pages of the *Atlantic Monthly* and the *Forum* and by the vigor of his editorial policy had transformed them into the glow of new life and lifted them financially from the red into the black. But he now had his own publishing company in Garden City, the Doubleday, Page, and Company, and his own magazine, the *World's Work*. He came to Wofford from a sort of exploratory tour of his native South, about which he was to write in his magazine. He was fairly beaming with what he had seen—signs of prosperity everywhere in the growing industrialism and improved methods of farming, the steady growth of nationalism, the hope and promise of the youth he had seen at several commencements. It was a happy Page that chattily shared his experiences with my other guests—a man who at last was seeing some of his dreams come true. His address the next day was warmly eloquent as he held before the graduating class the glory of the constructive development of the physical resources of the South and the nation. One might call his theme "The Idealism in Material Progress." In fact, one critical hearer remarked that Mr. Page had forgotten there might be a spiritual and intellectual South worth growing eloquent over.

I had invited to dinner with him after the address a company of some eight or ten leading visiting alumni, some of them men who were doing for South Carolina what others were doing for other sections of the South. To them he brought this story out of Texas: He was headed east after having made the commencement address at the University of Texas. On a crowded train he found a seat by a man who seemed to be a prosperous ranchman. He was reading Page's own magazine, the *World's Work*. Without knowing with whom he was talking, he informed the flattered editor that he regarded the *World's Work* as America's best periodical. Acquaintanceship being established on such an agreeable basis, it was easy to inquire where the editor was going. To Wofford College in Spartanburg, South Carolina. "Why, that's my college. When you get there, you'll find an old teacher named Carlisle. Tell him from me that when I came to Texas I tried every known way of going to hell; but, when I nearly arrived, in each instance I saw his long index finger pointed straight at me and heard once again one of those side remarks of his, that went into the heart of the meaning of right living, and I turned back, finally to stay back. For, tell him, I have built a little chapel on my ranch for my cowboys and their families, and I am the superintendent of the Sunday school."

After he had told his story, each man around the table had his own story to tell of a great teacher's art of helping men educate themselves. Page was profoundly impressed. He thought he had found at last one man who had discovered what education meant and the method of making it function in practical living. He wanted to know if Dr. Carlisle had written any books on the subject, or if anybody else had written about him as a teacher, his theories and practices. I had to say no. He must spend an hour with this man—would we let him stay over till the morning train? Of course we would!

He came back from his visit even more impressed. He was

reminded of some men he had had at Randolph-Macon and Johns Hopkins, Thomas R. Price and Basil L. Gildersleeve, for example; but these men were specialists, scholars in a more or less technical sense, while Dr. Carlisle was an educator in the broader sense, a teacher, a maker of men. Is there any way under the sun whereby others might learn from him his principles and the art of his practice?

Till far into the night we talked about the big matter of education and this teacher's evident mastery of it, and I saw Page, the militant idealist of the development of the material resources of the South become once again the crusading idealizer of its intellectual and spiritual resources. He had caught the contagion of a great personality who was doing just this in the narrow confines of a small denominational liberal arts college, and was influencing greatly the progress of an entire state and section. Could such a man be reproduced? Back at his editorial desk in New York he was still under the spell of the great teacher he had discovered. He concluded his running comment on the "March of Events," which discussed affairs of national and world interest, with this caption, "A Little Story of a Teacher," for nearly a double-columned page of comment. After describing the college and community and Dr. Carlisle, he went on to say:

And who is Dr. Carlisle? A man who went to the college as teacher of astronomy and moral philosophy in 1854 when it was founded, and is there yet. Doubtless neither philosophers nor astronomers regard him as a great contributor to their departments of learning. Yet it is doubtful whether there is an astronomer or philosopher in our whole land who has had so strong an influence on the young men with whom he has come in contact. They do not say that he taught them astronomy or philosophy, but they do bear testimony to his giving them in greater measure than any other man a right adjustment to life and a moral uplift.

Possibly the great business of teaching may get some hint from this simple story.

Yes, Mr. Page, it could if it would, but as one listens to the chatter and babble of the new vocabularies that have been invented since 1908 to conceal the real business of education, one would say that few hints have been taken from men like Carlisle.

Chapel attendance was required at Wofford five days in the week. From sheer force of long habit this practice was accepted without a murmur of protest. Of course, every now and then when some lad or lassie, editor of a college daily or weekly in the East or West, wrote a sharply critical editorial against compulsory chapel attendance, or compulsory anything else in our American democracy, as violating the principles of individual liberty and freedom of religious worship, our Wofford editor might chime in, but not very aggressively, and nobody paid very much attention to him, because everybody knew he couldn't get far in upsetting this Wofford custom. So what was the use?

Maybe it was because one could be sure of a full house any morning in the Wofford chapel, or convocation period, that every variety of promoter, or propagandist, or crusader for causes that would save the world was asking for the privilege of a few minutes for addressing the students. The sheer number of such requests was a constant source of amazement to me. Some group had to finance them, and they were always well groomed and well fed and stopped at the best hotels. There was never any evidence of the poverty of those tattered pilgrims of light who were giving their all to the cause. I used to ponder the ease with which funds could be extracted from well-to-do American men and women by showing them the rosy tints of some distant utopia. I never thought, however, that it was a bad idea to let Wofford students hear these "fifty-seven varieties" who were all for reforming mankind. Who knows what seed of fair fruitage would fall into fertile young minds, though much they heard might stir only a feeble dance in the molecules of the brain cells. So I let them in—I wish I had kept the list—from the blue-black Abyssinian, with the Oxford accent, who felt he was divinely called to prove that his people were not Negroid and that their faith, the Coptic, was the oldest and purest form of Christianity, to red-haired Rose Pastor Stokes, who seemed to feel if she could get a chapter of the Intercollegiate League of young socialists established at Wofford, a better future for the dispossessed of the world would be assured.

But occasionally there came one who left unforgettable impressions, making all the rest seem worth the gamble. In the early spring, March 21, 1909, I had a letter stating that President Charles W. Eliot would be coming our way and would be glad to address the students and community at the convocation hour. Certainly we would be glad to have him, and would count his visit a privilege and honor. He had just resigned after forty years of service as president of the nearest approach to a national university we had. He planned a rather extensive tour to emphasize this nationalism of Harvard and give a sort of personal stimulation to the loyalty of Harvard's widely scattered alumni. He would meet a few of them in Spartanburg and from neighboring communities, for since 1866 there had been a pretty constant trickle of Wofford graduates into the professional and graduate schools of Harvard. He wrote he would arrive about ten-thirty in the morning, Mrs. Eliot would be with him, and they would spend the day.

I met the train, and brought him, Mrs. Eliot, and Mr. Warren, his secretary, to my home on the Wofford campus. A stately man he was, with every mark of distinction about him, but with the simplicity and the directness that usually go with greatness. As we entered the yard my big setter dog came bounding to greet me as he always did. The president of Harvard wanted to know what kind of dog it was. Rather surprised that he didn't know, I merely said, "A bird dog."

"A bird dog; does he catch birds for you?"

"No, he finds them, and I kill them when they fly up, if I don't miss."

"And you kill wild birds!" was his reply. "We go into the

woods in New England, but we take with us a camera and notebook, and don't bring back anything dead."

Was he lecturing a young college president, or just expressing his views with that candor which was always a mark of his spoken and written utterances?

In the hall he bowed with the grace of an old-time gentleman to Mrs. Snyder, and inquired if they might not have a pot of tea in their room. The request made him at once at home with his hostess. He and Mrs. Eliot had their tea and an hour's rest before the address at the chapel period.

The chapel was crowded with students and townspeople who were eager to see and hear the most distinguished figure in American education. With that cameo-carved face, that height of figure, that ease of movement, he more than met expectations as he stepped upon the rostrum. He looked the part of the man who, for better or worse, had changed the whole course of undergraduate instruction during the past forty years, and seemed in his own person to embody the leadership of Harvard College in the field of higher education. The audience in the Wofford chapel on that spring morning, if they did not understand why Harvard was great, did know it had to be great with Eliot at its head.

On this twenty-first day of March, 1909, Charles W. Eliot was spending his seventy-fifth birthday on the Wofford campus. From the citizens of Spartanburg I presented him with a wreath of white carnations and a key of red carnations, the key to the city; and to Mrs. Eliot, from the ladies of the campus, a great bouquet of American Beauty roses. First, with a gesture toward her, quoting Andrew Carnegie, he said, "Behind every throne there is a power"; and for himself, "I only want it said of me—this American's life has been successful."

I gave a sketch of the significance of Harvard in American life, and presented him with only "Charles W. Eliot, president of Harvard College." That South Carolina audience at once caught the significance of this simple form of presentation and responded with an applause that meant they were recognizing him as the first citizen of their country. His address on "Public Spirit and Its Best Manifestations" was characteristic. Direct, simple, wise, practical in implication, it was unreservedly candid in thought. Possibly thinking of his surroundings, the chapel of a denominational college with its walls lined with portraits of distinguished ministers, he told what the church might do as one important manifestation of public spirit, closing with a quotation from the prophet Micah: "What doth the Lord require of thee, but to do justly, and to love mercy, and to walk humbly with thy God?"

His audience rose, applauding; and as Mr. Eliot turned toward those on the rostrum, Dr. James H. Carlisle, in his eighty-fifth year, six feet four inches tall, connected with Wofford from its foundation in 1854, president from 1875 to 1902, stepped forward to clasp President Eliot's hand and say in that rich, vibrant voice of his, and with deep emotion, "If figures do not lie, I was a youth in the dismal swamp of the multiplication table while you were a babe in your mother's arms. Rejoice, O young man, in thy youth, and let thy heart cheer thee and bring forth fruit in thine old age, and at eventide may there be light!"

There they stood, both tall men in every sense, dramatizing the historic forces that had divided their country and also at last had united it: Carlisle, of Scotch-Irish Covenanter South Carolina upcountry stock, was perhaps more of a Puritan in ideas and practice than was Eliot, descendant of the harsh Puritanism of early Massachusetts days. But both were one when any of the issues of life, public or private, entered the inner sanctuary of the conscience. Eliot came to the presidency of Harvard in 1869 when the North and East were reveling in the lush, if deceptive, prosperity of the post-Civil War days, and through its continuance for the next forty years he was able to leave to his successor a Harvard that not only had for the time being reformed American higher education, but had amassed financial resources sufficient to class it among the wealthier foundations of the world. Carlisle, signer of the

Ordinance of Secession, when he took over the presidency of Wofford in 1875, found the endowment and resources of the college quite gone, its buildings in a ruinous state of disrepair, the wealth of the South vanished in the tragedy of war, its people still crushed with the sense of defeat, their spirit all but broken under the humiliation of carpetbag and Negro rule; yet, making bricks without straw, barehanded as it were, he set himself to work to redeem and rebuild in the only way possible—by the process of training men in character and mind who would one day create another commonwealth, prosperous and happy, looking toward the future but not forgetting its heroic heritage from the past. And he succeeded, patiently working at the long day's task for fifty-five years. In so doing he earned the grateful appreciation of the people of the South; and as he stood by Eliot, in the thought of all he was of equal stature, and the two together were the greatest amongst us if the education of youth is our most important business.

I wish I had the Boswellian knack of recalling the conversation at the luncheon table, for we gave a "birthday party" to which we invited distinguished people, men and women, in honor of our guests. Just a few snatches of the things Eliot said stick now in memory. "How much land have you in your campus?" he inquired.

"Seventy acres."

"Don't sell a foot of it. Harvard College sold land by the acre which it had to buy back by the front foot. You know we college presidents must never forget that a college is immortal, and we must keep a long look ahead always. You know, your Wofford makes me think of our Harvard when I first knew it, and I feel that Wofford is a sort of contemporary ancestor of Harvard."

Not much to remember, to be sure, but what still remains is that I had Charles W. Eliot on my right that day and James H. Carlisle on my left, and that I heard great talk from two great men, and that American history was vividly alive in these two who had helped make it on college campuses.

13

OBSTACLE COURSE FOR
COLLEGE PRESIDENTS

IF ANYONE thinks the first ten years of a new college president's service are entirely rich in the romance of adventure into new fields and crowned with the satisfactions of accomplishment, he fails to consider many things that keep new presidents humble in their walk before God and man. Increasing the endowment of Wofford to well over $200,000; adding two greatly needed buildings to the facilities of the college as well as a fine (then) modern dormitory to reduce the living expenses of a majority of the students and break through, at least to a degree, the lines of social cleavage among them; seeing the faculty grow in numbers; knowing the college had been brought into a more understanding relationship with the church and its constituency—these were matters that could, pardonably, bring about a sort of presidential "strutting." But not for long at a time, because, first, every new president has to make his calling and election sure with his colleagues of the faculty. Probably, most of them, though they may like him, have never considered him as presidential timber, and in fact are no little surprised that the trustees overlooked that other man, who was older anyway and had been with the college longer. Also there are those who have deep convictions against selecting a president from the faculty at all, and for this view there are many and good arguments. Then, there are the older men, who, without being aware of it, have acquired a sort of vested interest in the institution. They are the guardians of the past and preservers of the *status quo*. Any change is a reflection on them, and they can easily become obstructionists, blocking any movement that has in it elements of what has not been done before.

Moreover, there is yet another group on many college faculties that every new president discovers he should do something about, and that group is those men who, just past middle age, have surrendered their ambition, have quit studying, and, finding a well-cushioned routine in which to loaf, are saying, "Soul, take thine ease." These too will keep watchful eyes on any new president, uneasy lest he disturb them in that measureless content in which they have wrapped themselves.

I have seen at other institutions the hampering, even explosive, tensions involved in these very human relationships. My kindly "demon" (*Daimon* is the word the Greeks had for it) told me to try, first of all, to win the affection and confidence of my colleagues as fellow workers in the same great cause: to be fellow workers effectively they must be friends as well to the man who by the chances of circumstance was also president. By the natural instincts of temperament I set about doing this with all the tact and understanding I had. To the accomplishing of this end, I made for myself two rules: (1) that I would be very economical in applying the privileges of prerogative, and (2) that I would always strive for the golden virtue of patience in my human relations, official and personal. Now the bare statement of these rules seems banal enough, platitudinous echoes out of the ancient copybooks. Certainly, whether I was born that way, I came to have no vanity of position and no sense of official prerogative, maybe too little, and I believe I could have stood for the model of Patience on a monument. And I know further I was all the happier because I was never conscious that presidential prerogatives were being invaded or usurped by anybody connected with the college, faculty or trustees. I imagine the members of both these groups were also happier. Anyway, he who has the last word on any issue can always afford to be patient, and he who is sensitive to the prerogatives of official position carries a sore and swollen thumb around with him and is, as I have seen, always getting hurt. I do not like to be hurt. So I have never suffered any pain from this source, as I know not a few of my presidential colleagues have.

These qualities, native or acquired, stood me in good stead as I faced the initial hurdles any new college president must in some way get over or by. There they were—comfortable middle age and stand-pat old age. In the course of time when I became one of the "nine old men" sitting in presidential chairs, there were about three stock questions that were put to me—who ought to have all the answers after forty years—by new presidents who were discovering their first worries: (1) What did you do with your old men, particularly those who wanted nothing changed? (2) How did you awaken the not so old, but the intellectually and spiritually dead on the faculty? (3) By what standards did you select your group of young instructors? The effect of such questions was to send me back to an address I made in the middle years of my administration at an educational gathering in Dallas, Texas. The chairman of the meeting flattered me into accepting his invitation by saying that Wofford had the reputation of having a strong, well-balanced, co-operative faculty, and that he wanted me to tell the college world how to secure and keep such a faculty. Now Dallas was far from home, and I knew I could therefore speak with the authority of an expert. To arrest the attention of my audience I began facetiously with, "There ought to be a few gentlemen on every college faculty." But for a moment or two I could hardly go on—plenty of real applause mixed with laughter. The address was headlined in the morning newspapers: "College president says there ought to be a few gentlemen on every college faculty!"

Just the other day I went into the Cleveland Science Hall. On the wall facing the entrance was a bronze tablet bearing this legend: "To the memory of Daniel Alston DuPré, Professor of the Natural Sciences at Wofford 1875-1930." For fifty-five years he was teacher of physics, chemistry, and geology in one college, and he taught them well. But the main thing was not how he taught or what he taught, but who did the teaching—"Uncle Dan," as his students came to name him with affectionate reverence with the passing years. His very name, Alston DuPré, told to all who knew South Carolina that he just couldn't help wearing without abuse the fine old name of "gentleman." His students recognized this, and the sheer fineness of him worked a magic on their youth to make them want to be like him, with his unaffected grace of manner, his unstooping integrity, the beauty of a mature courtesy that never forgot itself when dealing with their, at times, thoughtless boyishness, and his sense of honor that never needed to be asserted. If that more or less vague conception of what is supposed to happen to human beings during the four college years—called "education"—goes deeper than so many credits and quality points, majors, minors, deans' lists, and does something toward the shaping of human personality to the finer uses of life, then I say even yet, without equivocation and with no attempt at facetiousness: There must be a few gentlemen on every college faculty if youth is to carry on the culture of the race.

What to do with your old men? Why, capitalize them among the real assets of the institution. They represent in a living way its past; they are its traditions at their best; and it is they the alumni inquire about and visit when they come to the campus. So I paid special and sincere attention to these older men; told about them in public addresses; and took them with me to alumni gatherings. And as time went on and their infirmities increased, as tactfully as I could, I would ease them into teaching one course, with enough compensation—and I mean compensation, not a pension or retiring allowance—to give each a modest support, with the further assurance that their widows would also be provided with a small annuity. There was no system about this plan, no deducting of percentages from salaries, but rather a grateful college's way of taking care of its own for values received. And they were all worth it—these loved and honored men who stood before the alumni and friends of the college as living symbols of the fine and gracious life that all dreamed it stood for. What to do with your old men? Capitalize their service, their character, their personality; hold to them as long as life lasts; and memorialize them as among the enduring records of the institution. The dividends will be richly humane and satisfying. Daniel DuPré, James Augustus Gamewell, Arthur Gaillard Rembert, John G. Clinkscales—I saw them walking into the sunset, showing what kind of persons men become who through a long life have loved truth, and freedom, and honor, and courtesy, qualities still as valid as they were when Chaucer more than five hundred years ago ascribed them to his "verray parfit gentil knight." Their homes were meccas for visiting alumni, paying grateful tributes of affection and reverence to men who taught them science, Latin, Greek, mathematics, but also something that went deeper, something that called to an urge toward upright and serviceable living. Isn't this, I ask it again, one of the elements in what we are trying to say when we talk so much about a "liberal education"? If it isn't, it ought to be, and if a college president is not dumb and blind to what really counts, he will be greatly pleased to have such "old men" around, and will know what to do with them.

How does it happen—this dying at the top that perplexes college presidents as one of the major "obstacle courses" they must somehow hurdle? He is not over fifty. Most of his colleagues around him are just at the height of their effectiveness and influence, producing now and then articles that get published in scholarly magazines, winning no little fame as real teachers, and acquiring the reputation of being wonderful workers who not only inspire their students but also get plenty of work out of them. His training has been as good as theirs—excellent college record and graduate experience at a first-class university under good men. He was crowned with the doctorate that assured that the spirit and methods of research were his at least for a time. He started well, though one might feel from the beginning he was not going to set the college house

249

afire with enthusiasm. By and by faculty meetings bore him, and he becomes conspicuous for his frequent absences, and committee meetings are a waste of time; then he discovers that assigned readings and written reports or themes from his students are not important enough to bother with; he is also "poking fun" at the contributions his colleagues are making to learned journals as being "stuff" not worth printing. For him there are a rocking chair, a pipe, a magazine; and if his students accuse him of not looking over their examination papers, his only defense is that he doesn't need to, knowing beforehand what each will make, and an examination is no real test anyway. Other members of the faculty may be asking for new books in the library with tears in their eyes as if their departments cannot survive without them, while he has forgotten that there is a college library, or that publishers are still turning out new books, as far as either he or his students are concerned. Comes the long summer vacation; his colleagues, after a brief "breather" of a vacation, are off to several university centers for work in the libraries, or are hard at that piece of writing they must do before fall, while he disappears to mountain or seashore to recover what he has not lost—the physical or intellectual energies that he has not spent during the college year, as far as anybody knows.

It does not seem to take a new college president long to discover a few lost souls of this type wandering about the campus, and to inquire of his elders in the profession what to do about them. I could answer only out of a sense of failure. The disease here referred to is so subtle, so insidious, so gradual, the victim so agreeable, that he has reached the incurable stage before one is aware of it, before one discovers how really ill the patient is—so ill that only a surgical operation can relieve the institution. To perform the needed operation would be to bring down a committee of investigation and judgment from the American Association of University Professors and other learned groups who want to know how a man with the Ph.D. from X University could possibly be unacceptable anywhere! Has he stolen anything, or been guilty of immorality of the grosser sort that the law of "tenure" should be violated without due observance of long-established formalities that govern an institution of higher learning as it considers an instructor's rights without regard for its own, or rather those of its students? "Guilty of immorality"? What is "immorality" if it isn't failure not only to be a scholar but to be a growing scholar when dealing with the making of scholars out of even a few college boys? One wonders, with all the testing schemes invented by educators for keeping students unhappy, why they do not also invent a few fundamental methods for measuring the mental growth, or lack of it, in their professors. If there were even a little more certainty, the results arrived at with the professors rather than with students might avert some great tragedies that tell the story of the spiritual and intellectual death in life of men who once promised well—and new college presidents would have one less obstacle course to worry about.

Young instructors just introduced into the faculty are as hard to educate as freshmen. Nothing much can be done with the freshmen unless the college has the right men to do it with; and neither academic records, nor the degrees held, nor the institutions from which they were received are safe guides to go by when seeking a new instructor. I wish selecting one were as easy as looking over the paper biography of the prospect, or even those recommendations with great names attached. Every new college president, as I did, has to learn the hard way that over this road lies disaster, discovering that after the last word has been written about the man he needs, whom he has been investigating behind his back, there yet remains a sort of sum total of his fitness: his looks, his manner of dress, his social background; if married, the kind of woman he has chosen for a lifetime companion; and then his personality, for here is the mystery of all mysteries. Moreover, your new man must be considered not as a mere "filler-in," as if he were leaving next year, but as a long-run type, who will wear and last.

After learning in that bitter school of experience, I did not wonder that my new colleagues also inquired about methods of getting new and young blood infused into an old and aging faculty. I knew they had gone my way and had made enough mistakes to want to inquire of one who had doubtless made so many more as to have found ways of avoiding at least some of them. And so my colleagues thought that through length of service and hair made gray by blunders I had come at last to a "system"—everybody, even in education, where any sort of system is dangerous, wants to work by a system as a labor- and trouble-saving device. So the question would be, "What is your system for getting new men?" I probably felt I hadn't any that I could write about, and say, "Here it is!" But except in an avoidable "pinch," I did follow certain ways. To start with, I took nobody's statement as the last word. Experience very soon taught me not to do that. I must see the candidate; sit down with him at dinner; try to disarm him by the casualness of my conversation so that he might forget I was his prospective employer; talk about the college as if he were an interested friend; get around finally to his "specialty," his student comrades who went along with him, his teachers—those who meant most to him and why—what writing, if any, he had in mind, his hobbies and ways of recreation. All the time I tried to keep the two or three hours spent with him as the easy talk of an older scholar who was deeply interested in the accomplishments and ambitions of a younger scholar, being all the while careful that there should appear no "high-hat" attitude of a president hunting an employee. Even a hint of such an attitude not only is ungentlemanly, but tends to send into hiding the real person you are trying to discover.

But once you have him on the campus, don't lose him. He can get lost even in a small college, though he may have the distinguished label of his doctorate upon him. And the spirit and methods by which he won it, the chips from his dissertation workshop, the aspirations to be somebody in the field of scholarship, the pride he feels in the great men under whom he worked, his sense of discipleship and his obligation to create others, that article he wrote for one of the learned journals—these are matters the college president should discuss with his "freshman" instructors even if he has to do a little reading on the side in the field of their specialties. In the process he may be attaching to his institution for life that rarest of all jewels in its crown—a great scholar, a great teacher, a great person—and may be making his institution great, whether it muster on its roll a hundred or a thousand students, or whether its buildings be stately piles of imitated Gothic or ivy-covered towers which were inherited out of a past when it was the spirit that counted for more than the house in which it dwelt. The president who assists in the developing through the years of a really great college teacher (I do not say "effective" teacher—God forbid!) is overcoming the main hurdle in the success of his institution.

After I had been president of Wofford for twenty-five years, a friend put to me one of those very foolish questions: "What is the outstanding achievement of your administration?" Facetiously, I answered him according to his folly: "Keeping the faculty in a good humor with one another." He looked dazed, then laughed a little because I did; but the more I thought of what I had said, the more I was convinced that, if it were true that I had kept the faculty in a good humor with one another, it was really an "outstanding achievement." A college faculty gradually develops something of the intimacies of a family and then, naturally, the irritabilities of a family. The debates of faculty meetings, the contentions of committee groups, the petty jealousies, the small vanities, the inevitable rivalries that make us human and keep us from being saints, can easily enough banish all good humor from a college campus. The students, for whom the institution exists, become aware of faculty differences, making them matter for jocular remarks, wondering if their guides themselves do not stand in need of guidance. Reputable institutions have been so infected with poisonous divisive forces within the official family as to require a complete house cleaning and a period of fumigation to get a fresh start, causing one to inquire if the strongest argument against higher education isn't sometimes the behavior of those in charge—their lack of poise, balance, tolerance, and the common courtesies of civilized living. How these destructive discordances in college faculties could be maintained by apparently intelligent men, feudisms as bitter as those among mountaineers, is more than I can understand. Having had no practice in it at Wofford, I have no cure to offer for it, but I do know there is no obstacle course more obstructive or harder to get by than a faculty house divided against itself. The tragedy of it is that many a college president finds himself wasting much valuable time and thought to keep a faculty in good humor with one another.

The choices which the president must make represent further the obstacles he has to go over, through, or around. If his college is none too rich, he must be always deciding between the face of things and the soul of things, buildings or books, scientific apparatus or new chairs for the lecture rooms, extensive repairs or increases in professors' salaries, refurbishing the administrative building or promoting those two or three hardworking instructors. In these directions lie the deep inner conflicts that keep him ever perplexed. And he needn't think his measure is not being taken in terms of the choices he makes. That ambitious professor, one of his best men, conscientious to the last degree and highly efficient, whose department is overcrowded with students, wants a little help—an instructor costing not more than $1200—and is told by the president that he must cut expenses to the bone. But on the occasion of the professor's next visit to the president's office he finds that there are two new stenographers cluttering the already crowded space in near-by offices. What does he think? He doesn't tell the president, but he does raise the question with the president of another college—which he should not do, of course—as to the relative importance of stenographers and instructors in an educational institution. My guess is that his president will never be the same to him thereafter. Or yet another professor, all enthusiasm over the work he is trying to do, feels that with three hundred additional new books in the library he can make certain of his courses fairly hum—his students just must have them. But his president tells him that the college is virtually on the breadline, all expenses have to be cut, and there can be no more books this year. However, in a few days a carload of shrubbery is delivered on a campus already darkly shaded and overcrowded with shrubbery. He too has a way of talking with all who will listen about the relative value of books and shrubbery in that process called "higher education." His president made his choice in favor of shrubbery!

All through my presidential life I carried two conflicting dreams growing out of the questions just raised concerning what a college president should do with the all too limited funds he is free to spend. The first dream went this way: Suppose some good angel in the cause of education should unexpectedly drop into my lap a few million dollars with which to create the kind of liberal arts college I wanted according to my own heart—just enough money to do it with careful economies. I would first construct simple square substantial buildings in strict utility of purpose and surround them with a campus with the neatness that required only a minimum of expense for its upkeep. But I'd spend my money for the most competent instructors, selecting a limited student body with at least something like the same care, livable dormitories with appointments reduced to the barest terms, libraries and laboratories as nearly adequate as possible. "Use" would be the master word, but use in the service of intellectual and spiritual training, and over the gateway would be that ancient phrase, though a bit banal and worn now, "Plain Living and High Thinking." To such an institution the choicest youth of the land would want to come in such numbers that standards would have to be in a continuous process of being raised, and the best instructors from everywhere would be seeking places in this new kind of college of the liberal arts and sciences. This may be but the empty fabric of an impossible dream, but it has enough worth in it for someone some day to make it real.

A highly intelligent, widely traveled woman said every now and then she just had to drive through the Wofford campus to enjoy its old mellow beauty; that she not only was *seeing* a college, but was *feeling* one at this seat of ancient culture. "Beauty," "culture," feeling both as well as seeing buildings— these words and this conception seemed to melt away my dream of suave utilitarian substantiality to save the money my good angel dropped into my lap, and another dream entered in. "Beauty," "old culture"—these are things of the spirit, and they need a noble house in which to live. I recalled my feelings when I first saw the fresh newness of the University of Chicago and then of Duke. It brought to mind those ancient seats of learning in the old lands, Cambridge and Oxford. Then, too, I saw again the pillard fronts of the University of Georgia, the rotunda at the University of Virginia, and the twin ivy-covered towers of Wofford. My dreams of ultra-utilitarianism in buildings for educational uses vanished, or rather was fused into that other dream, and the conflicting choices merged into the conviction that the forces that help youth to discover its mind and become aware of the intangibles of the spirit should have a fair and appropriate home— material home, I mean. If the cathedral spire is the symbol of the soul's religious aspiration, so in no less gracious and beautiful a manner should youth see its own aspirations symbolized in buildings, in shaded vistas, in green-carpeted lawns, in noble trees, all mellowed by time and agelong associations into a sacredness of unforgettable memories. This too is higher education, and it need not be books *versus* shrubbery, but books *and* shrubbery, and the good angel of higher education, if there be any left, must provide for both.

In the last column of the *College World* might well appear this notice in the usual small type: "Lost—Mark Hopkins and his log. If any college has two of these museum pieces, and would care to dispose of one to a college of education for its collection of educational antiques, it would be appreciated. For obvious reasons, write X, care of this journal." There might be a few responses to this notice from old alumni of various American colleges, saying they had heard of him—in fact, at their own college, one or two of their professors had been called the "Mark Hopkins" of the institution, and they were the best they had. But when they talk to their sons and grandsons about these men and their greatness in the classroom and out, they wonder and wonder at a strange species that once lived on college campuses. They do not know this species, though the football coach does seem to have some of the qualities ascribed to it—enthusiasm, knowing each man on the squad individually, a knack at developing the best in each, a way of inspiring each member of the team to fight hard especially when the going is toughest, making everybody understand football and believe it is the greatest game that ever was, discovering men in the student body who never played the game, but who under his coaching turn out to be "stars." Is it possible that the American college has lost Mark Hopkins to the football field and the coach, that so-called "maker of men"? Better have him there than not at all on the college campus, even though he is, according to some educators, a legend of doubtful authenticity, and an evil influence in the attempts to bring him back.

I sometimes wish I might devise a required course for college professors—two courses, rather: (1) a preliminary course when they are entering upon their professorship; and (2) the same course after they have been teaching about ten years. They must hide their Phi Beta Kappa keys, and in dress and manner conceal all signs of their professorial business, and not betray themselves by talking. Then I would have them sit in, thus unknown, with a group of students from a half dozen colleges when they get around to discussing their instructors. This is something of what the professors would hear—I omit the profanity though it does add much to the course: "What's he teach for anyway?—shows no interest." "Got no opinion about anything." "Where'd he get that dry, drawling way of talking?" "Did you ever see him excited about anything?" "Doesn't care whether you learn or not." "Ask him a question about anything, and he tells you to do your own thinking. Has he the answer, or doesn't he want to be bothered?" "He may know his stuff, and just can't or won't put it across." "They say he's an authority in his line, but there's no authority in the way he dishes it out to us." "Does he know a thing outside it anyway?" "What's he hired for?" "You have to pinch yourself to keep awake in his class." "Now Old Man Blank (and the old man will be given an affectionate label)—you can't sleep in his class. The bell rings for the hour before you think you've been there fifteen minutes." "He's a honey for explaining things." "You'd think the future of the world depended on what he's teaching." "You just have to study for him. Well, you get as much excited as he does." "When he calls you back for a little confab, well, he knows all about it, and you are not the same man ever afterward."

Professor, could you take two hours of this and be the same man yourself ever afterward, assuming that you could understand the robust, gusty, picturesque language of youth? Maybe you would be like one whom I knew, a productive scholar of the first rank, who had one of his learned lectures to a select noncollege group recorded. When he heard it for himself as it came back to him, he could only say: "I am ashamed and humiliated. Can that throat-clearing, hesitant, flat, monotonously even voice be the voice I used in the classroom?" "No wonder," he might have said, "my students were inattentive, and so many of them failed. Why didn't I get hold of that twenty-five years ago when I might have been cured? Possibly when I was young, I was but a mimic of the dry, indifferent manner of my favorite graduate school instructor when in the stupidity of youth I thought that that manner and research scholarship were one and the same."

But that other man who brought the power of a great personality, whatever that is, into his teaching, created scholars, disciples who filled (across the continent) chairs in colleges and universities. He may not have written much, but his disciples have. And what is "productive scholarship" if it be not a biological capacity for repeating itself more richly in other minds? Those of this kind offer no obstruction courses to the college president, but those of that other kind do, and cause him to be forever raising the question as to why some men attempt to teach at all. Mark Hopkins, you'll be found some day, and rescued from the "Lost Column."

May it not be said that the issues of human destiny are determined by the kind of men who do the teaching in college and by the quality of the teaching itself? If the liberal arts and sciences are all we say they are in our more or less eloquent essays at their appraisement—the enrichment of the mind; the expansion of the spirit; the appreciation of truth, goodness, and beauty; the training of the capacity for thinking, the development of the whole personality for living in a free democracy—then should not there be a ruthlessness in selecting and holding to the men whose business is to make such values real for youth in those four unfolding years they spend on a college campus? These years represent youth's chance to appropriate these values for the uses of human society when they take it over, as they must. To miss this chance through defects due to their own incapacity, misunderstanding, and neglect, is bad enough, but to miss it through the ineptness, the cynical disinterestedness, the I-don't-give-a-hoot attitudes, the fumbling, aimless methods, the lack of passion on the part of those appointed to give them their chance, is a tragedy for which college authorities are responsible. Someday they will accept their responsibility in such a way as to select teachers who not only have scholarship and technical skill but also dedicated, as those divinely called, to the highest task to which one may commit himself. This, though, is just one of those dreams which come to every college president in certain flitting moments of consideration, but which he has not the courage to make real even on his own campus. If he only had the courage to do it, he might be counted among the great educational reformers.

All this may be just the thoughts of one college president after "the long day's task is done," but it does bring to mind the "Semicentennial Commencement" at Wofford in 1904. Fifty years is not a long span in the life of institutions, but somehow Wofford seemed old. Its buildings were of colonial architecture, and not in a good state of repair. Then, there was a sense of long history in the occasion—maybe because so much had been packed into this half century it was celebrating. And the celebration was strictly a family affair. No formal invitations were sent out, and the program of the exercises was almost exclusively of the alumni. To be sure, Bishop Charles B. Galloway, who preached the commencement sermon, was no Wofford man; neither, of course, was President Ira Remsen, of Johns Hopkins, who made the address dedicating the new science hall. But Bishop William Wallace Duncan, who read a paper on "Fifty Years of Wofford History," was of the class of '58. He came with his father, first professor of the classics, when the college opened in 1854. Professor J. A. Gamewell, son of a member of the board of trustees named in the will of the founder of the college, was present as a small boy when the cornerstone was laid in 1852, and was himself of the class of '72. Professor D. A. DuPré, '69, the son of the first professor of natural philosophy, came to the campus in 1854. The alumni orator, the Rev. R. D. Smart, graduated in 1868. Charles Forster Smith, '72, head of the classical department of the University of Wisconsin, made what was then called the "literary address," while Chancellor James H. Kirkland, '77, delivered the formal address to the graduating class.

The donor of the new science building, John B. Cleveland, was of the class of '69. Here is a list of distinguished alumni going back to the foundation of the institution (in living succession). Besides, it was a home-coming occasion for several hundred other alumni representing the leadership of South Carolina and other southern states—a very impressive array of men who had fought, some under Lee and Jackson, had lived through the poverty and humiliation of reconstruction, had helped redeem the state from the looting and oppression of carpetbaggers and ex-slaves, and had gone far toward rebuilding this old commonwealth economically and socially. I but hint at what produced this sense of history, not long history, but much history, in the mood and atmosphere that gave impressiveness to the simple dignity of Wofford's golden jubilee. This sense of history was further emphasized by the fact that there were present old men and women who could recall a tall, bent, gaunt man, Ben Wofford, the rich, parsimonious preacher, as he walked carefully along the streets of Spartanburg village, looking downward, but carrying in his mind a great purpose concerning the establishing of a college of the liberal arts and sciences in his native district. He was the son of a pioneer and fighting soldier in the Revolution, and could have heard in his infancy the guns of the conflict. As a preacher he had followed the immigrant trails over the Blue Ridge into the valleys of the Cumberland, the Tennessee, the Ohio—a circuit rider of the wilderness roads. He was much spoken of on this semicentennial occasion—a man who up to 1850 had given more at one time to denominational education than any other man in America, and had thereby turned over to his church a fully equipped institution.

But the real center of interest throughout the semicentennial days was not Benjamin Wofford but a teacher who came to the college to give instruction in mathematics and astronomy in 1854 when it first opened. James H. Carlisle was twenty-nine years old when he began his career at Wofford. He was now seventy-nine, and in a real sense it was his golden anniversary of service. To him all gave the homage of reverence and gratitude. In every spoken address tribute was paid to him, the teacher. The heads of great industrial enterprises, judges sitting on the bench, men directing the political affairs of the state, financiers, college professors and presidents, men in all walks of life who at last were looking toward the future to reconstruct a new South Carolina—his students talked among themselves of him as the greatest and best man they had ever known and as one who had taught them the meaning of life, giving to them standards for living and the inspiration to strive toward them.

Here was something to ponder, this glorification of the teacher in a state where glory has been mainly given to the statesman and the military hero—John C. Calhoun and Wade Hampton, for example. Yet men did not hesitate to rank this modest man with them, placing him while he yet lived in a niche beside them as deserving the gratitude of the commonwealth. He came to me once a little later, saying in an anxious, troubled manner: "There is a man calling himself a friend of mine, and he is a friend of yours too, who wants to write a biography of me. If you have an influence with him, please do all you can to stop him. What is there to write? I have been only a teacher." "Only a teacher!" If he wanted fame, he had it in large measure; if love, honor, gratitude gave him satisfaction, these too were his in large measure; if pardonable pride in the achievement of those he taught, his disciples, scattered as they were throughout the South and the nation, is one of the human emotions that may make men glad they have lived when at the end of their days they face the sunset—this also must have been his in largest measure.

This teacher—"only a teacher"—persists in my mind as I think of all the teachers I have known, particularly of the kind about whom college presidents have to worry; and James H. Carlisle somehow makes us all seem so small these days when men such as he are so greatly needed, as they were in those grim, hard, tragic fifty years of his life. What's the matter with us? In all the techniques of scholarship we are better trained than he was. That Ph.D. of ours guarantees this. But even in his day without it he sent more men questing the hard road toward it than we do now with it. We have our panels, forums, workshops, meetings of learned societies, but still we don't seem to be able to get the results he did in the quality of men our students become. In knowing all the details in our field, have we lost those wider horizons of life and failed to plumb the depths that give meaning to it? Are we just paddling about in grammatic flats and shallows, not venturing into those deeper currents where real human living is? Do we love the great books, the thinkers and philosophers, the dramatists, the poets, the essayists, the historians, the interpreters of the "course of things"? He did, and what's more, he loved those raw boys that faced him in the lecture room, seeing in each the kind of man he might be at his best, and he dedicated himself to the business of helping each to the high goal along the upper road:

> Of studie took he moost cure and moost heede.
> Nought o word spak he moore than was neede,
> And that was seyd in forme and reverence,
> And short and quyk and ful of hy sentence;
> Sownynge in moral vertu was his speche,
> And gladly wolde he lerne and gladly teche.

14

"THE LONG DAY'S TASK IS DONE"

1942

Two GIGANTIC wars within a period of twenty-five years are enough for any college president to find himself involved in. In the fall of 1917, the Student Army Training Corps took over, making of each eligible student an enlisted man in the Army, and furnishing preliminary preparation for officer training camps. A captain with six second lieutenants was in charge. His orders came from Washington, and the president of the college was never quite sure just what were his official relationships to the whole situation. He did manage, however, to get the swearing stopped on the drill ground in the presence of visiting mothers, and to say with authority when the commandant laid on his desk a telegram from the War Department ordering that in admissions to the Unit "no distinction be made in race, color, or creed": "Certainly, Captain, but remember, under regulations, all applicants must first be approved by this office." The captain understood and was much relieved. Moreover, when the question of daily chapel service came up, he yielded the point, though protesting that the Army "knew no religion," and gave Wofford the best chapel attendance it had ever had.

Instruction of course was reduced to its lowest terms—English, mathematics, physics, and history. The interesting thing was what was said by some of the colonels and professional educators: "You won't know your college when this war is over. The returning soldiers will demand something very different from the abstract stuff you have been dishing out to them. Get ready for drastic changes in the curriculum and the whole college setup if you want to survive!" Then, too, much was heard from some of the chaplains and ministerial visitants to army camps on the home front and from the Y.M.C.A. secretaries about what was to happen to the church and religion when the boys came marching home. "The church must be ready with a new kind of religion, a more practical kind, less emotional, less dogmatic, one that fits into a man's daily living —fewer creeds, more unity among denominations."

But alas! the boys came back demanding, not something new and radical in education and religion, or even in politics, but what they had left behind, and that without change. They fought not for a new world, but for the keeping of the old, and the American Legion became the most conservative, fundamentalist bloc under the flag. The high idealism with which they went to war and the noble emotionalism of the victory promptly gave place to the hard materialism of the back-to-normalcy conception of American life, which wrote for the United States a shameful decade of history, and today we are paying the price.

To be sure the intellectuals had a gorgeous time of it with their pessimistic post-mortems on Western civilization, and the writers of fiction found rich material in the Babbitts from the city of Zenith and the Jeter Lesters from Tobacco Road for showing how depressingly little man is after all—little in thought, speech, and living. The biographers didn't spare the great of the nation, but minimized them and their achievements, reducing them to the size of the smallest of us. Hitler's *Mein Kampf* and the Japanese estimate of us could well be quotations from books written by American men and women, purporting to be true pictures of American life and its meaning.

These poisons seeped of course into the college. In their poetry, stories, and essays at interpreting the course of events, the young intellectuals of the campus aped the moods, the attitudes, the profanities, and the obscenities of their famous elders who had brought the language and ways of the gutter into "polite" literature. In name at least, Wofford was a liberal arts college, doing its best to keep faith with the things that are lovely and of good report, so we let ourselves out to hold students to standards of decency and to the code of gentlemen in a day when at least the traditional code had become a by-word and a reproach. It occurred to me that the time had come to attempt an antidote to this sort of virus in American life. In 1929 the seventy-fifth year in the history of the college was approaching. Why not make it the occasion of a real celebration by giving a day or two to interpreting and emphasizing the significant things of the mind and the spirit, the things that added worth and dignity to the human personality, the enduring things for which Wofford and institutions like it are supposed to stand?

So the date was fixed, October 18 and 19, the latter being the birthday of the founder of the institution. Seventy-five years is a brief day compared with the ages of many other American colleges. Of course, we might have had a "synthetic" anniversary by going back to Bishop Asbury's Mount Bethel Academy set up in 1795 on a rugged hill in the Newberry District, and step by step through Mount Ariel, Tabernacle, and Cokesbury, tracing the history of Methodist education in South Carolina until it culminated in Wofford. Now a few institutions have acquired great age by picking up the odds and ends of wandering educational projects until finally one of them finds a fixed local habitation and continuous unbroken existence. But no, Wofford decided to accept the date of its founding with its opening in 1854, and to believe it had a history since then worth celebrating with significant ceremonies to which it might invite its comrades in the field of liberal education. More than one hundred institutions, from Harvard of 1636 to Anderson College, founded as recently as 1911, responded to the invitation to honor the occasion with representatives. The two-day celebration met all my expectations in its more or less spectacular processional aspects, in the social fellowship, in the number and quality of the alumni present, in the distinction and leadership of those who took part in the program and their understanding interpretation of the meaning of the occasion. The public program was built around discussions of the place of the liberal arts college in American education, the relation of the Christian church to education, the history of Wofford itself and its contribution, the alumni of the college and their responsibility to it. We felt glad and proud for Wofford during those two days. Things looked well for it in the coming years.

Even while the exercises were going on, I was pondering in stray moments this greater future. First, I was planning a leave of absence for five months to be spent in Europe—a sort of sabbatical it was to be. Then on my return I would settle down at last, become really an "educator," and make of Wofford an ideal small college of the liberal arts, selecting students with great care—students who might profit most by such an institution—and a faculty not only competent but dedicated with even a religious fervor to the great task of carrying out my plans. I was proud and happy, and eager to get at the realization of the purposes stirred by the celebration. But hasn't something been frequently said of what often happens to the "best laid schemes o' mice and men"? The decade of getting and spending, of coarse, crass materialism, of vanished ideals, of realism in life to the point of the exclusion of all spiritual values, of faith lost in the political and economic leadership that had kept us in a fool's paradise with slogans like "prosperity is just around the corner"—this ended in a crash that shook the foundations of the republic and left its financial structure in ruins. Great, powerful, rich, resourceful, boastful, courageous America was humbled, dazed, confused, defeated, whining, helpless, beneath the wreckage of what it thought was real wealth when, as a matter of fact, it was only the fool's gold of a deceptive inflation. No enterprise or institution of any kind escaped the devastating assaults of the sinister forces of destruction that nobody seemed to know how to combat.

267

I saw the invested funds of Wofford suddenly frozen tight and hard, its student body melting away at the rate of one hundred a year for the first year or two, the compensation of the faculty reduced below the living point, men with the highest degrees and the best training offering their services for room and board and $20 a month—at least one for just his room and board. Many of the faculty and trustees were gloomy and pessimistic, believing the college would, or even should, close its doors; and before it could be stopped, an indebtedness amounted to nearly $100,000, something that had never happened to Wofford before. And it all came with such suddenness and violence. The processes of accumulation were of course gradual, but nobody seemed to sense this gradual accumulation of destructive forces, and when they broke, it was of the nature of a terrifying surprise that few believed could come to the United States.

Up to this time, after nearly thirty years as president of this small southern college, I thought I had had every sort of experience possible, but here was something new. With a smile on my face, but grim and determined at heart, believing that the worthy things of life could not perish from the earth and that Wofford College was one of those worthy things, I set to work to salvage the endowment and once again to bring students to the campus. Slowly, through twelve hard, unresting years, the fight went on—not unhappy years because he who is fighting in worthy causes, though at times they seem but forlorn hopes always on the edge of being lost, is never unhappy. In June, 1942, I turned over to my successor a college free from debt, the professors' salaries restored to predepression levels, the endowments intact and distributing dividends, though much reduced, and a student body of 467, the largest strictly liberal arts group of men students in the state. But for the menacing storm that had already broken at Pearl Harbor things looked again well for Wofford.

In one of the darkest years of the depression, a colleague was retiring from the presidency of a college not unlike Wofford. He had been a scholar of the first rank and a great teacher of the classics. He had entered upon the presidency directly from the classroom, as I had done in 1902. Out of the none-too-happy experiences of trying to keep a college going under depression conditions—conditions that no doubt induced a nostalgic mood for the classroom I had left—I wrote him this letter:

What is it to be a college president anyway, and why are men willing to take such a job? To leave a congenial professorship to take charge of a small church college, and proceed to try to build something out of what is almost nothing in the face of criticism, misunderstanding, and the opposition of men whom you have saved from the logic of their own temperaments, to keep faith with standards of scholarship and sane ideals of religion, to do for the church what it seems the church really doesn't want done, to face your alumni all excited over the things that don't count, to have to be an eternal peacemaker among all sorts of conflicting human selfishnesses—why is a gentleman willing to bother with such things? Well, there are those boys of yours who will be writing to you to the end of your days in such a way as will make your heart glad and proud, and two or three times a year there will come to your desk a great piece of scholarship in the shape of a monograph or a big book, and on the very front page will be spoken to you such words of appreciation as will cause you to feel that you yourself have written the book. Then, too, in certain quiet hours, by a curious magic of the mind, you will be able to separate the gold from the dross and believe that after all you have been a faithful lover of things which are 'true, honest, and of good report;' and the light of this love will scatter the darkness of all those other things, and you will be well content that you have given life as generously as you could, without counting the costs, to the effort to establish foundations on which intellectual and spiritual sanity and security can be built!

Only a few years later, in June, 1942, I closed my letter of resignation with these words:

269

These have been happy years. The board of trustees has been co-operative to the highest degree and has given me freedom to do what I wanted to do, perhaps more freedom than I ought to have had. I do not know. But I do know that this is why I have remained at Wofford these more than fifty years, taking my stand here, because, unhampered, I was permitted by you to express what ability and purpose I had in trying to unite religion and learning in the training of men for the use and service of life.

And so: "The long day's task is done."

As I reread these two letters, I am reminded of a soft hazy day in late October, 1940, when we were called to the piazza of our home to find the yard crowded with hundreds of alumni. It was their annual home-coming day. Besides the lunch together, the reminiscing, the football game, they had this time the special feature of presenting to their president a silver service set commemorating his fifty years' connection with Wofford, 1890-1940. The set now rests on an antique sideboard, its dark mahogany furnishing a fitting background for the gleaming splendor of the silversmith's art. Into the waiter are cut these words:

For fifty years of extraordinary service to church and commonwealth, of masterly guidance of our Alma Mater with unswerving fidelity to the eternal verities of scholarship and character, of unfaltering leadership in perplexed realms of thought and life, of calm faith which brought strength to men in dark hours, of grace and charm whch add beauty to strength—we the sons of Wofford, his greatest debtors, present this gift to our beloved President, Dr. Henry Nelson Snyder, as a token of our pride in his high achievements, of our deep and abiding gratitude for all things so freely given to us and our sons, of our love grown deeper with the years, stronger with suffering and understanding, and which will be invisibly wrapped around him forever.

The author of these words is not singing a song in praise of a man's achievements but is interpreting something of his motives as he sought to apply the principles of discipline and training to youth for the uses of satisfactory and happy living.

And so, after "the long day's task is done," I come to the twilight. In this twilight of the long day there still lurk the shades of sinister figures—the Huey Longs, the Jeff Davises, the Vardamans, the Bleases, the Fergusons, the Talmadges, the Bilbos, and their kind; in the deepest shadows are the be-capped and berobed symbols of prejudice, and hate, and intolerance, flashing now and then a fiery cross. And when I see these again, I must think of that visit I had with David Coker in Hartsville, South Carolina. He had a pile of papers before him on a table.

"Sit down. These are the reports on my special farms. I have a standing offer to any farmer in Darlington County, guaranteeing him a living and a surplus, if he will conduct his farm according to my directions for three years, and here are some of the reports."

Now, everybody who knew David Coker, that master farmer and scientific producer of highbred seeds, would also know he would fulfill any promise he might make. So I inquired why every farmer in the county didn't take him up on his offer.

"They don't because of those twin enemies of human welfare and progress—ignorance and prejudice."

"But is there no cure for even these?" I asked of the wise man who loved men of low degree and wanted to lift them up.

"Yes," he replied, looking wistfully as into some far distance, "there is—sympathy, understanding, and patience."

And as one calls to mind men like him—farmers, bankers, industrialists, churchmen—scattered throughout the South, the twilight seems to brighten and the sinister figures to retreat deeper into the shadows. Then there also come to mind those others who built for the future during the long day—J. L. M. Curry, of the Peabody Board; R. E. Blackwell at Randolph-Macon in Virginia; W. W. Smith, who founded the Woman's College at Lynchburg; Charles W. McIver, E. A. Alderman, C. B. Aycock, John C. Kilgo, and W. P. Few in North Carolina; Harvey Cox and Warren Candler at Emory in Georgia;

Charles B. Galloway in Mississippi; R. S. Hyer, making the beginnings of Southern Methodist University in Texas; Holland N. McTyeire, L. C. Garland, and James H. Kirkland at Vanderbilt in Nashville; Bruce R. Payne at Peabody College; Charles Dabney at the University of Tennessee; and those crusaders out of New York, Wallace Buttrick, Robert Ogden, Wickliff Rose, and Walter Hines Page—and the twilight seems more like the morning of a new day. These worked in sympathy, understanding, and patience; and with them all men of good will and faith can take their stand in Dixie Land, knowing it is they who are still shaping the future of the South for better ways of thinking and living.

Date Due

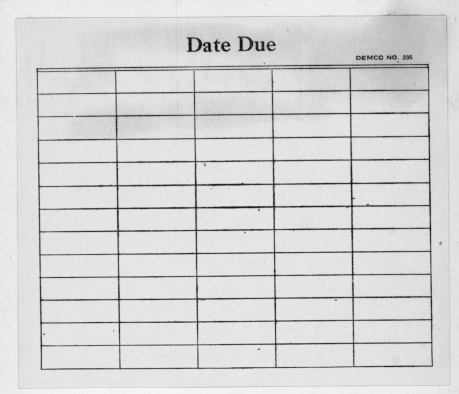